A MASTERCLASS IN DRAWING & PAINTING

THE HUMAN FIGURE

ANATOMY, THE NUDE, PORTRAITS & PEOPLE

A MASTERCLASS IN DRAWING & PAINTING THE HUMAN FIGURE

ANATOMY, THE NUDE, PORTRAITS & PEOPLE

Learn to depict the human form in pencil, charcoal, pastels, water paints, acrylics, oils and gouache
With expert step-by-step tutorials and over 35 projects shown in more than 800 photographs

SARAH HOGGETT & VINCENT MILNE

LORENZ BOOKS

This edition is published by Lorenz Books,
an imprint of Anness Publishing Ltd,
Blaby Road, Wigston, Leicestershire LE18 4SE;
info@anness.com

www.lorenzbooks.com; www.annesspublishing.com

A CIP catalogue record for this book is available from the British Library.

Publisher: Joanna Lorenz
Editorial Director: Helen Sudell
Project Editor: Rosie Gordon
Design: Nigel Partridge
Photographer: Martin Norris
Production Controller: Wendy Lawson

Parts of this book were previously published in *The Practical Encyclopedia of Drawing*, *The Practical Encyclopedia of Watercolour*, *The Practical Encyclopedia of Oils, Acrylics and Gouache*, and *How to Paint and Draw*.

ACKNOWLEDGEMENTS

The publishers are grateful to the following for permission to reproduce illustrations:
Gerry Baptist: p75r, 163b; Paul Bartlett: pp 63b, 164tr; Bridgeman Art Library: William Etty: p74l, 'Study for a Male Nude'; William Edward Frost: p72b 'Life study of the female figure'; Harold Gilman: p74b 'Nude on a Bed'. Gerald Cains: p162t; Trevor Chamberlain: p166t; Patrick Clossick: p167tr; David Curtis: p168tl; David Cuthbert: p72t; Douglas Druce: p35; Timothy Easton: p164b; Ted Gould: p166b, 167b; Elizabeth Harden: p73b; Hazel Harrison: pp 48–9, 75, 164; James Horton: p73tl, tr, 74t; Maureen Jordan: p76; Geoff Marsters: pp 64t, 168tr; Robert Maxwell Wood: p77; Vincent Milne: pp 32-4, 36–41, 43–47, 50, 51, 52-3, 54, 55b, 56–9, 66, 67b, 78l, 79, 80–89, 170–179; Ken Paine: page 165t, 169tl, b; Karen Raney: pp 69, 167tl; Ian Sidaway: pp 55t, 62, 64b, 65, 68, 162b, 163t; Sally Strand: p67t, 165b; Effie Waverlin: p 51b.

The publishers are grateful to the following artists for contributing step-by-step demonstrations:
Diana Constance: pp114–117, 214–219; Douglas Druce: pp 94–97, 104–107, 122–125, 142–147; Abigail Edgar: pp 98–103, 118–121, 202–207, 208–213, 226–231, 232–235, 236–239; Wendy Jelbert: pp 240–243; Vincent Milne: pp 90–93, 126–129, 136–141; 148–153, 192–197, 198–201; John Raynes: pp 108–113, 130–135, 154–159, 220–225, 244–247; Ian Sidaway: pp 186–191; Albany Wiseman: pp 180–185.

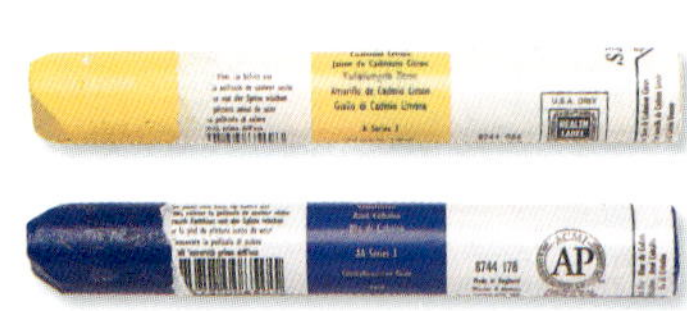

Contents

Introduction

There is a long-established tradition of drawing and painting the nude in Western art, from prehistoric times, when cave dwellers first used mineral pigments to create their simple representations of hunters and their prey, through the idealized marble sculptures of ancient Greece to the beautifully observed anatomical studies of great Renaissance artists such as Michelangelo and Leonardo da Vinci, and right up to the present day. Portraiture, too, has gone through many styles and changes over the centuries, from formal portraits intended as much to flatter the subject and show off a patron's wealth as to capture a realistic likeness, to 'warts and all' portraits that seek to convey, or lay bare, the character and personality of the sitter.

For many amateur artists, being able to produce good portraits and life drawings is the ultimate goal. Wouldn't it be lovely to be able to paint one's family and friends? At the same time, however, the subject is viewed with a certain amount of trepidation. There's a feeling that drawing and painting people is somehow harder than painting things like landscapes and flowers and, for beginners in particular, there's something quite intimidating about being faced with a live model.

In truth, one of the reasons that painting people is perceived as being so difficult is that our expectations, both as viewers and as artists, are somewhat different. No one will worry if you alter the position of a tree in a landscape, or if you don't put in every single petal of a flower. On the contrary, your changes will probably be put down to artistic licence – if they're noticed at all.

Paintings of people, on the other hand, are expected to be true, almost photographically accurate, likenesses. "It doesn't even look like him" is probably the most common criticism of a portrait – and a critique like that could well put you off life drawing for good. In the face of that, perhaps it's understandable that many amateurs decide to play it safe and stick to less contentious subjects such as still lifes and scenes of holiday destinations.

If you'd like to have a go at drawing and painting people, the material within this book is designed to provide a thorough introduction to everything you need to know. After a look at the tools and materials available, the book moves

▲ Always look at how the figure relates to the picture space. Here, although the background is relatively empty, the shadow is an important part of the composition and provides a strong horizontal line to counterbalance the figure of the child.

▼ Capturing a likeness is a gradual process. Build up the shapes and tones slowly, continually assessing the balance of the picture as a whole.

▼ Drawing the figure in motion is an interesting exercise in studying the human form. Choose a medium that allows you to work quickly – this will also help to convey the energy of the movement.

▲ Always ensure that the clothing and background are subdued so that they do not dominate the portrait.

on to a tutorials section, which sets out some of the technicalities of life drawing, touching on very simple anatomy for the artist as well as on more artistic concerns such as props, composition and lighting. If you're a complete beginner, work through this section page by page, as it will help you build up the confidence to tackle portraits and life studies on your own. Alternatively, if there are specific aspects of drawing and painting people that you feel you need a little help with, dip into the section for a refresher course whenever you need to.

The rest of the book is broken down into two parts, nudes and portraits. Each section begins with a gallery of works by professional artists that you can use as a source of ideas and inspiration, and ends with a series of step-by-step projects covering a whole range of poses and media.

Naturally, your own models may look very different to those who have sat for the projects in this book, and you will have your own ideas on compositions, room settings and so on – but don't be put off by that. You can learn a lot from the artists who have contributed to this book, and gain from their experience.

Although they work in a range of media, the one thing the artists all have in common is their ability to assess the essentials of the pose and translate it to the two-dimensional surface of the paper or canvas. Studying their step-by-step projects will give you all kinds of insights that you can use in your own work, from working out an effective composition to looking at the effect of light and shade on your subject and creating a lively and convincingly three-dimensional portrayal.

What comes after that? Well, it's up to you! The old adage 'practice makes perfect' really holds true in drawing and painting. Practise when you can – and don't wait until you have the time to create a full-scale portrait or life study, or you will never get started. Artists' sketchbooks are crammed full of studies made whenever they've got a few minutes to spare, and, whether they are preparatory sketches for a larger work or practice exercises to sharpen observational skills, the time this work takes is always valuably spent.

Drawing and painting people is an unending voyage of discovery. Every person is different; every pose is different; even shapes and relationships within the same pose may alter slightly as the work progresses, keeping you on the alert and making you continually reassess things. Even when you're drawing someone you know well, studying their features so intently may reveal to you things you'd never noticed before. And this is what makes portrait painting so endlessly fascinating.

▼ Less is very often more! If you're new to life drawing, keep the background plain so that you can focus your attention on the figure, resulting in a strong, simple portrait.

CARAN d'ACHE
NEOCOLOR II • 7500.030
NEOCOLOR II • 7500.210
DALER ROWNEY
OIL PASTELS

Materials

A good art supply store is like an Aladdin's cave, packed full of treasures. Huge boxes of soft pastels and pans of watercolour paint in every shade of every colour in the rainbow; row upon row of tubes of paint; pads of paper ranging in colour from pale biscuit to forest green; everything from nifty little gadgets for painting in the field to heavy studio easels: it's all too easy to get carried away and end up buying things you don't really need and may never use. This chapter sets out the pros and cons of the most popular media, and provides practical information on essentials, from selecting paper and brushes to stretching canvases, so that you can begin to feel confident navigating your way around the array of materials in your local art store.

You can also use this as an introduction to a medium that you might not previously have considered. If you've always worked in watercolour, for example, why not try oils or acrylics for a change? If you love the powdery texture of charcoal, why not give soft pastels a go? Or be bolder still and experiment with mixed media, perhaps combining pen and ink with soft watercolour washes. You'll be amazed at what you can achieve!

Monochrome media

For sketching and underdrawing, as well as for striking studies in contrast and line, there are many different monochrome media, all of which offer different qualities to your artwork. A good selection is the foundation of your personal art store, and it is worth exploring many media, including different brands, to find the ones you like working with.

Pencils

Pencils are graded according to hardness. 9H is the hardest down to HB and F (for fine) and then up to 9B, which is the softest. The higher the proportion of clay to graphite, the harder the pencil. A selection of five grades – say, a 2H, HB, 2B, 4B and 6B – is adequate for most purposes.

Soft pencils give a very dense, black mark, while hard pencils give a grey mark. The differences can be seen below – these marks were made by appying the same pressure to different grades of pencil. If you require a darker mark, do not try to apply more pressure, but switch to a softer pencil.

Water-soluble graphite pencils

There are also water-soluble graphite pencils, which are made with a binder that dissolves in water. Available in a range of grades, they can be used dry, dipped in water or worked into with a brush and water to create a range of watercolour-like effects. Water-soluble graphite pencils are an ideal tool for sketching on location, as they offer you the versatility of combining linear marks with tonal washes. Use the tip to create fine details and the side of the pencil to cover large areas quickly.

Graphite sticks

Solid sticks of graphite come in various sizes and grades. Some resemble conventional pencils, while others are shorter and thicker. You can also buy irregular-shaped chunks and fine graphite powder, and thinner strips of graphite in varying degrees of hardness that fit a barrel with a clutch mechanism.

Graphite sticks are capable of making a wider range of marks than conventional graphite pencils. For example, you can use the point or edge of a profile stick to make a thin mark, or stroke the whole side of the stick over the paper to make a broader mark.

Charcoal

The other monochromatic drawing material popular with artists is charcoal. It comes in different lengths and in thin, medium, thick and extra-thick sticks. You can also buy chunks that are ideal for expressive drawings. Stick charcoal is very brittle and powdery, and is great for broad areas of tone.

Compressed charcoal is made from charcoal dust mixed with a binder and fine clay and pressed into shape. Sticks and pencils are available. Unlike stick charcoal, charcoal pencils are ideal for detailed, linear work.

As with other powdery media, drawings made in charcoal should be sprayed with fixative to hold the pigment in place and prevent smudging.

Thick charcoal stick

Thin charcoal stick

Pen and ink

With so many types of pens and colours of ink available, not to mention the possibility of combining linear work with broad washes of colour, this is an extremely versatile medium and one that is well worth exploring. Begin by making a light pencil underdrawing of your subject, then draw over with pen – but beware of simply inking over your pencil lines, as this can look rather flat and dead. When you have gained enough confidence, your aim should be to put in the minimum of lines in pencil, simply to ensure you've got the proportions and angles right, and then do the majority of the work in pen.

Inks

The two types of inks used by artists are waterproof and water-soluble. The former can be diluted with water, but are permanent once dry, so line work can be worked over with washes without any fear of it being removed. They often contain shellac, and thick applications dry with a sheen. The best-known is Indian ink, actually from China. It makes great line drawings. It is deep black but can be diluted to give a beautiful range of warm greys.

Water-soluble inks can be reworked once dry, and work can be lightened and corrections made. Don't overlook watercolours and liquid acrylics – both can be used like ink but come in a wider range of colours.

Waterproof ink

Water-soluble ink

Liquid acrylic

Dip pens and nibs

A dip pen does not have a reservoir of ink; as the name suggests, it is simply dipped into the ink to make marks. Drawings made with a dip pen have a unique quality, as the nib can make a line of varying width depending on how much pressure you apply. You can also turn the pen over and use the back of the nib to make broader marks. As you have to keep reloading with ink, it is difficult to make a long, continuous line – but for many subjects the rather scratchy, broken lines are very attractive.

When you first use a new nib it can be reluctant to accept ink. To solve this, rub it with a little saliva.

Nibs

Dip pen

Sketching pens, fountain pens and technical pens

Sketching pens and fountain pens make ideal sketching tools and enable you to use ink on location without having to carry bottles of ink.

Technical pens deliver ink through a tube rather than a shaped nib, so the line is of a uniform width. If you want to make a drawing that has a range of line widths, you will need several pens with different-sized tubular nibs.

Sketching pen

Bamboo, reed and quill pens

The nib of a bamboo pen delivers a 'dry', rather coarse line. Reed and quill pens are flexible and give a subtle line that varies in thickness. The nibs break easily, but can be recut with a knife.

Rollerball, fibre-tip and marker pens

Rollerball and fibre-tip pens are ideal for sketching out ideas, although finished drawings made using these pens can have a rather mechanical feel to them, as the line does not vary in width. This can sometimes work well as an effect. By working quickly with a rollerball you can make a very light line by delivering less ink to the nib. Fibre-tip and marker pens come in an range of tip widths, from super-fine to calligraphic style tips and also in a wide range of colours.

Coloured drawing media

Coloured pencils contain a coloured pigment and clay, held together with a binder. They are impregnated with wax so that the colour holds to the support with no need for a fixative. They are especially useful for making coloured drawings on location, as they are a very stable medium and are not prone to smudging. Mixing takes place optically on the surface of the support rather than by physical blending, and all brands are inter-mixable, although certain brands can be more easily erased than others; so always try out one or two individual pencils from a range before you buy a large set. Choose hard pencils for linear work and soft ones for large, loosely-applied areas of colour.

Huge colour range ▲
Artists who work in coloured pencil tend to accumulate a vast range in different shades – the variance between one tone and its neighbour often being very slight. This is chiefly because you cannot physically mix coloured pencil marks to create a new shade (unlike watercolour or acrylic paints). So, if you want lots of different greens in a landscape, you will need a different pencil for each one.

Water-soluble pencils

Most coloured-pencil manufacturers also produce a range of water-soluble pencils, which can be used to make conventional pencil drawings and blended with water to create watercolour-like effects. In recent years, solid pigment sticks that resemble pastels have been introduced that are also water-soluble and can be used in conjunction with conventional coloured pencils or on their own.

Wet and dry ▼
Water-soluble pencils can be used dry, the same way as conventional pencils.

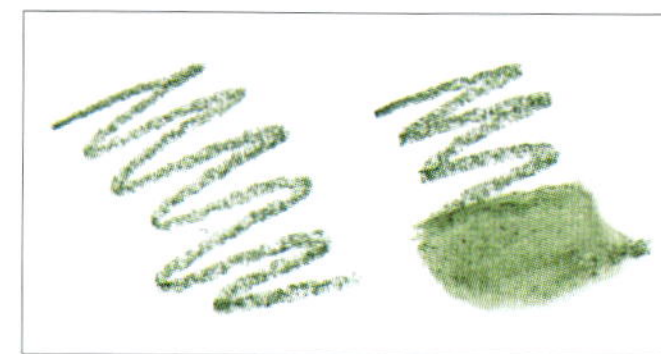

Conté crayons and pencils

The best way to use Conté crayons is to snap off a section and use the side of the crayon to block in large areas, and a tip or edge for linear marks.

The pigment in Conté crayons is relatively powdery, so, like soft pastels and charcoal, it can be blended by rubbing with a finger, rag or torchon. Conté crayon drawings benefit from being given a coat of fixative to prevent smudging. However, Conté crayons are harder and more oily than soft pastels, so you can lay one colour over another, letting the under-colour show through.

Conté is also available in pencils, which contain wax and need no fixing (setting); the other benefit is that the tip can be sharpened to a point.

Conté crayons ▼
These small, square-profile sticks are available in boxed sets of traditional colours. Drawings made using these traditional colours are reminiscent of the wonderful chalk drawings of old masters such as Michelangelo or Leonardo da Vinci.

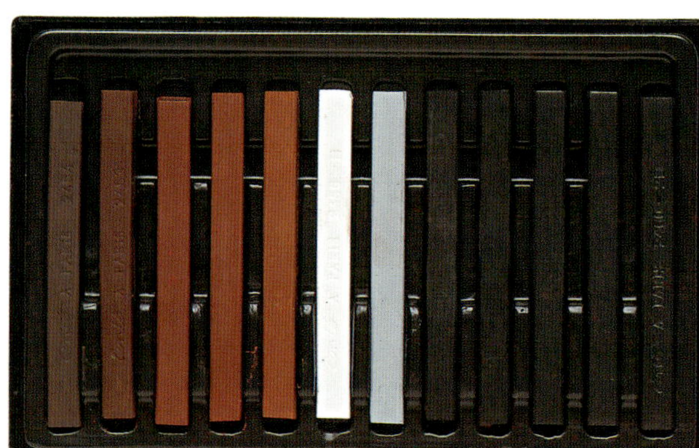

Conté pencils ▼
As they can be sharpened to a point, Conté pencils are ideal for drawings that require precision and detail.

Pastels

Pastel work is often described as painting rather than drawing as the techniques used are often similar to techniques used in painting. Pastels are made by mixing pigment with a weak binder, and the more binder used the harder the pastel will be. Pastels are fun to work with and ideal for making colour sketches as well as producing vivid, dynamic artwork.

Soft pastels

As soft pastels contain relatively little binder, they are prone to crumbling, so they have a paper wrapper to help keep them in one piece. Even so, dust still comes off, and can easily contaminate other colours nearby. The best option is to arrange your pastels by colour type and store them in boxes.

Pastels are mixed on the support either by physically blending them or by allowing colours to mix optically. The less you blend, the fresher the image looks. For this reason, pastels are made in a range of hundreds of tints and shades.

As pastels are powdery, use textured paper to hold the pigment in place. Spray soft pastel drawings with fixative to prevent smudging. You can fix (set) work in progress, too – but colours may darken, so don't overdo it.

Box of pastels ▼
When you buy a set of pastels, they come packaged in a compartmentalized box so that they do not rub against each other and become dirtied.

Hard pastels

One advantage of hard pastels is that, in use, they do not shed as much pigment as soft pastels, therefore they will not clog the texture of the paper as quickly. For this reason, they are often used in the initial stages of a work that is completed using soft pastels. Hard pastels can be blended together by rubbing, but not as easily or as seamlessly as soft pastels.

Oil pastels

Made by combining fats and waxes with pigment, oil pastels are totally different to pigmented soft and hard pastels and should not be mixed with them. Oil pastels can be used on unprimed drawing paper and they never completely dry.

Oil-pastel sticks are quite fat and therefore not really suitable for detailed work or fine, subtle blending. For bold, confident strokes, however, they are perfect.

Oil-pastel marks have something of the thick, buttery quality of oil paints. The pastels are highly pigmented and available in a good range of colours. If they are used on oil-painting paper, they can be worked in using a solvent such as white spirit (paint thinner), applied with a brush or rag. You can also smooth out oil-pastel marks with wet fingers. Oil and water are not compatible, and a damp finger will not pick up colour.

Oil pastels can be blended optically on the support by scribbling one colour on top of another. You can also create textural effects by scratching into the pastel marks with a sharp implement – a technique known as sgraffito.

Oil pastels ▼
Less crumbly than soft pastels, and harder in texture, oil pastels are round sticks and come in various sizes.

Pastel pencils

A delight to use, the colours of pastel pencils are strong, yet the pencil shape makes them ideal for drawing lines. If treated carefully, they do not break – although they are more fragile than graphite or coloured pencils. The pastel strip can be sharpened to a point, making pastel pencils ideal for describing detail in drawings that have been made using conventional hard or soft pastels.

Pastel pencils ▼
Available in a comprehensive range of colours, pastel pencils are clean to use and are ideal for linear work. Ideally, store them in a jar with the tips upwards to prevent breakage.

Watercolour paint

Watercolour paints are available in two main forms: pans, which are the familiar compressed blocks of colour that need to be brushed with water to release the colour; or tubes of moist paint. The same finely powdered pigments bound with gum arabic solution are used to make both types. The pigments provide the colour, while the gum arabic allows the paint to adhere to the paper, even when diluted.

It is a matter of personal preference whether you use pans or tubes. The advantage of pans is that they can be slotted into a paintbox, making them easily portable, and this is something to consider if you often paint on location. Tubes, on the other hand, are often better if you are working in your studio and need to make a large amount of colour for a wash. With tubes, you need to remember to replace the caps immediately, otherwise the paint will harden and become unusable. Pans of dry paint can be rehydrated.

Tubes of paint ▼
Tubes of watercolour paint are available in different sizes. It is worth buying the larger sizes for colours that you think you will use frequently. Keep the caps tightly sealed and rinse spilt paint off the tubes before storing them.

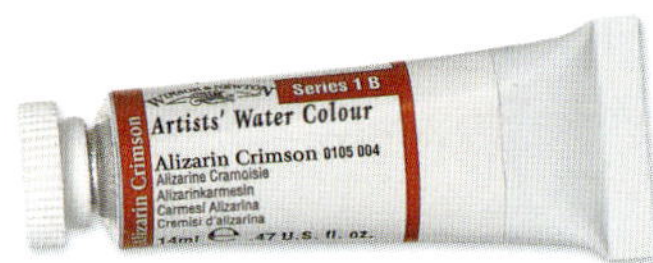

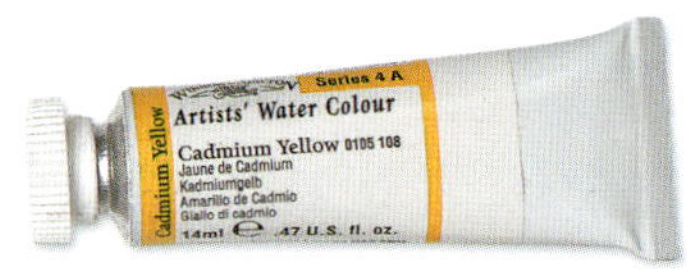

Grades of paint

There are two grades of watercolour paint: artists' and students' quality. Artists' quality paints are the more expensive, because they contain a high proportion of good-quality pigments. Students' quality paints contain less pure pigment and more fillers, and are usually available in a smaller range of colours than artists' quality paints.

If you come across the word 'hue' in a paint name, it indicates that the paint contains cheaper alternatives instead of the real pigment. Generally speaking, you get what you pay for: artists' quality paints tend to produce more subtle mixtures of colours.

The other thing that you need to think about when buying paints is their permanence. The label or the manufacturer's catalogue should give you the permanency rating. In the United Kingdom, the permanency ratings are class AA (extremely permanent), class A (durable), class B (moderate) and class C (fugitive). The ASTM (American Society for Testing and Materials) codes for light-fastness are ASTM I (excellent), ASTM II (very good) and ASTM III (not sufficiently light-fast). Some pigments, such as alizarin crimson and viridian, stain more than others: they penetrate the fibres of the paper and cannot be removed.

Finally, although we always think of watercolour as being transparent, you should be aware that some pigments are actually slightly opaque and will impart a degree of opacity to any colours with which they are mixed. These so-called opaque pigments include all the cadmium colours and cerulean blue.

Judging colours

It is not always possible to judge the colour of paints by looking at the pans in your palette, as they often look dark. In fact, it is very easy to dip your brush into the wrong pan, so always check before you put brush to paper.

Even when you have mixed a wash in your palette, appearances can be deceptive, as watercolour paint always looks lighter when it is dry. The only way to be sure what colour or tone you have mixed is to apply it to paper and let it dry. It is always best to build up tones gradually until you get the effect you want. The more you practise, the better you will get at anticipating results.

Appearances can be deceptive ▼
These two pans look very dark, almost black. In fact, one is Payne's grey and the other a bright ultramarine blue.

Test your colours ▼
Keep a piece of scrap paper next to you as you work so that you can test your colour mixes before you apply them.

Gouache paint

Made using the same pigments and binders found in transparent water-colour, gouache is a water-soluble paint. The addition of *blanc fixe* – a chalk – gives the paint its opacity. Because gouache is opaque you can paint light colours over darker ones – unlike traditional watercolour, where the paint's inherent transparency means that light colours will not cover any darker shades that lie underneath.

The best-quality gouache contains a high proportion of coloured pigment. Artists' gouache tends to be made using permanent pigments that are light-fast. The 'designers' range uses less permanent pigments, as designers' work is intended to last for a short time.

Characteristics of gouache

All of the equipment and techniques used with watercolour can be used with gouache. Like watercolour, gouache can be painted on white paper or board; due to its opacity and covering power, it can also be used on a coloured or toned ground and over gesso-primed board or canvas. Gouache is typically used on smoother surfaces than might be advised for traditional watercolour, as the texture of the support is less of a creative or aesthetic consideration.

If they are not used, certain gouache colours are prone to drying up over time. Gouache does remain soluble when dry, but dried-up tubes can be a problem to use.

Certain dye-based colours are very strong and, if used beneath other layers of paint, can have a tendency to bleed.

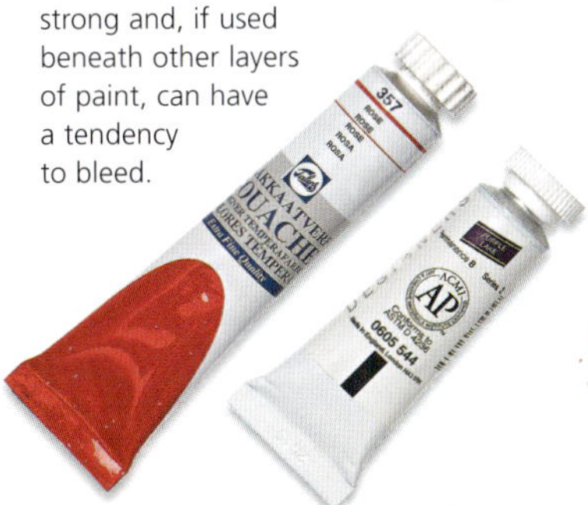

Gouache paint

Work confidently ▲
Gouache remains soluble when it is dry, so if you are applying one colour over another, your brushwork needs to be confident and direct: a clean, single stroke, as here, will not pick up paint from the first layer.

Muddied colours ▲
If you scrub paint over an underlying colour, you will pick up paint from the first layer and muddy the colour of the second layer, as here.

Wet into wet ▲
Like transparent watercolour paint, gouache paint can be worked wet into wet (as here) or wet on dry.

Removing dry paint ▲
Dry paint can be re-wetted and removed by blotting with an absorbent paper towel.

Change in colour when dry ▼
Gouache paint looks slightly darker when dry than it does when wet, so it is good practice to test your mixes on a piece of scrap paper – although, with practice, you will quickly learn to make allowances for this.

Wet gouache paint

Dry gouache paint

Oil paint

There are two types of traditional oil paint – professional, or artists', grade and the less expensive students' quality. The difference is that artists' paint uses finely ground, high-quality pigments, which are bound in the best oils and contain very little filler, while students' paints use less expensive pigments and contain greater quantities of filler to bulk out the paint. The filler is usually *blanc fixe* or aluminium hydrate, both with a very low tinting strength.

Students' quality paint is often very good and is, in fact, used by students, amateur painters and professionals.

The range of colours is more limited but still comprehensive, and each tube of paint in the range, irrespective of its colour, costs the same. Artists' quality paint is sold according to the quality and cost of the pigment used to make it. Each colour in the range is given a series number or letter; the higher the number or letter, the more expensive the paint. Various oils are used to bind and make the paint workable; linseed, poppy and safflower oil are the most common. The choice of oil depends on the characteristics and drying properties of the pigment being mixed.

Working "fat over lean" ▲
The golden rule when using oil paint is to work 'fat' (or oily, flexible paint) over 'lean', inflexible paint that contains little or no oil.

Tubes or tubs? ▼
Oil paint is sold in tubes containing anything from 15 to 275ml (1 tbsp to 9fl oz). If you tend to use a large quantity of a particular colour – for toning grounds, for example – you can buy paint in cans containing up to 5 litres (8¾ pints).

Glazing with oils ▲
Oils are perfect for glazes (transparent applications of paint over another colour). The process is slow, but quick-drying glazing mediums can speed things up.

Drawing with oils ►
Oil bars consist of paint with added wax and drying agents. The wax stiffens the paint, enabling it to be rolled into what resembles a giant pastel.

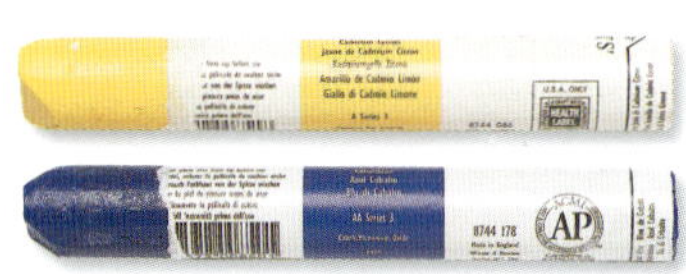

Water-mixable oil paint

Water-mixable oil paint is made using linseed and safflower oils that have been modified to be soluble in water. Once the paint has dried and the oils have oxidized, it is as permanent and stable as conventional oil paint. Some water-mixable paint can also be used with conventional oil paint, although its mixability is gradually compromised with the more traditional paint that is added.

Alkyd oil paints

Alkyd oil paints contain synthetic resin but are used in the same way as traditional oil paints and can be mixed with the usual mediums and thinners.

Alkyd-based paint dries much faster than oil-based paint, so it is useful for underpainting prior to using traditional oils and for work with glazes or layers. However, you should not use alkyd paint over traditional oil paint, as its fast drying time can cause problems.

Mixing colours with oils

Colour mixing with oils is relatively straightforward, as there is no colour shift as the paint dries: the colour that you apply wet to the canvas will look the same when it has dried, so (unlike acrylics, gouache or watercolour) you do not need to make allowances for changes as you paint. However, colour that looks bright when applied can begin to look dull as it dries. This is due to the oil in the paint sinking into a previously applied absorbent layer of paint below. You can revive the colour in sunken patches by 'oiling out' – that is, by brushing an oil-and-spirit mixture or applying a little retouching varnish over the affected area.

Acrylic paint

Acrylic paint can be mixed with a wide range of acrylic mediums and additives and is thinned with water. Unlike oil paint, it dries quickly and the paint film remains extremely flexible and will not crack. The paint can be used with a wide range of techniques, from thick impasto, as with oil paint, to the semi-transparent washes of watercolour. Indeed, most of the techniques used in both oil and watercolour painting can be used with acrylic paint. Acrylic paints come in three different consistencies. Tube paint tends to be of a buttery consistency and holds its shape when squeezed from the tube. Tub paint is thinner and more creamy in consistency, which makes it easier to brush out and cover large areas. There are also liquid acrylic colours with the consistency of ink, sold as acrylic inks.

You may experience no problems in mixing different brands or consistencies, but it is always good practice to follow the manufacturer's instructions.

◀ **Liquid acrylics**
Liquid acrylics are the consistency of writing ink.

Tubs ▶
Acrylic paint in tubs stores easily.

Tubes ▶
Acrylic paints in tubes are convenient to carry and use with a palette.

Characteristics of acrylic paint

Being water soluble, acrylic paint is very easy to use, requiring only the addition of clean water. Water also cleans up wet paint after a work session. Once it has dried, however, acrylic paint creates a hard but flexible film that will not fade or crack and is impervious to more applications of acrylic or oil paint or their associated mediums or solvents.

Acrylic paint dries relatively quickly: a thin film will be touch dry in a few minutes and even thick applications dry in a matter of hours. Unlike oil paints, all acrylic colours, depending on the thickness of paint, dry at the same rate.

Texture gels ▲
Various gels can be mixed into acrylic paint to give a range of textural effects. These can be worked in while the paint is still wet.

Mediums and additives ▲
A wide range of mediums and additives can be mixed into acrylic paint to alter and enhance its handling characteristics.

Adhesive qualities ▲
Many acrylic mediums have very good adhesive qualities, making them ideal for collage work– sticking paper or other materials on to the support.

Extending drying time ▲
The drying time of acrylic paint can be extended by using a retarding medium, which gives you longer to work into the paint and blend colours.

Glazing with acrylics ▲
Acrylic colours can be glazed by thinning the paint with water, although a better result is achieved by adding an acrylic medium.

Covering power
Acrylic paint that is applied straight from the tube has good covering power, even when you apply a light colour over a dark one, so adding highlights to dark areas is easy.

Shape-holding ability
Like oil paint, acrylic paint that is applied thickly, straight from the tube, holds its shape and the mark of the brush as it dries, which can allow you to use interesting textures.

Palettes

The surface on which an artist arranges colours prior to mixing and applying them to the support is known as the palette. (Somewhat confusingly, the same word is also used to describe the range of colours used by a particular artist, or the range of colours found in a painting.) The type of palette that you use depends on the medium in which you are working, but you will undoubtedly find that you need more space for mixing colours than you might imagine. A small palette gets filled with colour mixes very quickly and it is a false economy to clean the mixing area too often: you may be cleaning away usable paint or mixed colours that you might want to use again. Always buy the largest palette practical.

Wooden palettes

Flat wooden palettes in the traditional kidney or rectangular shapes with a thumb hole are intended for use with oil paints. They are made from hardwood, or from the more economical plywood.

Before you use a wooden palette with oil paint for the first time, rub linseed oil into the surface of both sides. Allow it to permeate the surface. This will prevent oil from the paint from being absorbed into the surface of the palette and will make it easier to clean. Re-apply linseed oil periodically and a good wooden palette will last for ever.

Wooden palettes are not recommended for acrylic paint, however, as hardened acrylic paint can be difficult to remove from the surface.

Holding and using the palette ▼
Place your thumb through the thumb hole and balance the palette on your arm. Arrange pure colour around the edge. Position the dipper(s) at a convenient point, leaving the centre of the palette free for mixing colours.

Wooden palette ▲
Artists working with oil paints generally prefer a wooden palette. Always buy one that is large enough to hold all the paint and mixes that you intend to use.

White palettes

Plastic palettes are uniformly white. They are made in both the traditional flat kidney and rectangular shapes. The surface is impervious, which makes them ideal for use with either oil or acrylic paint. They are easy to clean, but the surface can become stained after using very strong colours such as viridian or phthalocyanine blue.

There are also plastic palettes with wells and recesses, intended for use with watercolour and gouache. The choice of shape is entirely subjective, but it should be of a reasonable size.

White porcelain palettes offer limited space for mixing. Intended for use with watercolour and gouache, they are aesthetically pleasing but can easily be chipped and broken.

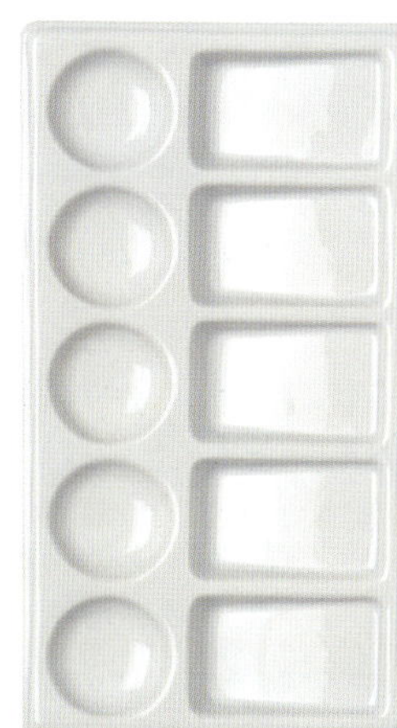

Slanted-well palette ▲
This type of porcelain palette is used for mixing gouache or watercolour. The individual colours are placed in the round wells and mixed in the rectangular sections.

Disposable palettes

A relatively recent innovation is the disposable paper palette, which can be used with both oils and acrylics. These come in a block and are made from an impervious parchment-like paper. A thumb hole punched through the block enables it to be held in the same way as a traditional palette; alternatively, it can be placed flat on a surface. Once the work is finished, the used sheet is torn off and thrown away.

Paper palette ▲
Disposable palettes are convenient and make cleaning up after a painting session an easy task.

Stay-wet palette

Intended for use with acrylic paints, the stay-wet palette will stop paints from drying out and becoming unworkable if left exposed to the air for any length of time. The palette consists of a shallow, recessed tray into which a water-impregnated membrane is placed. The paint is placed and mixed on this membrane, which prevents the paint from drying out. If you want to leave a painting halfway through and come back to it later, you can place a plastic cover over the tray, sealing the moist paint in the palette. This prevents the water from evaporating and the paint from becoming hard and unusable. The entire palette can be stored in a cool place or even in the refrigerator. If the membrane does dry out, simply re-wet it.

Stay-wet palette ►
This type of palette, in which the paint is mixed on a water-impregnated membrane, prevents acrylic paint from drying out. If you like, you can simply spray acrylic paint with water to keep it moist while you work.

Containers for water, solvents and oil

Although a regular supply of containers, such as empty jam jars, can be recycled from household waste and are just as good as a container bought for the purpose, several types of specially designed containers are available from art supply stores.

Among the most useful are dippers – small, open containers for oil and solvent that clip on to the edge of the traditional palette. Some have screw or clip-on lids to prevent the solvent from evaporating when it is not in use. You can buy both single and double dippers, like the one shown on the right. Dippers are useful when you want to work at speed.

Dipper ▼
Used in oil painting, dippers are clipped on to the side of the palette and contain small amounts of oil or medium and thinner.

Improvised palettes

For work in the studio, any number of impermeable surfaces and containers can be used as palettes. Perhaps the most adaptable is a sheet of thick counter glass, which you can buy from a glazier; the glass should be at least ¼in (5mm) thick and the edges should be polished smooth. Glass is easy to clean and any type of paint can be mixed on it. To see if your colours will work on the support you have chosen to use, slip a sheet of paper the same colour as the support beneath the glass.

Aluminium-foil food containers, tin cans, glass jars, paper and polystyrene cups also make useful and inexpensive containers for mixing large quantities of paint and for holding water or solvents. Take care not to put oil solvents in plastic or polystyrene containers, though, as the containers may dissolve.

Additives

Artists working with oils and acrylics will need to explore paint additives, which help attain various textures and effects in their work. Although oil paint can be used straight from the tube, it is usual to alter the paint's consistency by adding a mixture of oil or thinner (solvent). Simply transfer the additive to the palette a little at a time and mix it with the paint. Manufacturers of acrylic paints have also introduced a range of mediums and additives that allow artists to use the paint to its full effect.Oils and mediums are used to alter the consistency of the paint, allowing it to be brushed out smoothly or to make it dry more quickly. Once exposed to air, the oils dry and leave behind a tough, leathery film that contains the pigment. Different oils have different properties – for example, linseed dries relatively quickly but yellows with age so is only used for darker colours.

A painting medium is a ready-mixed painting solution that may contain various oils, waxes and drying agents. The oils available are simply used as a self-mixed medium. Your choice of oil or medium will depend on several factors, including cost, the type of finish required, the thickness of the paint being used and the range of colours.

There are several alkyd-based mediums on the market. They all accelerate the drying time of the paint, which can help to considerably lessen the waiting time between each application of paint. Some alkyd mediums are thixotropic; these are initially stiff and gel-like but, once worked, become clear and loose. Other alkyd mediums contain inert silica and add body to the paint; useful for impasto techniques where a thick mix of paint is required. Discussing your work with an art stockist will help you decide which additives you need.

Oils and thinners

There are a great many oils and thinners available. The more common ones are listed below.

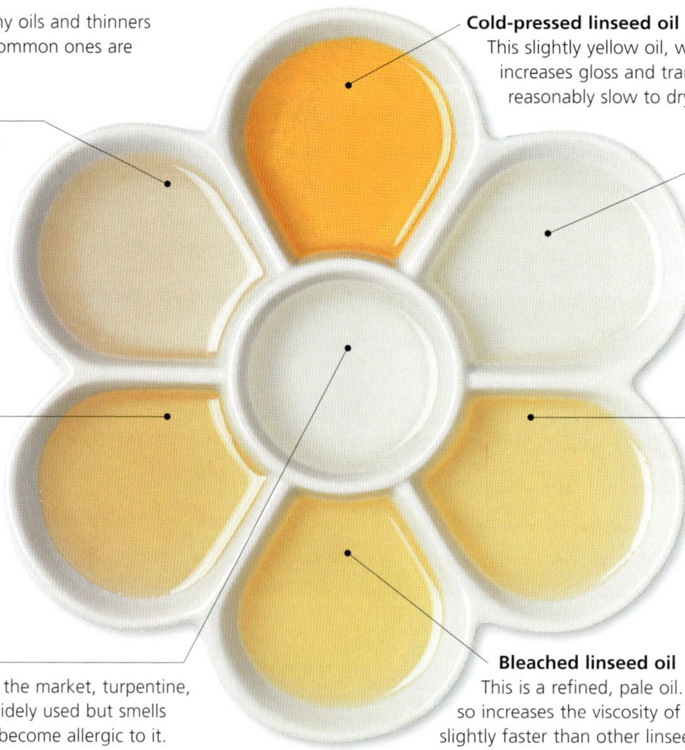

Poppy oil
Slow drying poppy oil is very pale and is traditionally used with pale colours to ensure that they do not yellow over time. Paint mixed with poppy oil has a beautiful buttery consistency.

Stand linseed oil
A pale oil that is slightly thicker than other linseeds. It is very slow to dry but leaves the paint with a tough, flexible finish.

Thinner
Of all the thinners on the market, turpentine, shown here, is very widely used but smells strong. Some people become allergic to it.

Cold-pressed linseed oil
This slightly yellow oil, when mixed with paint, increases gloss and transparency. It is reasonably slow to dry.

Safflower oil
Like poppy oil, safflower oil is traditionally used with light colours. It also slows down the drying time of the paint.

Refined linseed oil
Slow to dry and pale yellow in colour, refined linseed oil increases gloss and flow.

Bleached linseed oil
This is a refined, pale oil. It flows very easily, and so increases the viscosity of the paint. It dries slightly faster than other linseeds.

Thinners

The amount of thinner that you use depends on how loose or fluid you want the paint to be. If you use too much, however, the paint film may become weak and prone to cracking.

Ideally, any thinner that you use should be clear and should evaporate easily from the surface of the painting without leaving any residue.

Turpentine

Turpentine is the strongest and best of all the thinners used in oil painting. It has a very strong smell. Old turpentine can discolour and become gummy if exposed to air and light. To help prevent this, store it in cans or dark glass jars.

White spirit

Paint thinner or white spirit is clear and has a milder smell than turpentine. It does not deteriorate and dries faster than turpentine. However, it can leave the paint surface matt.

Oil of spike lavender

Unlike other solvents, which speed up the drying time of oil paint, oil of spike lavender slows the drying time. It is very expensive. Like turpentine and white spirit, it is colourless.

Low-odour thinners

Various low-odour thinners have come on to the market in recent years. The drawback of low-odour thinners is that they are relatively expensive and dry slowly.

Citrus solvents

You may be able to find citrus thinners. They are thicker than turpentine or white spirit but smell wonderful. They are more expensive than traditional thinners and slow to evaporate.

Liquin

Liquin is just one of a number of alkyd painting mediums that speed up drying time considerably – often to just a few hours. It also improves flow and increases the flexibility of the paint film. It is excellent for use in glazes.

Acrylic additives

Acrylic paints dry to leave a matt or slightly glossy surface. Gloss or matt mediums can be added, singly or mixed, to leave the surface with the desired finish. A gloss surface tends to make colours look brighter.

Gloss and matt mediums ▲
Both gloss (left) and matt (right) mediums are relatively thin white liquids that dry clear if applied to a support without being mixed with paint. Matt medium increases transparency and can be used to make matt glazes, but as a varnish can deaden colour. Gloss will enhance the depth of colour.

Flow-improving mediums

Adding flow-improving mediums reduces the water tension, increasing the flow of the paint and its absorption into the surface of the support.

One of the most useful applications for flow-improving medium is to add a few drops to very thin paint, which can tend to puddle rather than brush out evenly across the surface of the support. This is ideal when you want to tone the ground with a thin layer of acrylic before you begin your painting.

When a flow-improving medium is used with slightly thicker paint, a level surface will result, with little or no evidence of brushstrokes.

The medium can also be mixed with paint that is to be sprayed, as it assists the flow of paint and helps to prevent blockages within the spraying mechanism.

Retarding mediums

Acrylic paints dry quickly. Although this is generally considered to be an advantage, there are occasions when you might want to take your time over a particular technique or a specific area of a painting – when you are blending colours together or working wet paint into wet, for example. Adding a little retarding medium slows down the drying time of the paint considerably, keeping it workable for longer.

Gel mediums

With the same consistency as tube colour, gel mediums are available as matt or gloss finishes. They are added to the paint in the same way as fluid mediums. They increase the brilliance and transparency of the paint, while maintaining its thicker consistency. Gel medium is an excellent adhesive and extends drying time. It can be mixed with various substances such as sand or sawdust to create textural effects.

The effect of modelling paste ▼
Modelling pastes dry to give a hard finish, which can be sanded or carved into using a sharp knife.

The effect of heavy gel medium ▼
Mixed with acrylic paint, heavy gel medium forms a thick paint that is useful for impasto work.

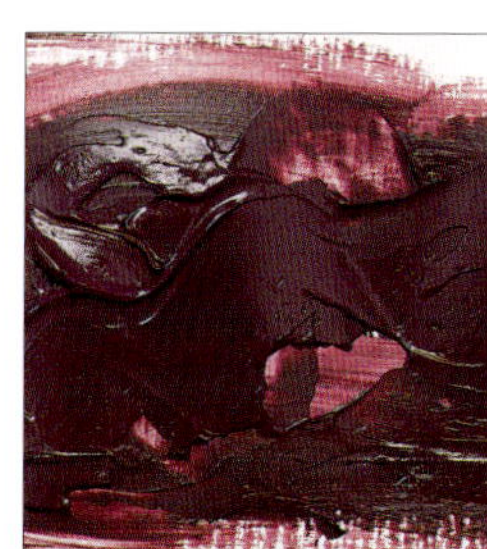

Paintbrushes

Oil-painting brushes are traditionally made from hog bristles, which hold their shape well and can also hold a substantial amount of paint. Natural hair brushes are usually used for watercolour and gouache, and can be used for acrylics and fine detail work in oils, if cleaned thoroughly afterwards.

Synthetic brushes are good quality and hard-wearing, and less expensive than either bristle or natural-hair brushes. However, they can quickly lose their shape if they are not looked after and cleaned well.

Cleaning brushes

1 Cleaning your brushes thoroughly will make them last longer. Wipe off any excess wet paint on a rag or a piece of newspaper. Take a palette knife and place it as close to the metal ferrule as possible. Working away from the ferrule towards the bristles, scrape off as much paint as you can.

2 Pour a small amount of household white spirit (paint thinner) – or water, if you are using a water-based paint such as acrylic or gouache – into a jar; you will need enough to cover the bristles of the brush. Agitate the brush in the jar, pressing it against the sides to dislodge any dried-on paint.

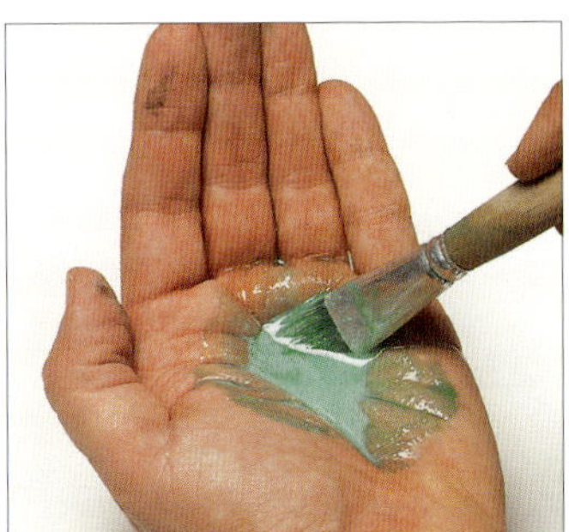

3 Rub household detergent into the bristles with your fingers. Rinse in clean water until the water runs clear. Reshape the bristles and store the brush in a jar with the bristles pointing upward, so that they hold their shape.

Brush shapes

Brushes for fine detail ▶
A rigger brush is very long and thin. It was originally invented for painting the straight lines of the ropes and rigging on ships in marine painting – hence the rather odd-sounding name. A liner is a flat brush which has the end cut away at an angle. Both of these brushes may be made from natural or synthetic fibres.

Rigger brush

Liner brush

Wash brushes ▶
The wash brush has a wide body, which holds a large quantity of paint. It is used for covering large areas with a uniform or flat wash of paint. There are two types of wash brush: rounded or 'mop' brushes, which are commonly used with watercolour and gouache, and flat wash brushes, which are more suited for use with oils and acrylics.

Rounded or "mop" brush

Flat wash brush

Flat brushes ▼
These brushes have square ends. They hold a lot of paint, which can be applied as short impasto strokes or brushed out flat. Large flat brushes are useful for blocking in and covering large areas quickly. Short flats, known as 'brights', hold less paint and are stiffer. They make precise, short strokes, ideal for impasto work and detail.

Large flat brush

Short flat brush

Round brushes ▼
These are round-headed brushes that are used for detail and for single-stroke marks. Larger round brushes hold a lot of paint and are useful for the initial blocking-in. The point on round brushes can quickly disappear, as it becomes worn down by the abrasive action of the rough support. The brushes shown here are made of natural hair.

Large round brush

Small round brush

Other paint applicators

Brushes are only part of the artist's toolbox. You can achieve great textual effects by using many other types of applicator, from knives to rags.

Artists' palette and painting knives

Palette knives are intended for mixing paint with additives on the palette, scraping up unwanted paint from the palette or support, and general cleaning. Good knives can also be found in DIY or decorating stores.

You can create a wide range of marks using painting knives. In general, the body of the blade is used to spread paint, the point for detail and the edge for making crisp linear marks.

Regardless of the type of knife you use, it is very important to clean it thoroughly after use. Paint that has dried on the blade will prevent fresh paint from flowing evenly off the blade. Do not use caustic paint strippers on plastic blades, as they will dissolve; instead, peel the paint away.

Steel knives ▲
A wide range of steel painting and palette knives is available. In order to work successfully with this method of paint application, you will need several.

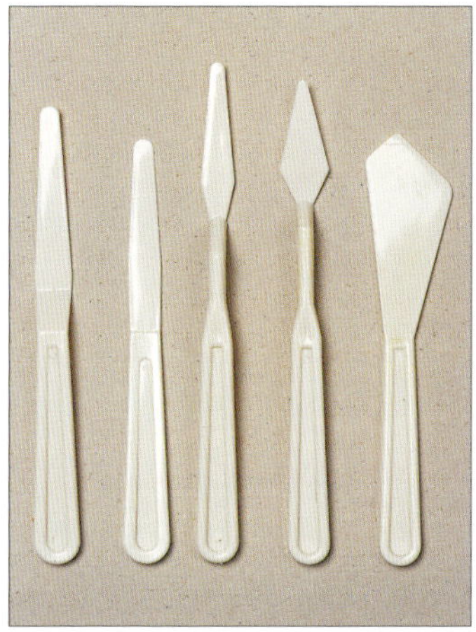

Plastic knives ▲
Less expensive and less durable than steel knives, plastic knives manipulate watercolour and gouache paints better than their steel counterparts.

Paint shapers

A relatively new addition to the artist's range of tools are paint shapers. They closely resemble brushes, but are used to move paint around in a way similar to that used when painting with a knife. Instead of bristle, fibre or hair, the shaper is made of a non-absorbent silicone rubber.

Foam and sponge applicators

Nylon foam is used to make both foam brushes and foam rollers. Both of these are available in a range of sizes and, while they are not intended as substitutes for the brush, they are used to bring a different quality to the marks they make.

Sponge applicators and paint shapers ▶
Shapers can be used to apply paint and create textures, and to remove wet paint. Foam rollers can cover large areas quickly. Sponge applicators are useful for initial blocking in.

Natural and man-made sponges
With their pleasing irregular texture, natural sponges are used to apply washes and textures, and are invaluable for spreading thin paint over large areas and for making textural marks. They are also useful for mopping up spilt paint and for wiping paint from the support in order to make corrections. They are especially useful to landscape artists. Man-made sponges can be cut to the desired shape and size and used in a similar fashion.

Alternative applicators

Paint can be applied and manipulated using almost anything. The only limitations are set by practicality and imagination. The cutlery drawer and tool box are perhaps a good starting point, but you will no doubt discover plenty of other items around the home that you can use. Cardboard, pieces of rag, wood, wire wool and many other seemingly unlikely objects can all be – quite literally – pressed into service.

Supports

A 'support' is the name for the surface on which a drawing or painting is made. It needs to be physically stable and resistant to deterioration from the corrosive materials used, as well as the atmosphere. It should also be light enough to be transported easily. Importantly, choose a support with the right texture for the media, marks and techniques you intend to use.

Drawing papers

Drawing papers vary enormously in quality and cost, depending on whether the paper is handmade, machine-made or mould-made. The thickness of a paper is described in one of two ways. The first is in pounds (lbs) and describes the weight of a ream (500 sheets). The second is in grams (gsm), and describes the weight of one square metre of a single sheet. Sheets vary considerably in size.

Many papers can also be bought in roll form and cut to the size required. You can also buy pads, which are lightly glued at one end, from which you tear off individual sheets as required. One of the benefits of buying a pad of paper is that it usually has a stiff cardboard back, which gives you a solid surface to lean on when working on location and means that you don't have to carry a heavy drawing board around with you. Sketchbooks have the same advantage.

The most common drawing paper has a smooth surface that is suitable for graphite, coloured pencil and ink work. Papers intended for use with watercolour also make ideal drawing supports. These papers come in three distinctly different surfaces – HP (hot-pressed) papers, which are smooth; CP (cold-pressed) papers, also known as NOT, or 'Not hot-pressed' papers, which have some surface texture; and rough papers which, not surprisingly, have a rougher texture.

Art and illustration boards are made from cardboard with paper laminated to the surface. They offer a stable, hard surface on which to work and are especially useful for pen line and wash, but can also be used with graphite and coloured pencil. They do not buckle when wet, as lightweight papers are prone to do, and are available in a range of sizes and surface textures, from very smooth to rough.

Coloured paper ▲
The main advantage of making a drawing on coloured paper is that you can choose a colour that complements the subject and enhances the mood of the drawing. Coloured papers can be used with all drawing media.

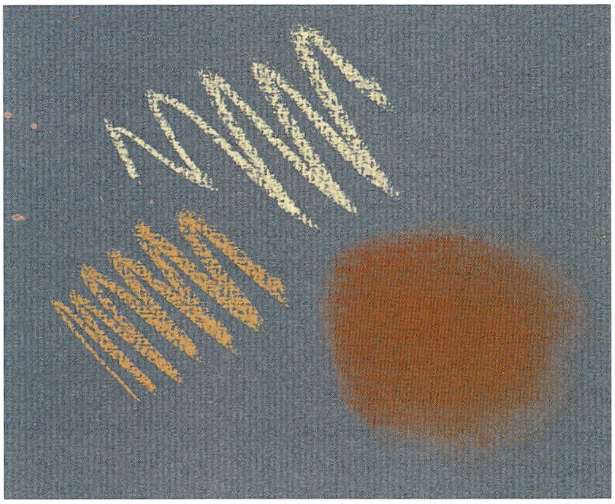

Pastel papers ▲
Papers for use with pastels are coated with pumice powder or tiny cork particles that hold the pigment and allow for a build-up of colour. They are available in a range of natural colours that complement the pastel shades.

Preparing your own surfaces

It is both satisfying and surprisingly easy to prepare your own drawing surfaces. Acrylic gesso, a kind of primer that is used to prepare a surface such as canvas or board when painting in oils or acrylics, can also be painted on to paper to give a brilliant white, hard surface that receives graphite and coloured pencil beautifully.

To make a surface that is suitable for pastels, you can mix the gesso with pumice powder. You can also buy ready-made pastel primer.

To create a toned or coloured ground, simply tint the gesso by adding a small amount of acrylic paint to it in the appropriate colour.

Painting papers

Papers for use with paints need to be carefully chosen. Some hold paint well, other papers are textured or smooth, and of course there are many different shades – all these factors will affect your final artwork.

Canvas paper and board ▶

Artists' canvas boards are made by laminating canvas – or paper textured to look like canvas – on to cardboard. They are made in several sizes and textures and are ideal for use when painting on location. However, take care not to get them wet, as the cardboard backing will disintegrate. They can also be easily damaged if you drop them on their corners. They are ready sized and can be used for painting in both oils and acrylics.

Paper and illustration board

Although best suited to works using water-based materials, paper and illustration board, provided it is primed with acrylic primer, can also be used for painting in oils.

Watercolour papers provide ideal surfaces for gouache work. The papers are found in various thicknesses and with three distinct surfaces – rough, hot-pressed (which is smooth) and NOT or cold-pressed, which has a slight texture. Watercolour boards tend to have either a rough or a hot-pressed surface. Illustration board tends to be very smooth and is intended for use with gouache and linework.

Tinted papers ▼

Although they are sometimes frowned upon by watercolour purists, tinted papers can be useful when you want to establish an overall colour key. Ready-made tinted papers are a good alternative to laying an initial flat wash.

Oil and acrylic papers

Both oil and acrylic papers have a texture similar to canvas and sheets can be bought loose or bound together in blocks. Although they are not suitable for work that is meant to last, they are perfect for sketching and colour notes.

Stretching paper for watercolours

Papers come in different weights, which refers to the weight of a ream (500 sheets) and can vary from 90lb (185 grams per square metre or gsm) to 300lb (640gsm) or more. The heavier the paper, the more absorbent. Papers that are less than 140lb (300gsm) in weight need to be stretched before use.

1 Dip a sponge in clean water and wipe it over the paper, making sure you leave no part untouched. Make sure a generous amount of water has been applied over the whole surface and that the paper is perfectly flat.

2 Moisten four lengths of gum strip and place one along each long side of the paper. (Only gummed brown paper tape is suitable; masking tape will not adhere.) Repeat for the short edge of the paper. Leave to dry. (In order to be certain that the paper will not lift, you could staple it to the board.)

Canvas

Without doubt, canvas is the most widely used support for both oil and acrylic work. Several types of canvas are available, made from different fibres. The most common are made from either cotton or linen, both of which can be purchased ready stretched and primed to a range of standard sizes (although there are suppliers who will prepare supports to any size) or on the roll by the yard (metre) either primed or unprimed. Unprimed canvas is easier to stretch.

Cotton duck ▼
Cotton duck has a more regular (some people might say more mechanical) weave than linen. It is also less expensive than linen.

Linen canvas ▼
Linen canvas is made from the fibres of the flax plant, *Linum usitatissimum*. The seeds of the plant are also pressed to make linseed oil, used by artists. Linen canvas is available in a number different textures and weights, from very fine to coarse. The fibres are stronger than cotton fibres, which means that the fabric is less likely to sag and stretch over time.

Stretching canvas

Canvas must be stretched taut over a rectangular wooden frame before use. For this you will need stretcher bars and wooden wedges.

Stretcher bars are usually made of pine and are sold in pairs of various standard lengths. They are pre-mitred and each end has a slot-in tenon joint. Longer bars are morticed to receive a cross bar (recommended for large supports over 75 x 100cm/30 x 40in).

1 Tap the bars together to make a frame. Arrange the canvas on a flat surface and put the frame on top. Staple the canvas to the back of the frame, ensuring it stays taut.

2 Tap wooden wedges lightly into the inside of each corner. These can be hammered in further to allow you to increase the tension and tautness of the canvas if necessary.

Priming canvas

Canvas is usually sized and primed (or, increasingly, just primed) prior to being worked on. This serves two purposes. The process not only tensions the fabric over the stretcher bars but also (and more importantly in the case of supports used for oil) seals and protects the fabric from the corrosive agents present in the paint and solvents. Priming also provides a smooth, clean surface on which to produce work.

In traditional preparation, the canvas is given a coat of glue size. The most widely used size is made from animal skin and bones and is known as rabbit-skin glue. It is available as dried granules or small slabs. When mixed with hot water the dried glue melts; the resulting liquid is brushed over the canvas to seal it.

Increasingly, acrylic emulsions are used to size canvas. Unlike rabbit-skin glue, the emulsions do not have to be heated but are used diluted with water.

The traditional partner to glue size is an oil-based primer. Lead white, which is toxic, together with titanium white and flake white, are all used in oil-based primers. To penetrate the canvas the primer should be the consistency of single cream; dilute it with white spirit (paint thinner) if necessary.

Traditional primer can take several days to dry, however; a modern alternative is an alkyd primer, which dries in a couple of hours.

Primers based on acrylic emulsion are easier to use. These are often known as acrylic gesso, although they are unlike traditional gesso. Acrylic primer should not be used over glue size, but it can be brushed directly on to the canvas. Acrylic primers can be used with both oil and acrylic paint, but oil primers should not be used with acrylic paints.

Primer can be applied with a brush or a palette knife. With a brush the weave of the canvas tends to show.

If you want to work on a toned ground, add a small amount of colour to the primer before you apply it. Add oil colour to oil primer and acrylic colour to acrylic primer.

Boards

Several types of wooden board make good supports for oil and acrylic work. Wood gives off acidic vapours that are detrimental to paint (for an example of how wood products deteriorate with age, think how quickly newspaper yellows). The solution is to prime the board with acrylic gesso, or glue canvas to the surface; a technique known as marouflaging. There are three types of board in common use: plywood, hardboard (masonite) and medium-density fibreboard (MDF). Plywood is made up of a wooden core sandwiched between a number of thin layers of wood glued together. Hardboard is a composite panel made by hot pressing steam-exploded wood fibres with resin, and is less prone to warping than solid wood or plywood. MDF is made in the same way, with the addition of a synthetic resin. It has a less hard and glossy face side than standard dense hardboard. All these boards come in a range of sizes. If used at a size where they begin to bend, mount rigid wooden battens on the reverse to reinforce them.

Priming board

Wood was traditionally sized with rabbit-skin glue and then primed with a thixotropic primer in the same way as canvas; nowadays, most artists use ready-made acrylic primer or acrylic gesso primer, which obviates the need for sizing. Acrylic primer also dries much more quickly.

Before you prime your boards, make sure they are smooth and free of dust. You should also wipe over them with methylated spirits to remove all traces of grease.

Using a wide, flat brush, apply primer over the board with smooth, vertical strokes. For a very large surface, apply the primer with a paint roller. Allow to dry. When it is dry, rub the surface of the board with fine-grade sandpaper to smooth out any ridges in the paint, and blow or dust off any powder. Apply another coat of primer, making smooth horizontal strokes and again allow to dry. Repeat as many times as you wish, sanding between coats.

Covering board with canvas

Canvas-covered board is a light painting surface that is useful when you are painting on location. It combines the strength and low cost of board with the texture of canvas. You can use linen, cotton duck or calico, which is cheap. When you have stuck the canvas to the board let it dry for two hours in a warm room. Prime the canvas with acrylic primer before use.

1 Arrange the canvas on a flat surface. Place the board on the canvas. Allowing a 5cm (2in) overlap all around, cut out the canvas. Remove the canvas and using a wide, flat brush, liberally brush matt acrylic medium over the board.

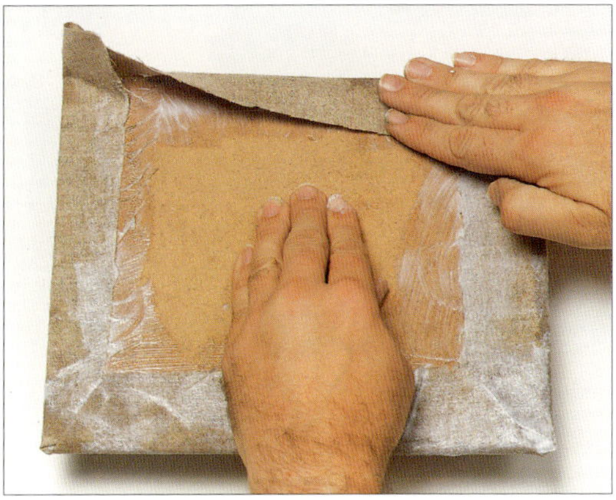

2 Place the canvas on the sticky side of the board and smooth it out with your fingertips, working from the centre outwards. Brush acrylic medium over the canvas to make sure that it is firmly stuck down. Place the board canvas-side down on an bowl so that it does not stick to your work surface. Brush acrylic medium around the edges of the board. Fold over the excess canvas, mitring the corners, and brush more medium over the corners to stick them firmly.

Additional equipment

There are a few other pieces of equipment that you will probably find useful in your painting, ranging from things to secure your work to the drawing board and easels to support your painting, to aids for specific painting techniques.

Boards and easels

The most important thing is that the surface on which you are working is completely flat and cannot wobble as you work. If you use blocks of watercolour paper, then the block itself will provide support; you can simply rest it on a table or on your knee. If you use sheets of watercolour paper, then they need to be firmly secured to a board. Buy firm boards that will not warp and buckle (45 x 60cm/18 x 24in is a useful size), and attach the paper to the board by means of gum strip or staples.

It is entirely a matter of personal preference as to whether or not you use an easel. There are several types on the market, but remember that watercolour paint is a very fluid liquid and can easily flow down the paper into areas that you don't want it to touch. Choose an easel that can be used flat and propped at only a slight angle. The upright easels used by oil painters are not really suitable for watercolour painting.

Other useful items

Other useful pieces of equipment include a scalpel or craft (utility) knife: the fine tip allows you to prise up pieces of masking tape that have become stuck down too firmly without damaging the paper. You can also use a scalpel to scratch off fine lines of paint – a technique known as sgrafitto. Absorbent kitchen paper is invaluable for cleaning out paint palettes and lifting off or softening the colour before it dries.

As you develop your painting style and techniques, you may want to add other equipment to the basic items shown here. You will probably assemble a selection of props, from bowls, vases and other objects for still lifes, to pieces of fabric and papers to use as backgrounds. Similarly, you may want to set aside pictures or photographs that appeal to you for use as reference material. The only real limit to what you can use is your imagination.

Box easel ▼
This easel includes a handy side drawer in which you can store brushes and other paraphernalia, as well as adjustable bars so that it can hold various sizes of drawing board firmly in place. Some easels can only be set at very steep angles, which is unsuitable for watercolour, so do check before you buy.

Table easel ▲
This inexpensive table easel is adequate for most artists' needs. Like the box easel it can be adjusted to a number of different angles, allowing you to alter the angle to suit the technique you are using. It can also be stored neatly.

Eraser ▲
A kneaded eraser is useful for correcting the pencil lines of your underdrawing, and for removing the lines so that they do not show through the paint on the finished painting.

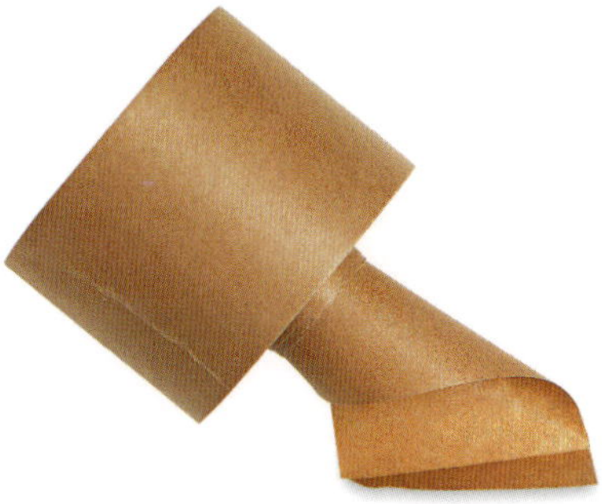

Gum strip ▲
Gummed brown paper strip is essential for taping stretched lightweight watercolour paper to a board, to ensure that it does not buckle when the water is applied. Leave the paper stretched on the drawing board until you have finished your painting and the paint has dried, then simply cut it off, using a scalpel or craft (utility) knife and a metal ruler, and discard. Masking tape cannot be used in place of gum strip for the purpose of taping stretched watercolour paper.

Gum arabic ▲
Adding gum arabic to watercolour paint increases the viscosity of the paint and slows down the drying time. This gives you longer to work, which is often what you need when painting detail or referring to a reference photo while you are painting. Add a few drops of the gum arabic to your paint and stir to blend. Gum arabic also imparts a slight sheen on the paper, which can be useful for certain subjects, and it increases the intensity of the paint colour.

Masking fluid and masking tape ▲
One of the most basic techniques in watercolour is masking. It is used to protect white areas of the paper so that they do not get splashed with paint, or when you want the white of the paper to represent the lighter areas of your subject. Depending on the size and shape of the area you want to protect, masking fluid and masking tape are the most commonly used materials. Masking tape can also be used to secure heavy watercolour paper to the drawing board.

> **Tips:**
> • Store small painting accessories such as sponges and rolls of tape in lidded boxes to keep things tidy.
> • Store bottles upright and always put the lids back on immediately after use to prevent spillage. Wash sponges immediately after use.

Sponge ▲
Natural or synthetic sponges are useful for mopping up excess water. Small pieces of sponge can be used to lift off colour from wet paint. Sponges are also commonly used to apply paint, with the pitted surface of the sponge creating interesting textures on the paper.

Mahl stick ▼
A useful piece of equipment when oil painting at an easel, the malh stick is a rod of wood (bamboo) with a soft leather ball at one end. It can be positioned over the work and leant on, to steady the painting hand and protect your work from being smudged.

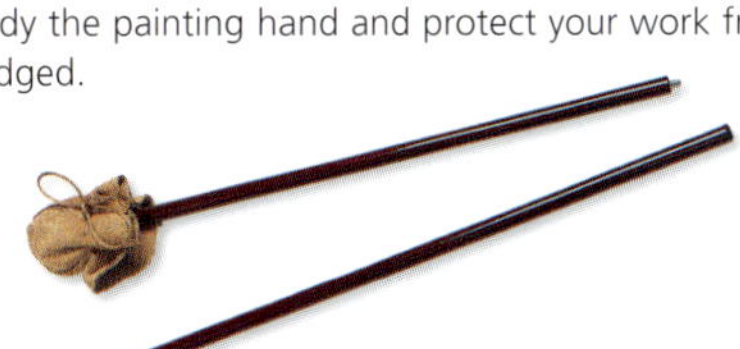

Tutorials

This chapter consists of a series of lessons on the technical aspects of drawing and painting people. Careful observation lies at the basis of all good representational drawing and painting. We begin by looking at the basic shape of the human head and at how to measure and place the features. This is followed by an introduction to simple human anatomy: you do not need a detailed knowledge, but if you understand basic skeletal and muscular structures you have a much better chance of being able to 'read' your model's pose and interpret it accurately. We then move on to drawing and painting individual features in more detail.

Of course, good portraits and nude studies are about much more than simply getting a good likeness. The composition, lighting, props and background that you choose are an integral and essential part of the whole, as is capturing the personality of your subject. The last part of this chapter examines all these topics and is packed with ideas and useful tips that you can incorporate into your own work.

The head

One of the most common mistakes that beginners make when they are drawing a portrait is to try to put in too much detail in the very early stages. The most important thing to remember is that, as with any subject, you need to start by getting the basic shape right.

Although every head is different, and you have to learn to carefully observe your subject and measure the individual parts and the distances between them, it is nevertheless possible to set out some general guidelines that you can use as a starting point.

Start by practising viewing the head from straight on, to get used to looking at the general shape. From this angle the head is not a perfect circle, as often seen in children's drawings, but an egg shape, so begin with that.

Drawing the basic shape of the head

Draw this basic shape, keeping your initial marks quite light so that you can alter them if necessary. Build up the shape from the inside, making a series of curved marks that go around the shape and across it, so that you start to build up a three-dimensional sense of the form rather than a contour. In this way your hand is also working rhythmically, building up the shape without getting engrossed in the detail.

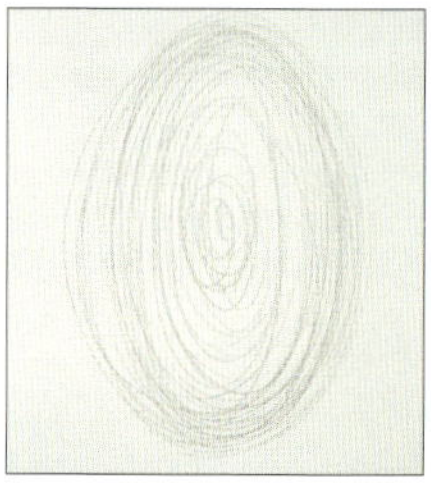

1 Start by drawing a series of curves.

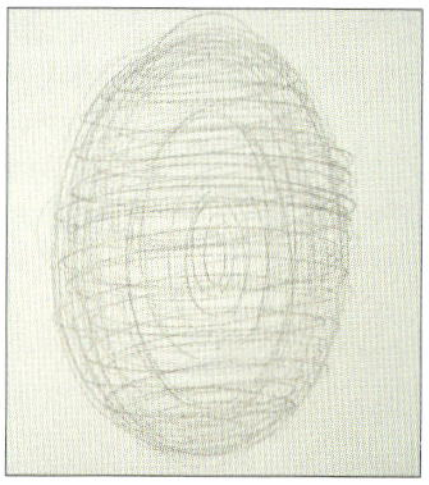

2 Then add more spherical movements.

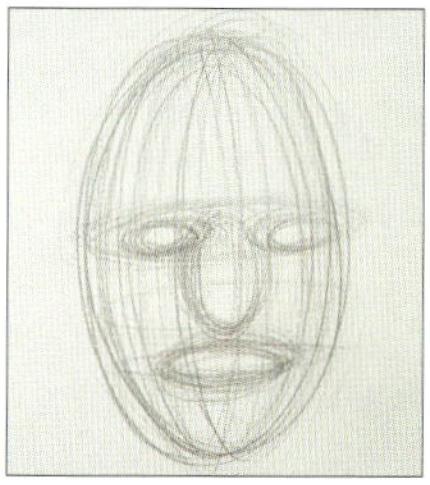

3 Add spheres and ovals for the features.

Positioning the facial features

Once you're used to the basic shape of the head, you can then begin to look at where the individual features of the face are positioned. Draw a line dividing the face from top to bottom, passing between the eyes, down the bridge of the nose, through the centre of the mouth and chin and through the neck. All the facial features are positioned symmetrically on either side of the face, so you can use this central line to check that you are placing them correctly.

Now lightly draw a series of lines across the face to mark the position of the facial features – the corners of the eyes, the top and bottom of the nose and the corners of the mouth. (Even the most experienced of artists often draw lines like this, which are known as 'construction lines', in the early stages of a portrait.) However, the exact positions will vary from one person to another, so careful measuring is essential.

General guidelines ▶
Although everyone's face is different, you can use these basic guides for assistance. Remember that these rules apply only when the head is viewed from straight on.

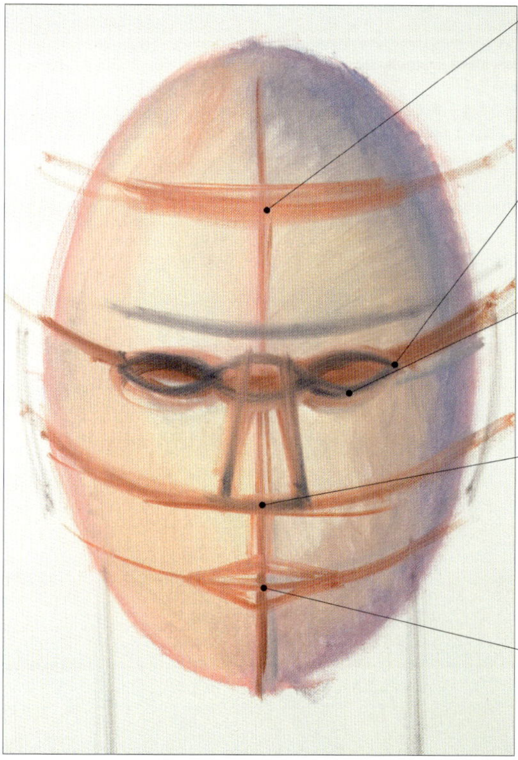

The hairline is the point at which the front plane of the face moves to the top plane of the skull.

The corners of the eyes are roughly level with the tips of the ears.

The base of the eye socket is located approximately halfway down the facial area.

The base of the nose is roughly halfway between the eyes and the base of the chin, and level with the lobes of the ears.

The mouth is less than halfway between the base of the nose and the tip of the chin.

The features in an inverted triangle

Another useful way of checking the position of the facial features is to draw an inverted triangle. There are two ways of doing this. You can either draw a horizontal line across to the outer corner of each eye and a line down from the corner of each eye to the chin (shown right, in blue) or alternatively, draw lines down from the outer corners of the eyes to the middle of the lips (shown right, in red). If the mouth extends beyond the side edges of the triangle, or the chin is below the apex, then you have probably positioned them incorrectly and need to re-measure – although, of course, people vary considerably, so you must judge with your eye as well.

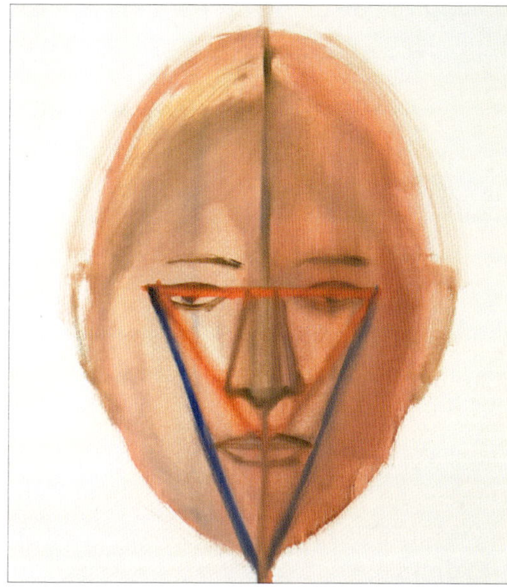

Inverted triangles as construction lines ▶
In most people, all the facial features should be contained within these inverted triangles, so you can use them to check that you haven't made the mouth too wide or placed the chin too low down.

The head from different viewpoints

If you look at your sitter from above or below, then the relative positions of the features will alter. Measuring becomes even more important and you must train yourself to do this rather than rely on any prior knowledge of where the features are in relation to each other. Put in the central axis through the face, as before, then take careful measurements to establish where the features should be placed exactly – and keep measuring as you draw to ensure you are still on track.

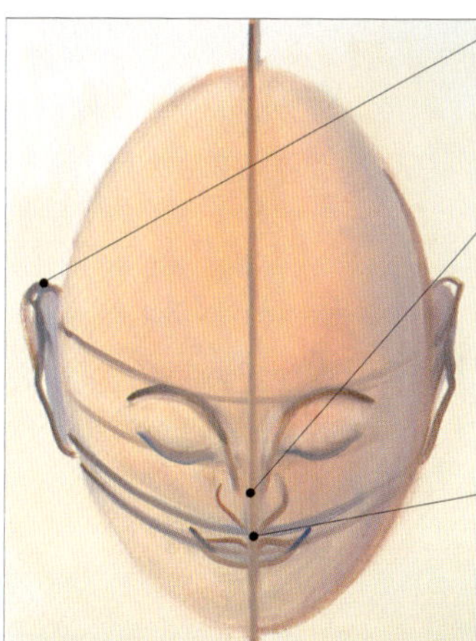

Head tilted forwards ▲
When the head is tilted forwards – as it might be, for example, if your model is reading a book – you can see more of the cranium and less of the facial features.

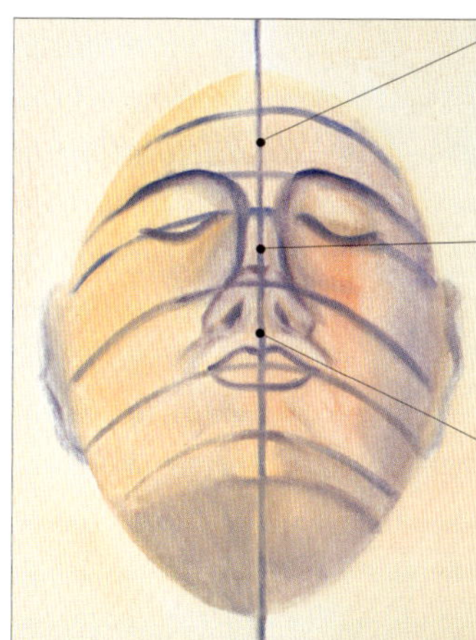

Head tilted backwards ▲
When the model is looking up and his or her head is tilted backwards, you can see very little of the cranium. The lower part of the face, from nose to chin, takes up a larger proportion of the facial area.

▶

Making the head look three-dimensional

In addition to placing the facial features correctly, you also need to make the head look three-dimensional. To do this you need to create a sense of the major planes – the front, the sides, the top and the underside. No matter what subject you're drawing, a good principle is to try to think of it as a basic geometric shape – a sphere, a box, a cylinder or a cone. You will find that even the most complicated of subjects can often be looked at in this way. So think of the skull as a box. Draw (lightly) a box around the basic egg shape, noting where the different planes occur.

The number of planes that you see will vary depending on your viewpoint. From straight on, you see only one plane – the front. But if you look at the head from the side on and from the same eye level, you will see two planes – the side and the front. And if you look at the head from above or below, you will see three planes – the top (or underside), side and front.

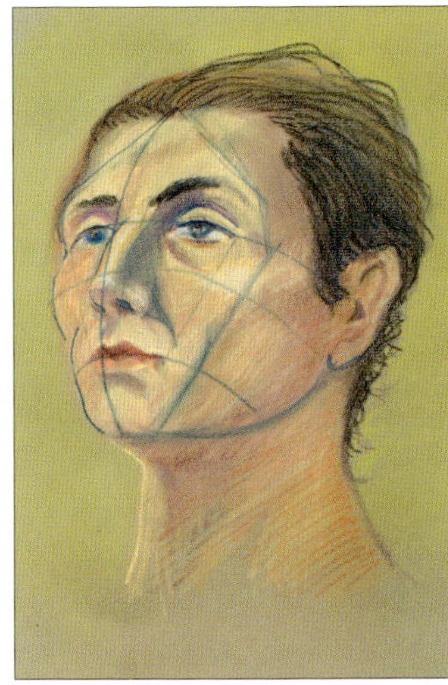

Visible planes depending on viewpoint ▲
In making this sketch, the artist was positioned slightly to one side of the model. As a result, we can see two major planes (the side and the front) and, as the model's head is tilted upwards, a suggestion of a third plane underneath. Marking the position of the different planes, however lightly, is a good idea for beginners.

Drawing the major planes of the head

1 Draw the egg shape of the face inside a box and draw a central perpendicular and horizontal axis.

2 Now draw the box at different angles (but don't worry too much about the perspective at this stage). Depending on your viewpoint and the tilt of the head, you will see different planes and perhaps even different numbers of planes.

Drawing the minor planes of the head

Up to now we've only looked at the very simple planes of the sides of the enclosing box. Within the head, however, there are many more planes that you need to capture. The nose is perhaps the most obvious, as it juts forward from the front of the box: it has four major planes – two sides, the top and the underside. But there are other less extreme planes, too – for example, within the forehead, across the cheekbones and under the chin. Try exploring your own face with your fingertips to see where these changes in plane, which define the underlying bone structure, occur. They are gradual but essential if you are to create a convincingly three-dimensional rendition of your subject.

Minor planes ►
This sketch demonstrates breaking up the surface of the face into a number of different planes, depending on the underlying bone structure. Here we can clearly see the top plane of the head; the other major planes have been subdivided into smaller planes.

Using tone to create a three-dimensional impression

Up to this point, we've looked primarily at drawing the head using only line. Thinking of the head as a box, rather than a flat two-dimensional object, is the first step. Now you should begin to use tone – cross-hatching in pencil, shading with the side of a stick of charcoal or pastel, or applying a light wash in watercolour or acrylics – to create a sense of light and shade.

Changes in tone occur when the planes of the face and head change direction – for example, if your model is lit from the side, the side of the face nearest the light source will be light, while the side furthest away from it will be dark – and there will be a whole host of mid-tones in between.

The images here show a plaster-cast head of the French writer and philosopher Voltaire, lit from different directions. Where light falls directly on the subject, very little detail is discernible. But on the sides that are turned away from the light, strong shadows are formed – and these show up the muscle formation and bone structure, making the cast look three-dimensional.

Lit from the left, almost full profile ▼
Here, the light was positioned to the left of the plaster cast and slightly above it. As a result, the forehead is brightly illuminated: the artist left the paper untouched in this part of the drawing. On the left side of the head, (the right side as we look at the drawing), a mid-tone is used to draw deep shadows that reveal the sunken cheeks and indentations in the skull. The slab of the neck is drawn using a tone that is even darker, as virtually no direct light hits this part of the cast.

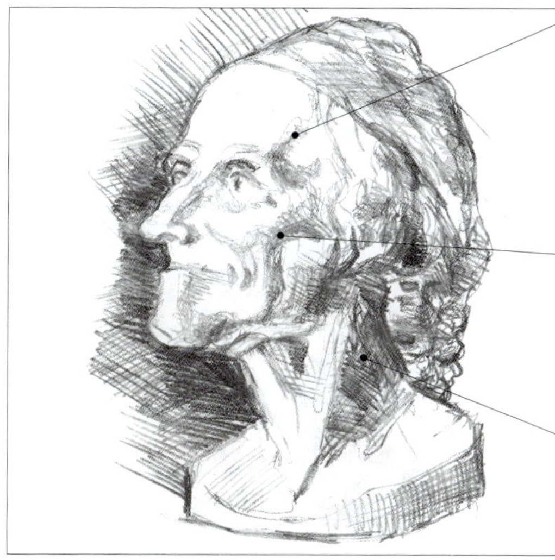

Light pencil marks indicate the change in plane from the brightly lit front of the skull to the shadowed side.

A mid-tone reveals the planes of the cheekbones.

Very little direct light reaches the side of the neck and so a very dark tone is used here.

Lit from left, almost full face ▲
Here, the cast was turned to show more of the face. The light is shining from the left, so everything on the other side of the rather prominent nose is in shadow.

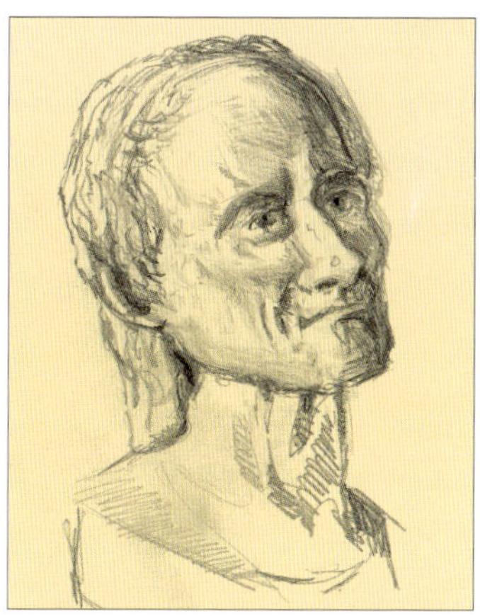

Lit from left, three-quarters view ▲
Here the light was again positioned to the left – but slightly lower, almost level with the cast – and the cast was turned further to the right, emphasizing different features.

Lit from front, full face ▲
With the light in front and slightly to the right, the right side of the face is shaded. Note how the lighting flattens out the features: the cheekbones, in particular, look less angular.

The skull bones and muscles

You do not need to know the names of all the bones and muscles in the skull, but by knowing something of the skull's proportions, shapes and rhythms, you will have a much better understanding of how the flesh can reveal a true sense of the underlying form. If you have access to a model of a skull, draw it. If you do not, practise by referring to anatomy books.

The bones of the skull

The skull has both convex and concave surfaces. Convex forms protrude and are visible beneath the surface of the flesh at the brow, the cheeks and chin and jaw. The concave cavities are not visible on the surface: the eye sockets, for example, appear huge, but they are filled with the eyes and surrounding flesh of the eyelids.

Unlike most of the other bones in the body, the skull is not covered by large amounts of muscles and tissue – so the form of the head and face closely follow the form of the skull beneath. Once you know the general shape of the skull, you will then have some idea of the shapes to look for when drawing or painting the head – although the relative sizes, shapes and distances between different areas of the skull vary considerably from one person to another.

The structure of the skull ▼
The skull consists of only two separate parts – the mandible (or jawbone) and the cranium (which encloses the brain). Shown here are the bones that are most relevant to the artist. It is important to remember, however, that every individual's skull is slightly different. It is these differences that play an important part in making us recognizable as individuals.

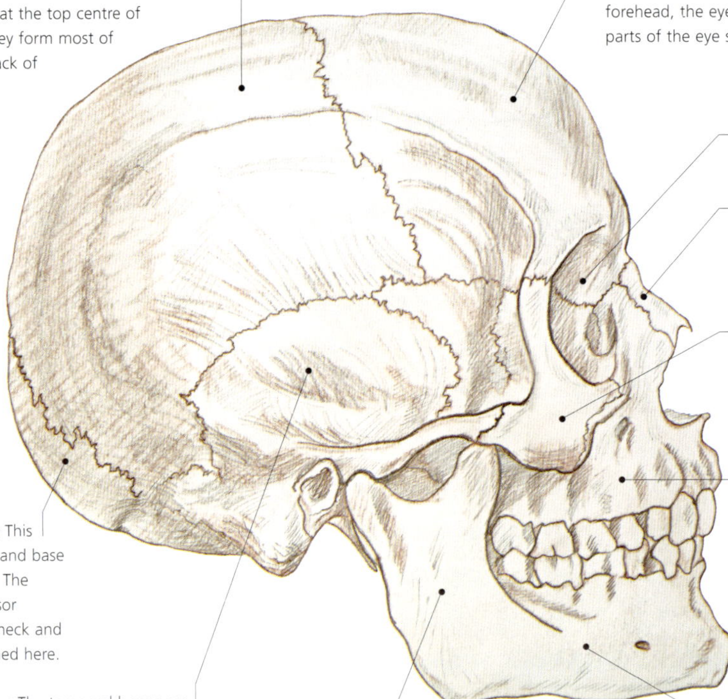

Parietal bone There are two parietal bones, joined together at the top centre of the cranium. They form most of the sides and back of the cranium.

Frontal bone The frontal bone forms the forehead, the eyebrow ridges and the upper parts of the eye sockets.

Orbital cavity This is the eye socket.

Nasal bones The two nasal bones form the bridge of the nose.

Zygomatic bones These are the cheek bones and form part of the lower rims of the eye sockets.

Maxillae The two maxillae form the upper jaw and extend into the eye sockets; they also join with the nasal bones to form the bony shape of the sides of the nose.

Occipital bone This forms the back and base of the cranium. The powerful extensor muscles of the neck and spine are attached here.

Temporal bones The temporal bones are at the side of the skull and include the external ear hole.

Ramus Each ramus of the mandible has two upward-pointing projections, one of which articulates with the temporal bone to form the mandibular joint, making it possible for the lower jaw to move.

Mandible This is the lower jaw and comprises a rounded V-shaped body and a ramus on each side that projects upwards.

The muscles of the head

In some areas of the head it is the muscles, rather than the bones of the skull, that determine the surface form. These muscles that move the facial features and give the face a range of expressions are known as the mimetic muscles. In most of the mimetic muscles, very little force is required. The muscles of mastication, which act on the mandible, are capable of exerting considerable force; the masseter is the most prominent of these.

The mimetic muscles ▼
Knowing a little bit about where the mimetic muscles occur and the effect that they have on the surface of the skin can help you to read and capture your model's mood and expression. For example, you will know which muscles are working to make a smile. Remember, when you create a portrait you are not just drawing or painting a face – you are trying to express a personality.

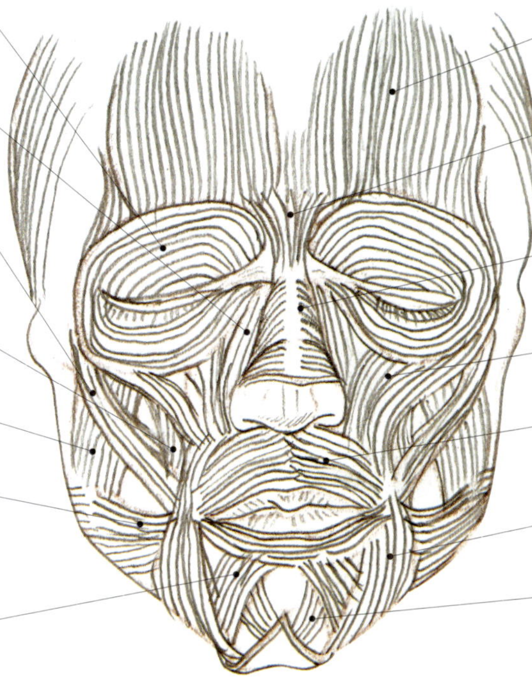

Orbicularis oculi Is concerned with blinking and closing the eyelid.

Levator labii superioris alaeque nasi Raises the nostrils and upper lip and slightly lifts the tip of the nose.

Zygomaticus major Lifts the corner of the mouth up and sideways.

Levator anguli oris Lifts the mouth upwards.

Masseter Lifts the mandible and closes the jaws.

Rissorius Works with the zygomaticus major to create the folds around the mouth when you laugh or smile.

Depressor labii inferioris Pulls the lower lip downwards.

Occipitofrontalis Moves the skin of the forehead and eyebrows.

Procerus Creates the fold in the top of the nose and wrinkles the bridge of the nose.

Nasalis Pulls the sides of the nose downwards and backwards.

Levator labii superioris Lifts and furrows the upper lip.

Orbicularis oris Closes and purses the mouth.

Depressor anguli oris Pulls the mouth downwards.

Mentalis Produces the horizontal furrow between the chin and lower lip.

Frowning man ◄
When you frown, the skin on your forehead wrinkles; the occipitofrontalis muscle, which is located just below the surface of the skin, enables this movement. The procerus creates the fold at the bridge of the nose. Also, the chin may lower; the mouth may pucker.

Laughing girl ►
When you laugh or smile, your mouth stretches out to the sides; at the same time, deep folds are created on either side of the base of the nose; this is achieved through the movement of the rissorius and zygomaticus major muscles. The eyes and brow also move.

The facial features

Once you've mastered the position of the facial features, have a go at drawing each one by itself. In addition to giving you much-needed practice in observing and drawing what you see, this will also give you an insight into just how different people's appearances can be. The differences between one eye and its neighbour, the crookedness or straightness of the bridge of the nose or the fullness or thinness of someone's lips – all these are part of the individual's unique appearance. If you can't persuade anyone to pose for you, do a self-portrait or draw from photographs.

The eyes

The eyeball is a spherical form and it is important to make it look rounded. The way to do this, as with any rounded form, is to use light and dark tones to imply the curvature of the surface, which requires very careful observation on your part. The darks are strongest where the form comes forward, usually around the pupil. The upper eyelid generally casts a band of shadow across the upper part of the eye.

The highlights are strongest near the top of the iris, close to the pupil, as this is the zenith of the curvature of the eye. In oils, you can either let the darks dry first and then put in the highlight; alternatively, you can work wet into wet and put in the highlight in thicker paint with a rapid, light brushstroke. In watercolour, you need to leave a point of light, or use masking fluid to keep a spot of the paper white.

Another option with both oil and watercolour paint is to lift out the highlights.

The white of the eye is not pure white; it is often shadowed and may reflect a bright highlight. The eyelashes are larger and more visible on the upper lid than on the lower lid. Do not try to paint or draw every single eyelash; instead, put in a dark line to give an impression of eyelashes.

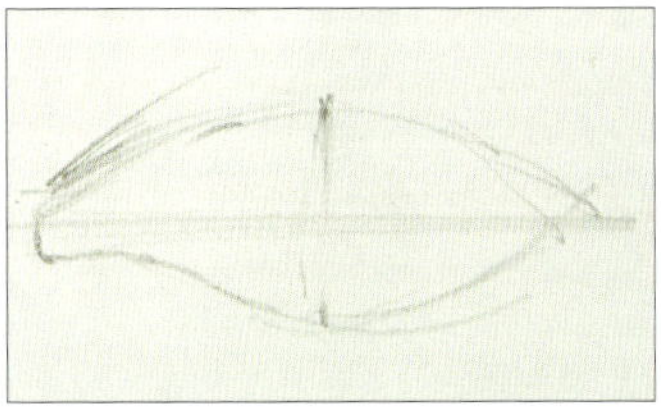

Central axis ▲
To start with, establish a central axis running through both eyes, so that you do not position one higher than the other. Establish the corners of each eye, measuring the space between the eyes.

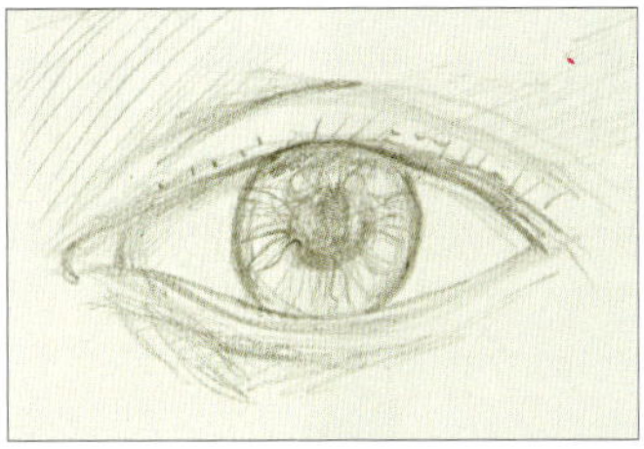

The shape of the eye ▲
Then look at the shape of the individual eyes – how far open or closed are they? Draw the visible part of the iris; remembering that we rarely see the complete circle of the iris, as the upper lid usually obscures the top – especially in older people.

Shadows in the eye ▲
Pay attention to the lights and darks: the upper lids and eyelashes usually cast a shadow on to the eye. Here, a shadow is cast in the socket and underneath the brow. There is a faint bluish shadow in the eye, which accentuates the white.

The nose and nostrils

At first glance, the nose looks a rather complicated shape to draw, so simplify things by thinking of it initially as a matchbox turned on its side; this makes it easier to see the individual planes. The nose has four distinct planes – the bridge, two side planes moving from the bridge to the cheeks, and the plane underneath the tip of the nose where we see the dark of the nostrils.

On the lower nose there are so many changes in direction, from convex to concave, that it may be difficult to see the separate planes. The way that these convex and concave forms face into or away from the light source means that the nostrils always appear dark – but these contrasts in tone are relative to the other areas of shadow under the nose and on the upper lip. Take care not to make them too dark and flat – look carefully at the colours and tones within the shadow.

Highlights usually appear at the edge where two planes meet, as at the junction between the bridge and side planes of the nose and on the tip of the nose. There will also be reflected mid-tones in the plane underneath, around the dark of the nostrils.

The shape of the nose ▲
Although the nose may have many curves and bumps within it, try to think of it as a box shape, like an upended matchbox, in which the individual planes – the two sides, the bridge and the underside – can be clearly defined.

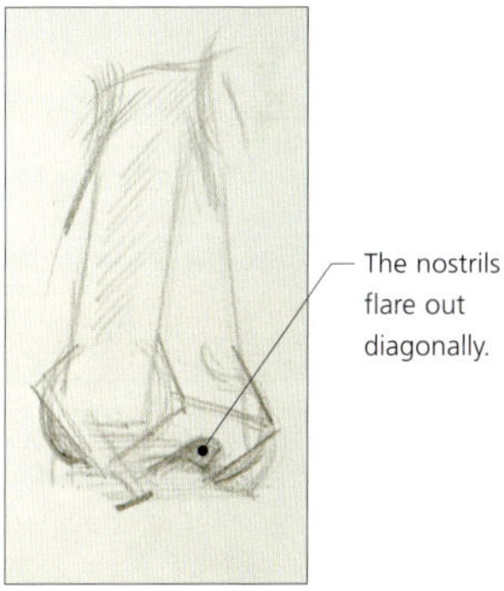

The shape of the nostrils ▲
The nostrils have planes that catch the light and cast shadows. The dark part of the nostril should be considered as part of the underside of the nose.

Highlights ▲
Areas of light appear on the bridge, in the nostrils and at the end of the nose.

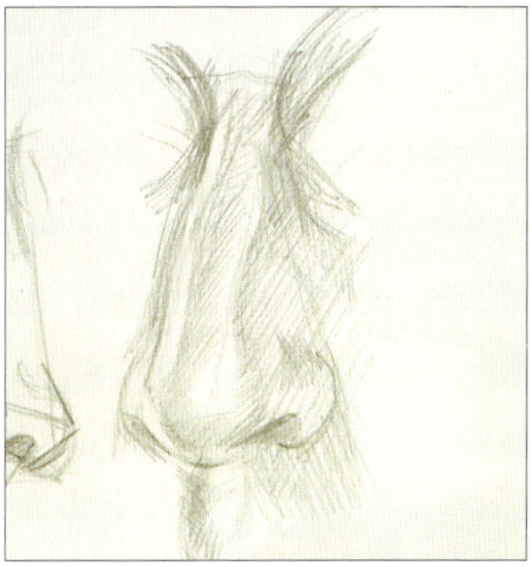

The planes of the nose ▲
Most people's noses change near this point on the bridge of the nose – the transition from bone to cartilage. Light reflects into the shadow under the nose and on the upper lip. Look very carefully: this is not solid shadow.

The mouth

Regardless of whether a person's lips are thin or full, they are pushed outwards by the teeth and follow the curve of the teeth – even though, from the front, the lips appear to be almost on a straight axis. The top lip often appears darker than the bottom lip because the plane of the top lip angles away from light above. (You can see this more clearly if you look at someone's mouth from the side.)

The philtrum is the groove of flesh in the upper lip, which gives the top lip its shape in the middle. This 'valley' of light and dark can be very useful with the right lighting: it signals direction and brings a sense of sculptural relief to an area that often has shadows cast by the nose.

Although you might think of the lips as a flat splash of colour across the lower half of the face, it's important to observe their shape – and, of course, that shape is affected by what lies beneath them.

The upper lip follows the groove of the philtrum, which descends from the nose. When we smile, the upper lip turns outwards and flattens against the teeth, and the philtrum changes shape.

If you make the line between the lips too dark, it can come forwards in the picture rather than recede, so look carefully at the tone of the two lips to see if the top lip overlaps the bottom one, in the centre below the philtrum.

Without lipstick, the lips are not necessarily different in colour to other colours in the face. Use the same colour for both lips, adjusting the tone as necessary. Usually the upper lip is darker than the bottom lip. There are also highlights in the lower lip; sometimes these can be created by using white, sometimes a totally different colour is required. A crimson mixed with yellow ochre or white in differing proportions usually gives a distinct lip colour. A darker colour in the lips may be an earth tone or a deeper purple.

Shape of the mouth ▼
There is a huge difference between the shapes of different people's mouths. To establish the shape, find the corners and use the philtrum in the upper lip to find the centre of the mouth.

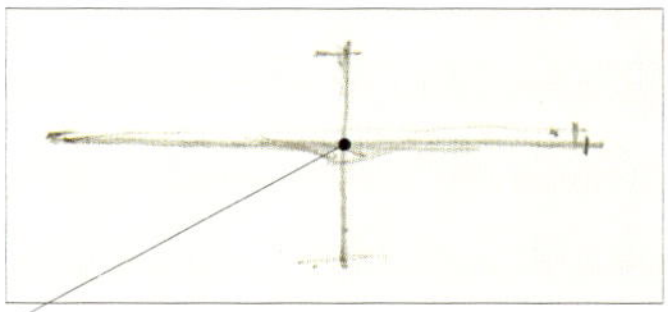

Axis

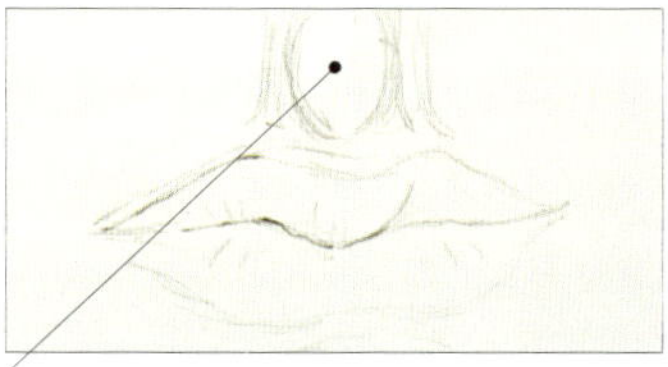

Philtrum

Lip shape and tone ▼
Lips are not a flat shape. Note how the upper lip overhangs the lower one. The top lip is darker than the lower one, as it slopes inwards, facing away from the light source.

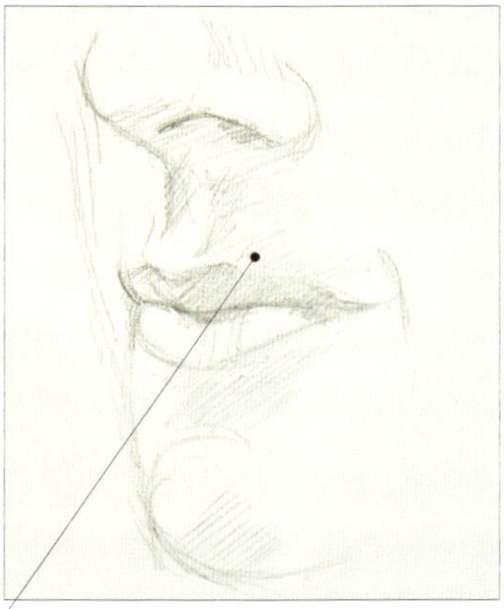

Light catches the edge of the upper lip

Folds around the mouth ▼
There is a faint line (in young people) or a deep fold (in older people) running from the nose around the mouth, dividing the mouth and cheek. The philtrum is also clearly visible: use contrasts of tone to make the recesses obvious. There may also be slight undulations below the lower lip. The folds around the mouth are more apparent in older people.

The ear

When you make studies of ears, make sure you work in strong light so that you can see the sculptural, shell-like, three-dimensional rhythms. Shadows give you the sense of the form of ears, especially in the interior. Try to model the form of the ear using light and dark tones.

To place the ear correctly, look to see where the ears align with other features such as the eyes or mouth, and look at the distance between the features. Start by taking a light diagonal line from the base of the lobe to the top of the ear to establish the length. The upper part of the ear is wider than the lower. Carefully observe the length of the lobe; it is longer in older people. Look at the shadow behind and below the ear and note how hair moves around the top and behind.

The interior of the ear always appears darker than the surrounding flesh – but if you make the interior of the ear too dark, you destroy the sense of where these recesses are and they jump forwards in the picture. Always look at the tonal contrasts – the amount of half tones and light that are around these darker areas.

Shape and structure of the ear ▼
Think of the ear as being like a seashell in the way that the outer ear spirals in to the centre. Look for the lights and darks in the different surfaces of the ear. The top of the ear and the ear lobe are the fleshiest parts and invariably appear lighter. The recesses of the inner part of the ear are in shadow.

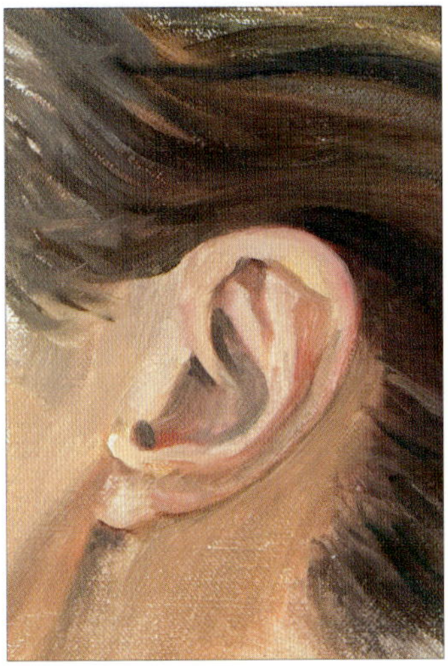

Examine your own reflection ▼
Look at your reflection in a mirror and see what shapes you can see in the ear. The shapes and angles will vary depending on your viewpoint. Note, for example, how the bony cartilage of the inner ear appears to jut out in this individual when he is viewed from this particular angle.

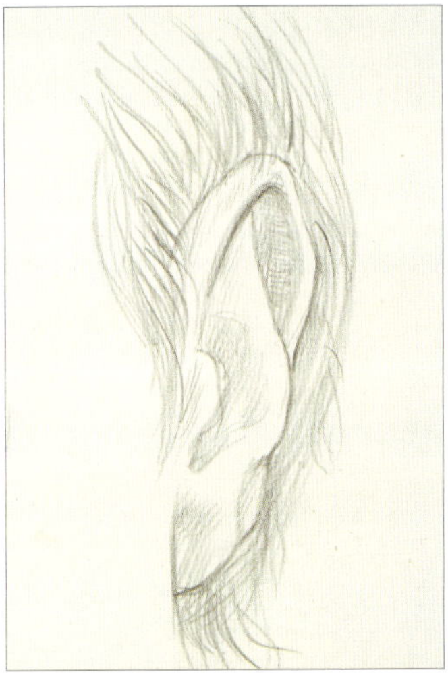

Shadows ▼
Look at the shadow underneath the lobe as this shaded area shows the relief of the ear.

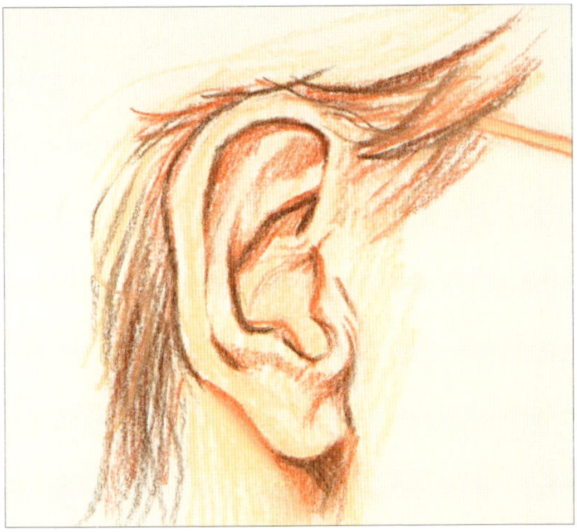

Hair around the ear ▼
Look at the way the hair falls around the ear: it may obscure the ear, but always remember the structure underneath.

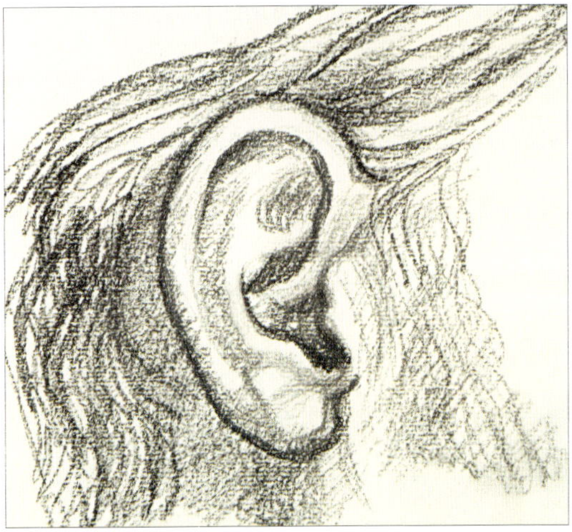

Measuring and proportions

No matter what subject you're drawing or painting, you need take careful measurements so that the relative sizes of different elements are correct. You also need to check continually as you work to make sure that you keep the proportions true to life. After a while, you'll find that this becomes second nature – but if you're a beginner, it's important to make a conscious effort to measure and check everything before you put it down on paper. Remember, too, to make your initial marks quite light so that you can make adjustments if need be. Even experienced artists find that they need to make revisions – and this is particularly true in portraiture and life drawing, where the position of the model will inevitably shift slightly during the course of the pose.

Taking measurements

Choose a unit within your subject against which you can measure everything else. That unit can be anything you like – the width of the eyes, the length of the nose, the distance between the bridge of the nose and the chin, for example.

With this method, it's absolutely vital that you keep your arm straight, so that the pencil remains a constant distance from the subject. Close one eye to make it easier to focus, and concentrate on looking at the pencil rather than at your subject.

The subject ▶

Here, the subject is a small statue, but the principle remains the same whatever you are drawing.

1 Close one eye and, holding a pencil at arms' length, measure the chosen section of your subject – here, the distance from the forehead to the chin. Align the top of the pencil with one end of the section you are measuring and move your thumb up or down the shaft of the pencil until it is level with the other end of the distance being measured.

2 Then transfer this unit of measurement to the paper. The unit of measurement is relative to the scale of your drawing. You will need to double or treble the ratio. Next, use the same unit of measurement to compare the size of other parts of the subject. Here, the distance across the widest part of the statue is the same as the measurement taken in Step 1.

The proportions of the human body

Artists have tried for centuries to define the proportions of the human body, but in reality proportions vary from one individual to another just as features vary. However, the head is a standard 'unit of measurement' that is often used in assessing proportions. Generally speaking, the average adult is roughly seven and a half heads tall. The height of his or her head fits seven and a half times into the total height of the body. It is important to stress that these proportions are average. Nonetheless, if you know the 'norm', you will find it easier to assess how far your model conforms to or departs from it.

Children, however, are another matter. In babies, the head takes up a larger proportion of the whole and a young baby's total height may be only about four times the height of the head, with about three-quarters of the height being the head and abdomen. The limbs then grow dramatically in the early years; by the age of three, the legs make up about half the total height.

Although the head is a standard and accepted unit of measurement, you can use anything you choose. For example, in a sitting pose the head may be seen in perspective, which will make it difficult to use it as a unit against which to judge other parts of the body. In a portrait where the model's hand supports the chin, for example, you could compare the length of the head to the hand. Or you could look at the length of the forearm in relation to the thigh. The important thing is that you check and measure sizes as you work.

If we look at further sub-divisions, more general guidelines emerge. In a standing figure, the pubic area is just below the mid-point of the body; the legs make up nearly half the total height. If the hands are hanging loosely by the sides, they will reach the mid-point of the thighs, while the elbows will be roughly level with the waist. When you're drawing or painting the figure, look for alignments such as this to check that you're placing limbs and features correctly. You can also put in 'landmarks' such as the nipples as guides, although there is no substitute for repeated and careful measuring.

There are also some differences in body shape between the sexes. Men's shoulders are generally wider than women's and their legs longer. A female pelvis is wider at the top.

General proportions ▼
See how proportions change with age. In this sketch, the adult male figure is seven-and-a-half heads tall and the woman is just over seven heads. The boy is just over six heads tall; the young child is just over four heads, while the baby is just under four – so his head takes up a much larger proportion of his total height than it does in adults.

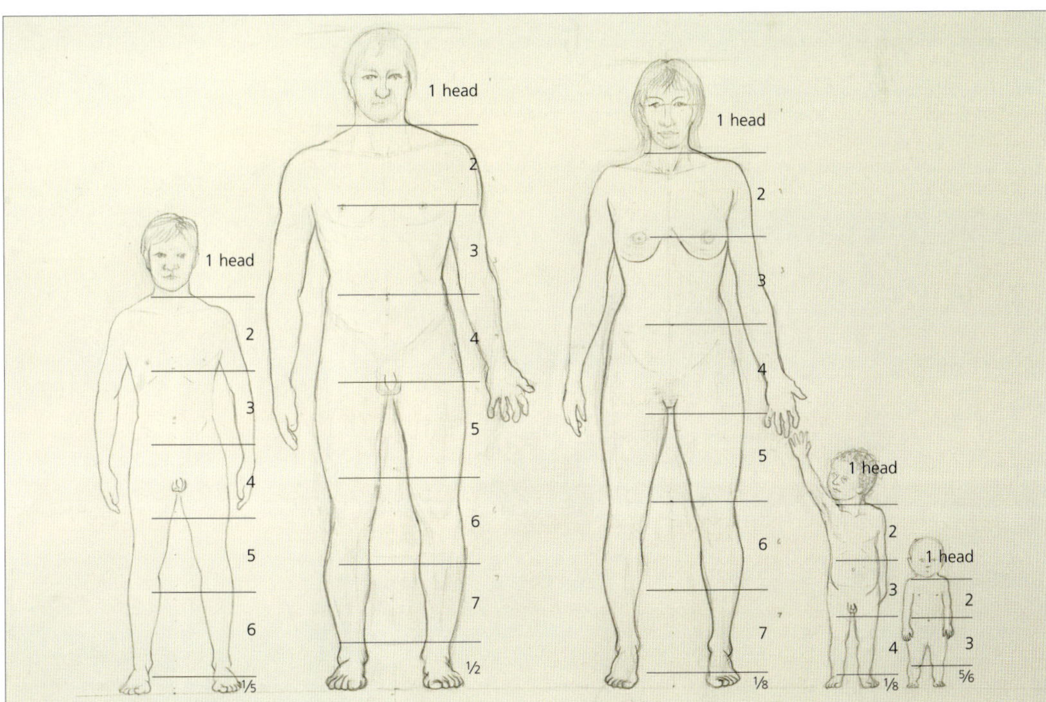

Simple anatomy

Beginners often make the mistake of trying to draw or paint every detail that they see, rather than deciding what is really important in a pose. You don't need to capture every crease in the skin or every bony protuberance – but if you understand something of what's happening beneath the surface, you have a better chance of being able to pick out the essentials.For artists, the most important bones are those that are visible near the surface of the skin. Divide the body into sections; spine, shoulder blades, rib cage, bones of the arms and hands, pelvis (hips), and the bones of the legs and feet.

The spine

The spine, or vertebral column, is the most important support structure in the body. People often tend to think of it as being a fairly rigid, straight structure, so you may be surprised by how much it curves. In a normal upright posture there are four curves, which correspond to the different sections of the spine and describe a double S-shape: viewed from the side, the cervical vertebrae (the vertebrae in the neck) curve outwards; the thoracic vertebrae, which support the ribs, curve inwards; the lumbar vertebrae, which link to the pelvis, curve outwards again; and the vertebrae in the coccyx curve inwards. When you're analyzing a standing pose, the way the spine curves is critical. People often overlook the curve in the vertebrae of the neck, in particular, which makes the head jut forwards.

In a relaxed, reclining pose, the weight of the model will be supported by the pelvis, so the spine will sag or gently curve under the pull of gravity. In most models you will clearly see a depression running down the centre of the back, which shows you the position of the spine. Look at the protruding bones of the scapula and pelvis to help work out the balance of the pose.

The body's flexibility depends on the movement of the spine, so the next thing to look at is how the spine attaches to the shoulder girdle, rib cage and pelvis.

The shoulders

Making up the shoulder girdle are the scapula, or shoulder blade (a triangular-shaped bone that lies on the back of the thorax, the collarbone or clavicle, and the acromion, which is the outermost shoulder bone. When drawing or painting the nude, look for the bony upper edge of the scapula as this indicates the tilt of the shoulders. The clavicle is also prominent and tends to catch the light, forming a kind of visual link between the rib cage and the shoulder girdle.

The rib cage

The bones that form the rib cage are suspended from the thoracic vertebrae. The rib cage, inside which are vital organs such as the heart, liver and lungs, is wider at the bottom than at the top. Viewed from the front or side, the individual bones and overall shape of the rib cage can be clearly seen in thin individuals, although in many people a layer of fatty tissue makes them less obvious.

The pelvis

Attached to the base of the spine is the pelvis. Women tend to have a wider pelvis than men. The portions that jut outwards are known as the iliac crests and, from both the front and back view, these are useful 'landmarks' to watch out for. From the back you can also see the two small dimples of the rather grandly named 'posterior superior iliac spines': these, too, are useful landmarks, as they indicate the tilt of the pelvis.

The limbs

Now let's consider the limbs. The long bone of the upper arm is the humerus. The upper half of the humerus is almost cylindrical, but it flattens and widens in the lower half, near the elbow. There are two main bones in the forearm – the radius and the ulna – and these cross over one another as you rotate your hand. The ulna, in particular, is prominent at both the elbow and the wrist and provides a useful point against which you can judge the position of other features.

In the hand, look for the joints across the back of the hand and the fingers (the metacarpals and phalanges), as they help you establish the different planes of the hand.

In the legs, the hip bone juts out beyond the edge of the pelvis. The femur, or thigh bone, is the longest bone in the body. In the lower leg, the two main bones are the fibula and the tibia (shin bone). The patella, or knee cap, is prominent, as are the bones on the inside and outside of the ankle (the knobbly base of the tibia and fibula).

Bones visible beneath the skin ▼

In thin models with little fatty tissue you will probably be able to see many of the major bones of the body. Below, the underlying skeletal structure is highly evident at the point where the muscle in the neck (the sternocleidomastoid muscle) meets the collarbone and at the bony protrusions of the sternum and rib cage.

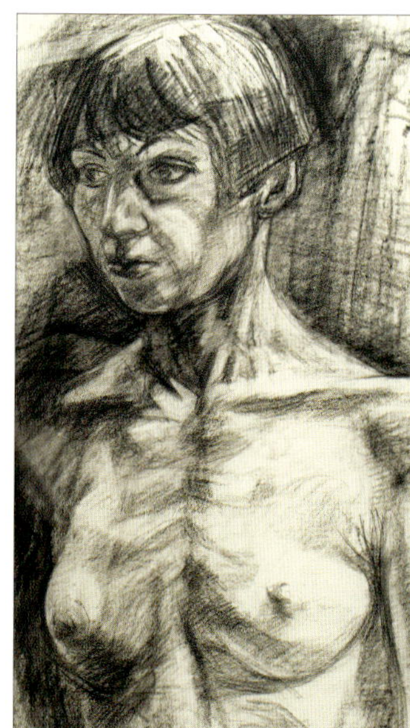

The skeleton ►
This is a slightly stylized sketch of the main bones of the skeleton that you need to be aware of as an artist.

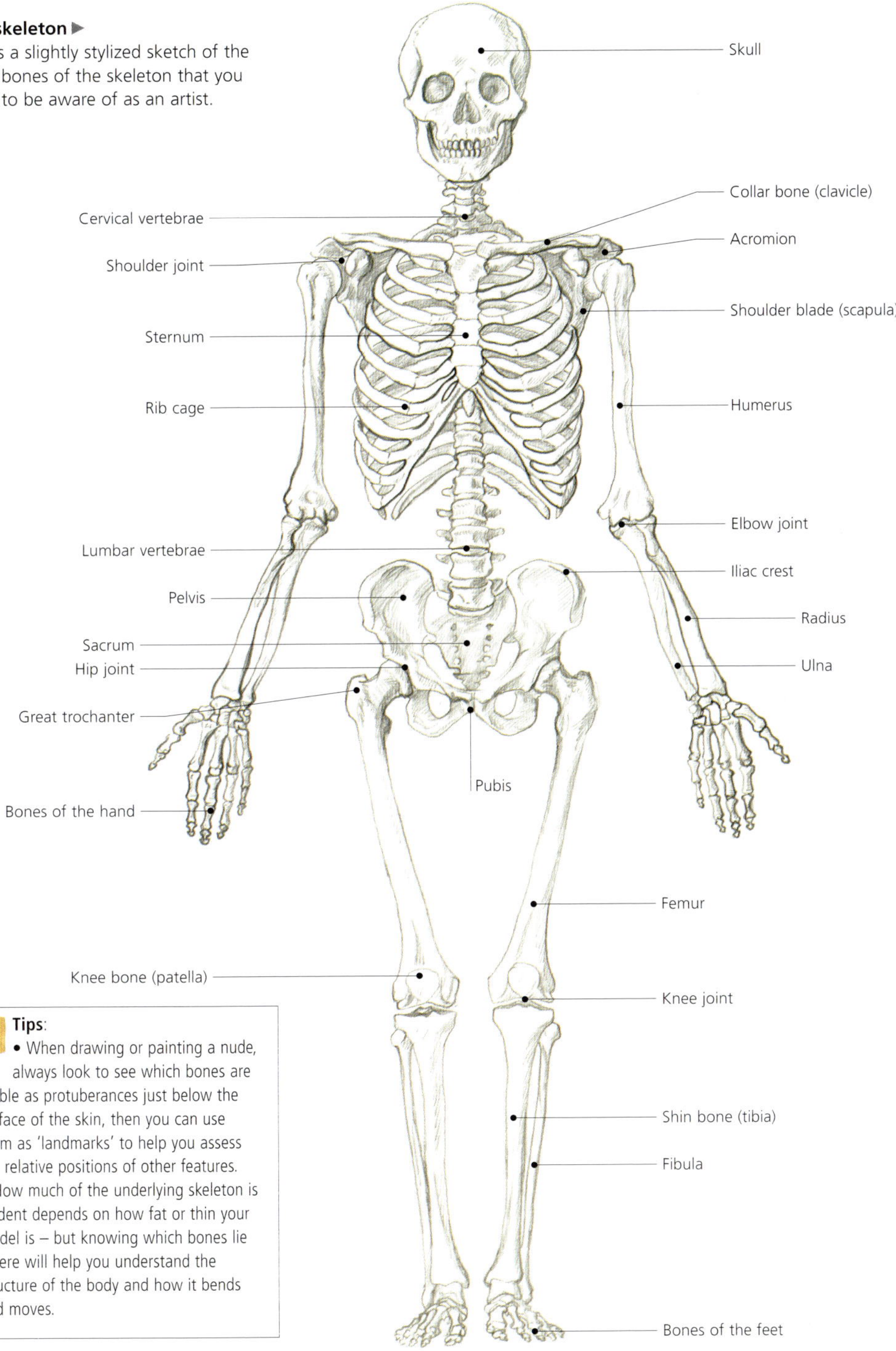

Tips:

- When drawing or painting a nude, always look to see which bones are visible as protuberances just below the surface of the skin, then you can use them as 'landmarks' to help you assess the relative positions of other features.
- How much of the underlying skeleton is evident depends on how fat or thin your model is – but knowing which bones lie where will help you understand the structure of the body and how it bends and moves.

The muscles

As with the bones of the skeleton, muscles are of interest to artists only insofar as they affect the surface of the body, and naturally we see them more prominently in people of an athletic build. Nonetheless, it is still useful to have a basic knowledge of the main muscle groups and how they work. You can convey the effect of muscles on surface form through careful use of tone. Try copying illustrations of the muscles from books on anatomy so that you get an understanding of the direction in which the muscles run and the range of movements that they allow; in doing so, you will be better able to create a sense of movement and tension in your work.

So what are the muscles that can we see under the surface – and how do they contribute to the movement, postures and shapes of the body?

Muscles of the back and torso

The **platysma** covers the shoulder girdle, the neck and the lower part of the face. It is only evident in extreme expressions of anguish or pain.

The **sternocleidomastoid** is the most prominent muscle in the front of the neck. It is one of the muscles that turns and bends the head to the side.

The dominating muscles of the back are the **trapezius** muscles – large triangular muscles attached to the back of the skull and the vertebrae. They cover the back between the shoulder blades and also extend over the shoulder to join the clavicle (collarbone) at the shoulder joint. They stabilize the shoulder girdle and move the shoulder blade and clavicle.

The **deltoid** muscle covers the shoulder and is attached to the bones of the shoulder girdle and humerus. It flexes and rotates the arm.

The **infraspinatus, teres major** and **teres minor** muscles cover the scapula and are visible between the deltoid and the latissimus dorsi. They rotate the arm and lift the arm backwards.

The **latissimus dorsi** covers a large area of the lower back and wraps around the side of the trunk to create the back fold of the armpit. It is thin, so the underlying bones are usually visible. It brings the shoulder blades together, pulls the shoulders down and back and lowers the raised arm.

The **pectoralis major** is the chest muscle. It lowers the raised arm, abducts and rotates the arm inwards, and lowers the shoulder forwards. It helps with respiration and forms the front fold of the armpit.

The **serratus anterior** lifts the ribs, moves the shoulder blades and enables elevation of the arm.

The **external obliqu**e lies on the side of the trunk and is part of the superficial abdominal musculature. It flexes and rotates the trunk.

The **gluteus maximus, gluteus medius** and **minimus** form the buttocks. The gluteus maximus functions when we climb or stand from a sitting position. It extends and rotates the hip joint and stabilizes the pelvis. The gluteus medius rotates, flexes and abducts the upper hip. The **tensor fasciae latae** flexes the hip joint, stabilizes the femur and rotates the leg.

The stomach muscles, the **rectus abdominis**, run down from the lower ribs through the centre of the body to the pubis. Look for this line when drawing a figure from the front, as it is a useful central axis that you can use as a guideline. It flexes the trunk and supports the internal organs.

Muscles of the back ▼

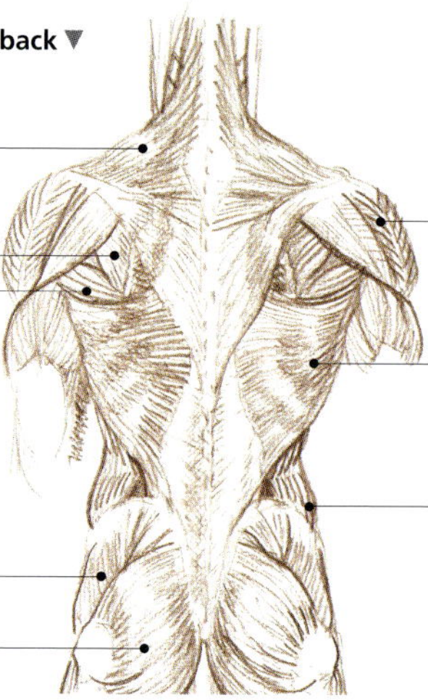

Muscles of the torso ▼

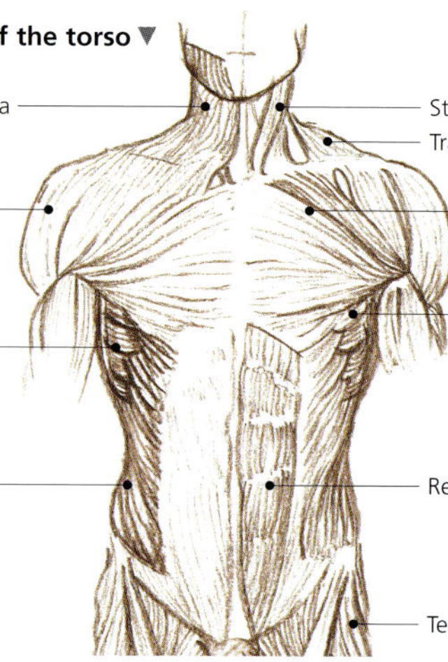

Muscles of the arms

When the palm of the hand is facing forwards, the muscles in the front of the arm are flexors (they bend the arm), while those at the back are extensors (they straighten the arm). In the upper arm, the **biceps** flexes and rotates the limb. Located under the biceps, the **brachialis** flexes the elbow. The **triceps** extends the lower arm at the elbow and moves the shoulder blade.

In the lower arm there are three groups of forearm muscles, which act upon the bones of the forearm, wrist and fingers. They are named as extensors, flexors or abductors and are shown individually on the sketches. Three muscles move the thumb; three extensors are in the back of the hand; and there are ten muscles in the palm.

Muscles of the arm ▼

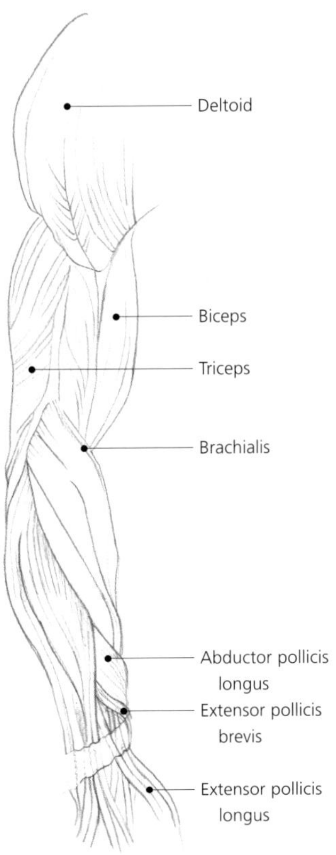

Muscles of the leg

The **biceps femoris, semitendinosus** and **semimembranosus** (commonly known as the hamstrings) are superficial flexor muscles in the rear of the thigh. They extend the hip joint, flex the knee joint and rotate the leg.

The **gracilis** muscle arises in the pubis and extends into the tibia. When the thigh is abducted, it is visible at the back of the knee along with the semitendinosus and sartorius.

The **sartorius** runs from the iliac spine and diagonally across the thigh, into the tibia. It flexes the knee and rotates the leg.

The quadriceps femoris group is made up of the **rectus femoris, vastus intermedius, vastus medialis** and **vastus lateralis**. They all extend the knee joint. The rectus femoris also flexes the upper leg at the hip joint.

The **tibialis anterior** and **extensor digitorum longus** are surface muscles on the front of the leg; the tendons run into the foot.

The **peroneus longus** and **brevis** run along the side of the leg; the tendons run through to the ankle.

The triceps surae is a muscle group at the back of the leg and is composed of the **soleus** and the **gastrocnemius**. These muscles lift the weight of the body when we are standing on our toes, as well as when we are standing or walking. The soleus tendon at the back of the leg and heel is called the **Achilles tendon**. The gastrocnemius lifts the heel and flexes the knee joint.

Muscles of the front of the leg ▼

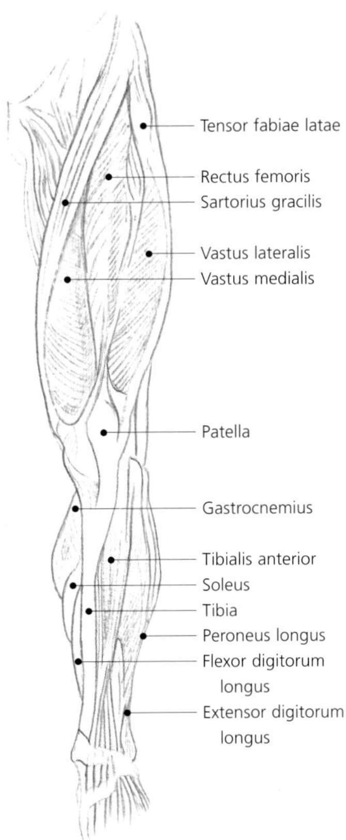

Muscles of the back of the leg ▼

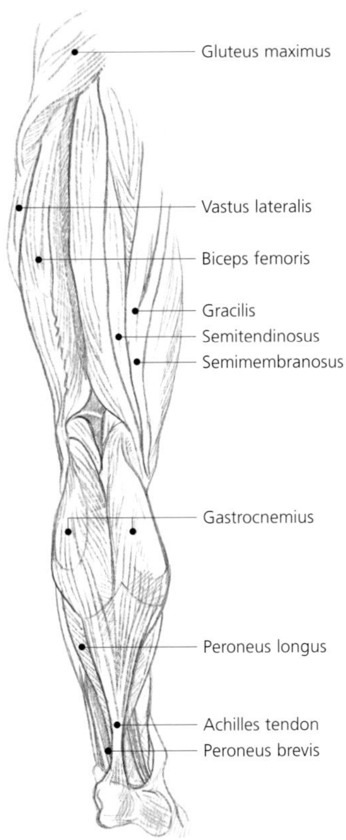

Balance and movement

Maintaining our balance is something that we do instinctively most of the time: our bodies naturally make tiny adjustments as we move to prevent us from falling over. When you're drawing or painting, however, things don't come quite so readily! It's all too easy to produce something in which the figure looks as if it's leaning to one side.

Establishing balance

You need first of all to determine the 'line of balance' of the pose – and the way to do this is to drop an imaginary plumb line down to the point on the ground where the weight of the body falls. The line that you choose depends on the angle from which you're viewing the figure: from the front, start from the hollow space at the base of the neck, between the collarbones; from the side, take a line down from the ear hole; from the back, take a line down from the base of the neck. Hold a pencil or brush vertically in front of you, aligning with one of these points; the weight-bearing point should intersect that vertical line. Draw this line lightly in the early stages of your work for reference.

If the model is standing with all his or her weight on one leg, the weight-bearing point will be the arch of the foot that carries the weight. It's more likely, however, that the weight will be unevenly distributed, as it is not comfortable to stand with all your weight on one leg; in this case the weight-bearing point will be in between the feet. Even if the model is leaning to one side or bending over, this will apply.

Knowing the shapes of the main bones of the skeleton will also help you to establish the balance of the pose. Look for the bones that lie near the surface of the skin. From the back, the shoulder blades show the shoulders' angle and the depressions of the posterior superior iliac spines reveal the pelvic tilt. The twist of the spinal column is also useful. From the front, the tilt of the shoulders and pelvis show the torso position, while the collarbones show the angle of the shoulders.

The muscular support around the skeleton creates a system of tension within the body. Muscles form pairs. When one contracts, the other relaxes and stretches – and this enables the body to maintain its balance. If the weight is on the right foot, then the upper body will shift over this leg to maintain balance and the shoulder girdle will tilt down to the right; the pelvis will then tilt to the left. If a model extends his or her arm upward, the lower leg will lift back to balance it. Look for these movements in every pose. When opposing muscles are in equal tension, the body is still; when the tensions are unequal, the body moves.

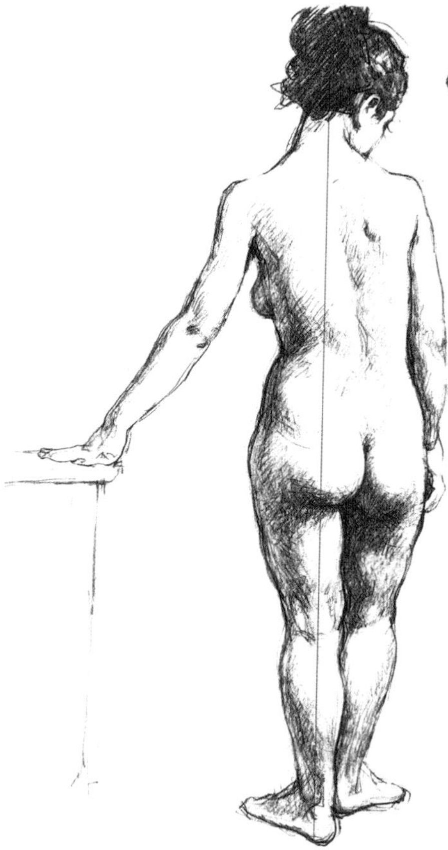

Weight on one foot ▲
Here the weight is mainly on one foot, with a little of it taken by the hand resting on the table. The balance line, or imaginary plumb line, starts at the centre of the base of the neck and runs through to the centre of the weight-bearing foot.

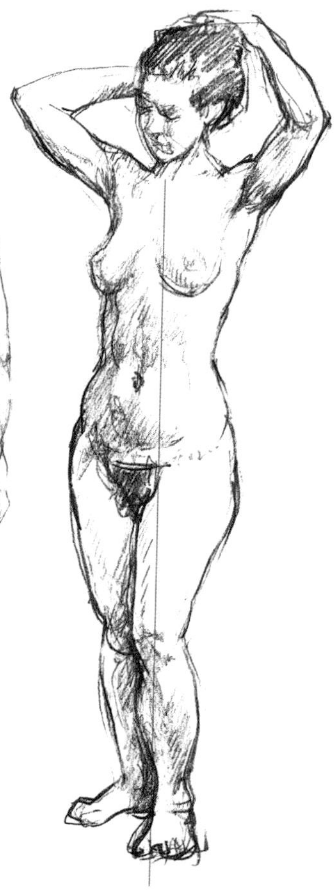

Weight distributed between the feet ▲
Here, the model's weight is more evenly distributed, but there is still more weight on her left foot than on her right. Consequently, the balance line falls nearer the left foot – the one that is maintaining the balance.

Weight on the right leg ▶
Here, the weight is more on the model's right leg than on her right arm. The balance line runs through the centre of the weight-bearing leg. The shoulders and hips slope in opposite directions to maintain the balance of the body.

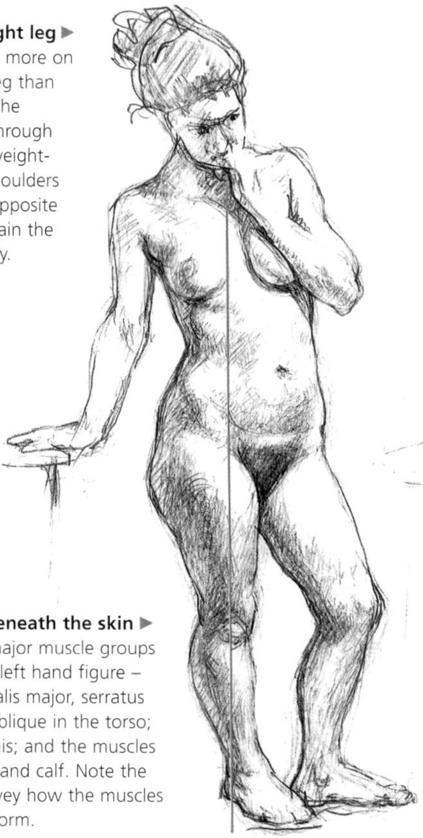

Weight taken by the arms ▼
In this pose, very little weight is taken by the feet, so the balance line falls some way outside them.

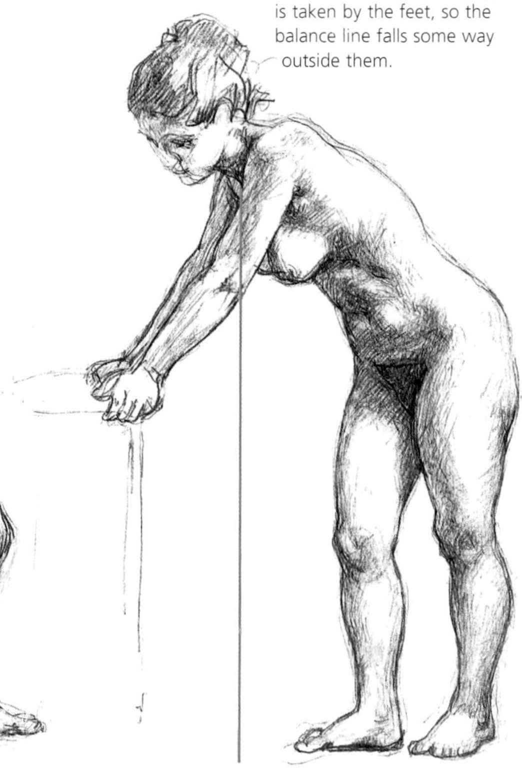

Muscles visible beneath the skin ▶
A number of the major muscle groups can be seen in the left hand figure – the deltoid, pectoralis major, serratus anterior, external oblique in the torso; the rectus abdominis; and the muscles of the upper thigh and calf. Note the use of tone to convey how the muscles affect the surface form.

Portraying movement

Balance and movement are closely interrelated: balance is a matter of arresting the movement of the body, while movement occurs when the body's natural point of balance is upset. Often, the only way we know that a figure in a painting is moving is because we know that the pose could not be held without the figure falling over: the artist has 'frozen' a split second in time, as in a still photograph.

Looking at still photos is a good way of analyzing how a figure is moving – but don't rely too heavily on them as reference sources as there's a danger that your drawings and paintings will look very static. You're also more likely to simply copy what's there instead of really thinking about how the body is moving. Try drawing from life, instead.

Start with a relatively slow movement, such as someone walking, and try to analyze the repeated motions that occur, jotting down small marks until you feel you've got the rhythm of the movement fixed in your mind. Gradually move on to faster motions – running, dancing – perhaps even drawing from the television or a DVD. As they say, practice makes perfect!

The moving form ▶
To depict the figure in motion, you need to use a medium that actively discourages detail. This figure has been drawn with a brush and diluted Chinese ink, with a few deft touches of charcoal line. The definition is minimal, yet the drawing is an elegant description of the fluid lines of body and arms.

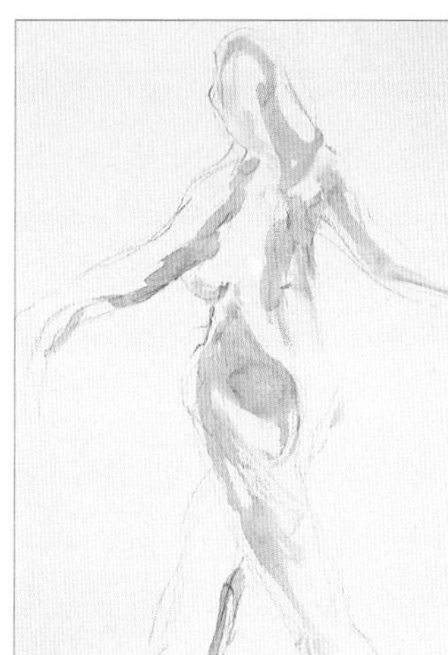

The figure in perspective

Perspective sounds like a dauntingly technical term and (like anatomy) you will find books that go into a lot of detail, setting out complicated 'rules' and measuring systems. What it really boils downs to, however, is training yourself to observe accurately and put down on paper what you can actually see.

The important thing to remember is that forms appear larger or smaller depending where they are in relation to your viewpoint. This is one of the ways in which you can create an impression of scale and distance in your drawings and paintings and make things look three-dimensional.

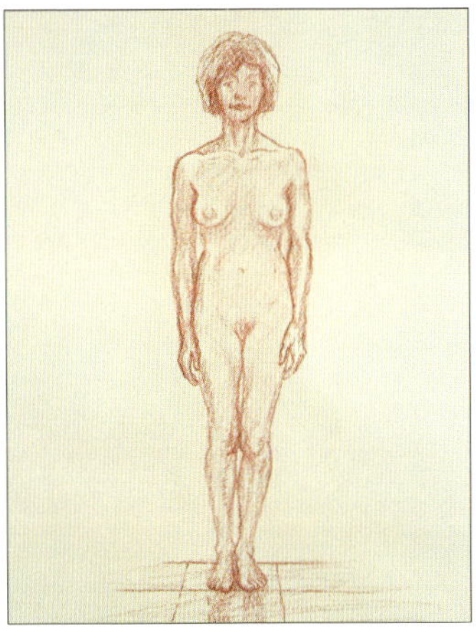

Equidistant features ◄
In this sketch, the model is standing with her feet together, arms hanging straight by her side. Both hands look more or less the same length, as do both feet. This is because both hands and both feet are the same distance away from the viewer.

Features at different distances from the viewer ►
In this sketch, the model has brought a foot forward and has stretched out one arm as if to shake someone by the hand. The hand and foot that are nearest appear slightly larger than those that have not moved – even though they are, in reality, the same size.

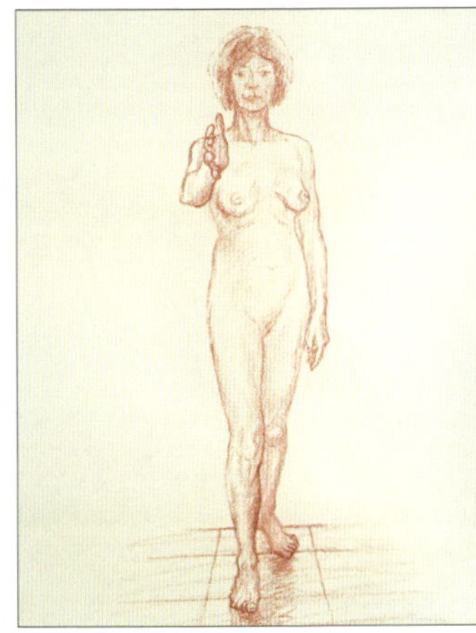

One-point perspective

The first rule of perspective is that all parallel lines, when viewed from anywhere other than straight across your vision, appear to converge on the horizon. The point at which they converge is known as the 'vanishing point'. Vanishing points are always situated on the horizon line, which runs across your field of vision at eye level. If you are higher than your subject, then the vanishing lines will slope up to the horizon; if you are lower than your subject, they will slope down.

The same applies to a human figure viewed in perspective. If, for example, your model is lying on the floor with his or head further away from you than the feet, then the head will appear to be compressed in length – a phenomenon known as foreshortening.

Contour lines on their own are not always enough to create a sense of volume, so think of the figure as being in a box. As the sides of a box run parallel to one another, this will make it easier for you to judge the degree of convergence.

Parallel lines converge ►
The artist has drawn a grid underneath the figure, as if the model is lying on a tiled floor. Our experience tells us that each square of the grid is the same size, but because the parallel lines of the grid are receding away from us towards the vanishing point above the forehead (on the horizon of our vision), the lines appear to converge – and hence the squares diminish in size the further they are from the viewer. Note, too, how the head is foreshortened as it is furthest away.

Two-point perspective

If you then change your viewpoint so that two sides of your model become visible, then you are dealing with what is known as two-point perspective. Imagine, then, that you're looking at a seated figure not from straight on but from slightly to one side. You can see one side of the body and something of the front – in other words, two major planes. In this scenario, two vanishing points come into play. The parallel lines of each plane converge at a different vanishing point. Those on the right converge at a vanishing point on the right; those on the left converge at a vanishing point on the left. As in one-point perspective, if you are higher than the subject the vanishing lines will slope up to the horizon; if you are lower than your subject, they will slope down.

If you're a beginner, you may find it easier to lightly enclose your subject in a box, so that you can see which features run parallel to the edges and assess where the vanishing point(s) could be placed. With practice, you'll be able to omit this stage.

Two vanishing points ▼
Here we can see two planes – the side and front. The parallel lines of each plane converge at a different vanishing point. To create a realistic impression of distance, you need to make the edges of the dais slope inwards towards the appropriate vanishing point. Similarly, features need to diminish in scale: note, for example, how the right foot appears smaller than the left foot because it is further away.

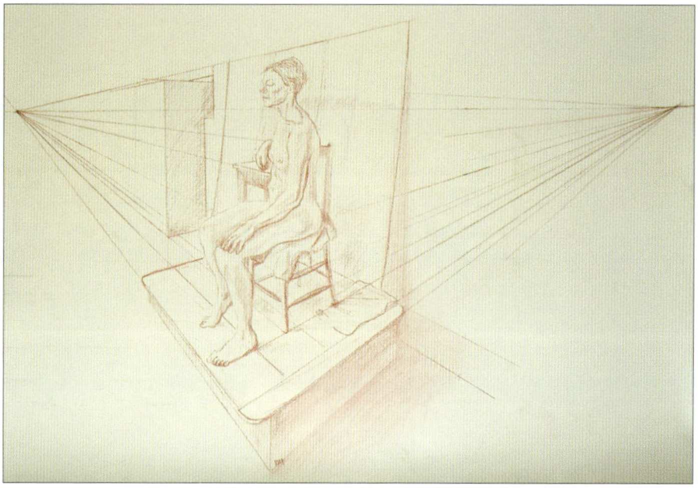

Multi-point perspective

In many compositions with more than one figure, in particular, the models will probably be arranged at different angles to each other and you may well see more than two major planes. It is possible (though time-consuming!) to plot all the vanishing points mathematically, but if you remember the basic principle – that each plane of each subject has its own vanishing point – and rely primarily on your own observations and on measuring one part of the body against another, then you will be well on the way to success. Practise your skills with one subject before moving on to multiple figures.

Foreshortened figure ►
The head, body and limbs are seldom all viewed in profile, except in simple standing poses. When seen at a tangent, any element will appear diminished in length, or foreshortened, as it recedes away from you, while the width is little affected along the span. With extreme foreshortening, you can expect to see some overlaps: for example, a foreshortened head seen from above might show the chin overlapped by the nose.

From this viewpoint, the model's right shoulder appears much broader than the left – though they are, of course, the same size.

Viewed from a relatively high eye level, the torso appears shortened in relation to the model's legs.

The hair

When drawing or painting hair, you must consider it as part of the head as a whole, rather than as a separate entity. Start by thinking about the overall shape and mass of the hair before you concern yourself with colour and texture. If someone has long, thin hair, it may hang down over the head, face and shoulders, showing the form underneath rather like a tight-fitting garment on the body. Big, curly hair, on the other hand, can almost double the volume of the head as a whole, and it can be hard to imply the shape of the cranium beneath.

Use the hair to help you search out the different planes within the head. Since the hair follows the contours of the scalp and therefore the different planes of the skull, even straight, very thin hair contains highlight and shadow areas as one plane changes direction into the next. Coarse, wavy hair may contain many transitions from light to dark as it undulates over the surface of the skull. Try to see hair as a series of blocks, rather than individual strands. These blocks reflect light in different ways, depending on the colour and type of hair. In straight, dark hair that clings closely to the scalp, the highlight may look like a bar of light; in wavy hair, each curl will have its own pattern of highlights and dark areas, so the highlights over the head as a whole will be much more fragmented.

The way that you convey these areas of light and shade depends, of course, on your choice of medium. A pencil drawing may include cross hatching to create different tones, erasing to lift out the highlights and lines illustrating the movement of strands or clumps of hair. If you are using soft pastels, use the side of the pastel for broad areas beneath any light strands and put in the lights on top as a final series of touches. You could also lightly brush or wipe a paper tissue over the broad areas to create softer effects.

If you are using oils or acrylics, you might choose to put in the darks first and use a rag (or a damp brush) to wipe them out, applying a lighter colour on

Wavy hair ▲
Here, the model's hair was pulled back over her scalp and tied up on the top of her head – but it still escapes in unruly waves! The bulk of the dark hair on the shaded side of her head was put in using the side of a charcoal stick, with bold, curling strands conveying the direction of hair growth. On the lighter side of her head, the artist left the original dark ochre colour of the paper showing through, just as he did in the mid-toned areas of the model's skin. You can also see some fleck of pinks and purples in the hair. You might think this is an unusual colour choice, but the artist selected them for their tonal values, rather than for their actual colour: they relate to the light and dark areas in the skin. Another reason for choosing them was that the model was from Hawaii and he wanted to create a sense of hot, tropical colours, just as Gauguin did so famously in his wonderfully vibrant paintings of Tahitian women.

top, making the subsequent layers thicker so that they do not merge with the underpainting. In watercolour, you normally work from light to dark so you need to establish the lightest tones first and then add the darks on top, allowing each layer to dry before the next.

Whatever medium you use, exploit the contrasts between warm and cool colours in order to convey the areas of light and dark within the hair. Hair picks up some reflected colour from its surroundings: you may see green/blue tones in blonde hair, hints of blue in black hair, and red or blonde in brown hair, depending on the light.

Sleek, shiny hair ▼
Here, the hair closely follows the contours of the scalp, but the artist has taken care to use different tones to convey the changes in plane. Note the blue highlights on the top of the head, for example, while the side nearest us is in shadow and is therefore darker in tone. A crimsony purple oil paint serves as a mid-toned ground colour for the hair. The artist then applied a darker violet on top; with the addition of white, this same violet becomes a cool half light in the highlights in the back of the hair, behind the ear. The yellow background is reflected into the hair, so adding yellow ochre to the violet both lightens it and gives a complementary colour contrast which emphasizes the glossy quality of the hair.

Long flowing hair ▼
The key to drawing hair like this is to think of it not as a solid mass nor as a wild array of individual strands, but to aim for something in between: try to capture the general direction of hair growth without putting in every strand – and remember to look at how the hair follows the contours of the scalp. With charcoal and other monochrome media, you're limited to a small range of tones. Here, the mid tones are created by smudging the charcoal with the tip of a finger and the light tones by lifting off pigment with a torchon or kneaded eraser.

The hands and feet

Hands and feet are notoriously difficult to draw. One of the reasons for this is that people do not look at the hand or foot as a single unit; instead of being able to schematize the form into simple planes, they get too caught up in drawing details such as individual fingers and toes with too much prominence and tend to make them too big. Study them carefully until you are confident in your observational skills.

To find out about the basic anatomy, start by drawing your own hand or foot. Place your hand on paper, trace around the outline, and then 'fill in' the missing information – the veins, wrinkles of the knuckles and so on – using line. This gives a flat image. If you shine a light on your hand from the side, you will throw these details into relief; you can then describe the hand's surface using tone, which is much more interesting.

Schematize the shapes into simpler forms and define the planes. A clenched fist, for example, is a rough cube shape: there are four changes in plane on the back of the hand and fingers, plus two on the sides of the hand. Try to analyze the foot in the same way.

Then look at the surface anatomy – the veins, wrinkles, lines and folds. Flex your fingers or rotate your ankle and see how the tendons fan out. The tendons that you can see are the long tapering ends of the flexor muscles in the forearm (or, in the foot, the long tendons of the muscles running down the front of the lower leg). Look at how light catches the veins and wrinkles, but do not give them too much definition; if you make them too strong, they become too dominant and the sense of the form underneath gets lost.

The colour of hands and feet may also be different from other areas of the body. Hands are exposed to light, while feet are generally not exposed to the same degree. The skin's colour may also change because of its texture.

The planes of the hand ▲
Here we can see three main planes – the back of the hand, the side of the hand, and the section between the base of the fingers and the first knuckle. Tucked out of sight but implied, there are two further planes on the fingers – between the first and second knuckles, and the second knuckle and fingernail. Use tone to suggest the changes of plane: here, the brightest section is the side plane, with the back of the hand, and then the first segment of the fingers becoming progressively darker in tone as the planes turn away from the light source.

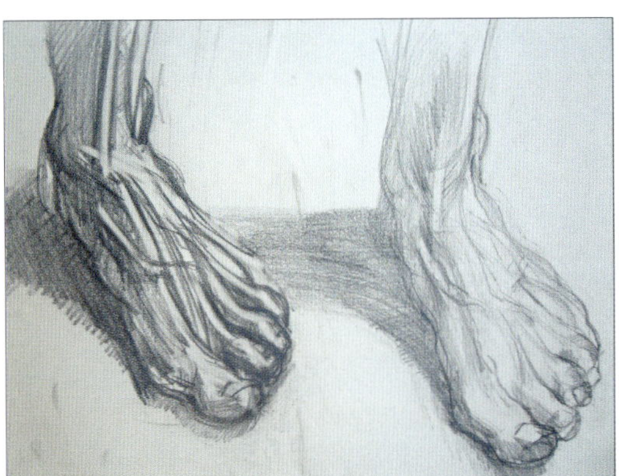

Visualizing forms under the surface ▲
Here you can see the muscles and tendons beneath the skin. The artist has used his knowledge of anatomy and studied the foot, shading in the raised and shadowed areas.

Underlying structure ▲
You may see the wrinkles and creases on your hand as a pattern of flowing lines, but don't forget that this is only the surface detail: what's more important is what lies underneath.

Cupped hands ▲
The different planes of the hands and fingers can be clearly seen, with subtle differences in tone (delineated with a flat brush) conveying the shape of the hands and the way the fingers curl around the coffee mug. The shadows cast on the mug by the fingers, as well as the highlights on the fingernails, reveal both the direction and the intensity of the light, while the dark, plain background allows the hands to stand out clearly. Note, too, how the amount of fingernail that is visible varies according to whether the fingers are angled towards or away from our view.

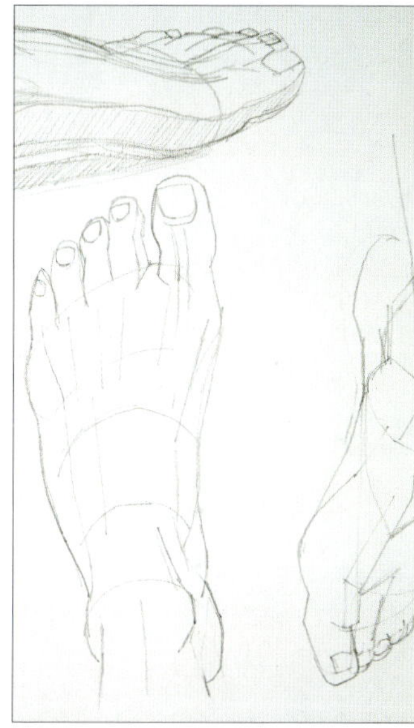

The planes of the feet ▲
These sketches show how the foot is broken down into a series of simplified planes. It is important to do this and to analyze the tones of the sections when you're depicting the foot, as it makes it easier for you to think of the whole unit and make it appear three-dimensional.

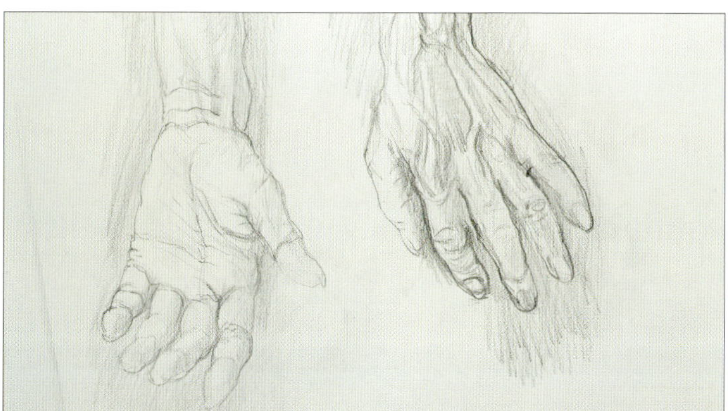

The palm and back of the hand ▲
The bony knuckles, tendons and veins are much in evidence on the back of the hand. Look at how they catch the light, as this will help you to convey their form and structure. Drawing the fleshy palm of the hand is a little more difficult, as there are fewer structures to guide you, but you will still see creases across the palm and around the knuckle joints that indicate the changing planes.

Creating light and shade ▲
In this charcoal sketch the highlights that convey the different planes of the feet and legs have been expertly created by wiping off charcoal with a kneaded eraser.

Colours and colour palettes

Although you may come across tubes of paint labelled 'flesh colour' in your art supplies store, in reality there is no such thing! Skin colour varies enormously from person to person and, of course, nobody's skin is a uniform colour all over. Take a look at your reflection in a mirror, or hold your hand up in front of you: you will soon see that, even on a relatively flat area, your skin colour actually contains many variations.

Things get even more complicated when we bring tone into the equation. Introducing tone is the main method artists use to make their subjects look solid and three-dimensional. A brightly lit area of skin will appear lighter in tone than one that is in shadow. In portraiture and figure painting, the transition from one plane to another – and hence from one tone to another – is often very subtle, and you need to be able to create a wide range of tones from every colour in your palette.

Mixing colours

Once you've selected your basic palette for a painting, it's a good idea to pre-mix a few tones, combining the same mixture of colours with different amounts of white (or water, in the case of watercolour) to achieve a light, mid and dark tone for each colour. You can then mix the subtle half tones around those main tones as required.

When mixing colours, use a large surface as a palette to prevent the colours from becoming muddied or jumbled. Try to begin and end with clearly defined tones and colours.

You can make any soft pastel lighter by adding white, but usually you will find such a huge range of ready-made colours in both soft pastels and coloured pencils that you do not necessarily need to darken or lighten them. However, it is worth experimenting to find out how different colours can mix optically on the paper.

Applying paint to the surface

However well you mix a colour on the palette, it will probably appear different when placed next to other colours on the support. If you are using a wet-into-wet technique (oils, acrylics, gouache and watercolour can all be used in this way), colours will mix into each other on the painting. You will need to be aware of this and work with a deft hand to prevent unwanted bleeds of colour.

If you are painting in layers and letting each colour dry, then the colour underneath will have an influence – a dark colour underneath will darken the top shade.

You can develop a painting in more opaque layers, putting thicker paint on thinner undercoats (the 'fat over lean' technique used in oil painting), then wiping off with a cloth or scraping through with a palette knife to create colour variations. Whatever technique you employ to apply paint, knowing how to use tonal values and warm and cool hues will help you control and evaluate the effects on the surface as they occur. The only way to know this is through practice.

Basic palette plus colour mixes for portrait opposite ▼
The basic palette shown below consists of the colours that the artist selected to make the portrait opposite. It is made up of just nine colours, which are shown down the left-hand side. Next to these colours you can see how each has been modified by combining it with one or more colours from the same basic palette. It's surprising how many different colours and tones you can create in this way.

Look at the painting and try to see where the different mixes occur. As you practise colour blending you will become adept at getting your tones right, even though at first it may seem a daunting element of portraiture. Just use scrap paper to experiment on before you colour your portrait.

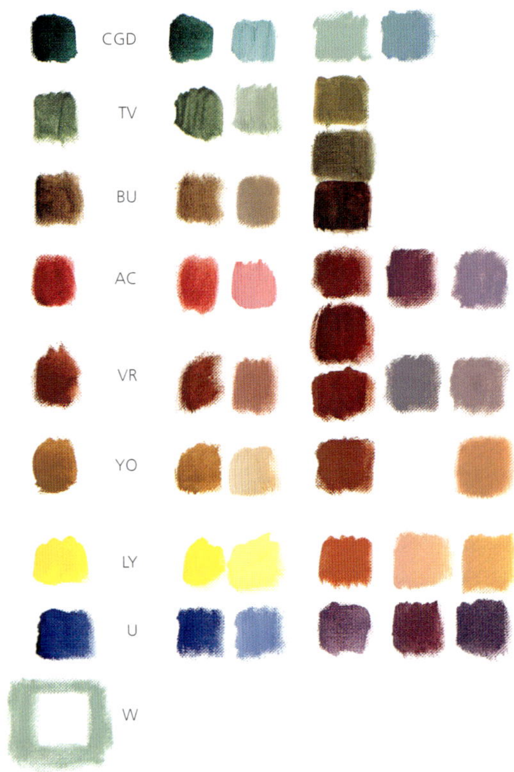

Key

CGD	Chrome green deep	YO	Yellow ochre
TV	Terre verte	LY	Lemon yellow
BU	Burnt umber	U	Ultramarine
AC	Alizarin crimson	W	Titanium white
VR	Venetian red		

Pale skin, painted in oils ▼

In this oil portrait of a woman with very pale skin, the artist toned the canvas with a warm earth mix of Venetian red and yellow ochre, so that he could allow the same mix to show through for the hair and parts of the skin (in the forehead, for example). White was used to lighten the skin tones and crimson to create the darks, with the addition of blues to make bluish and purplish (cool and warm) grey where appropriate. (Note how the interplay of warm and cool tones in the flesh helps to create a sense of modelling.) Terre verte was used as a dark mid tone in the shadow under the chin. White was used as a pigment to give the flesh body and to lighten and make cooler the colour of the flesh.

The forehead has three tones – light in the middle (a warm hue – b), a mid-tone on the left (a warm hue – a) and a dark on the right in the shadow of the hair (c). In both the mid and dark tones, the coloured ground is visible through scumbled and wiped-off areas. The dark tone and colour of the hair in the shade (d) contrasts with a light ochre (e).

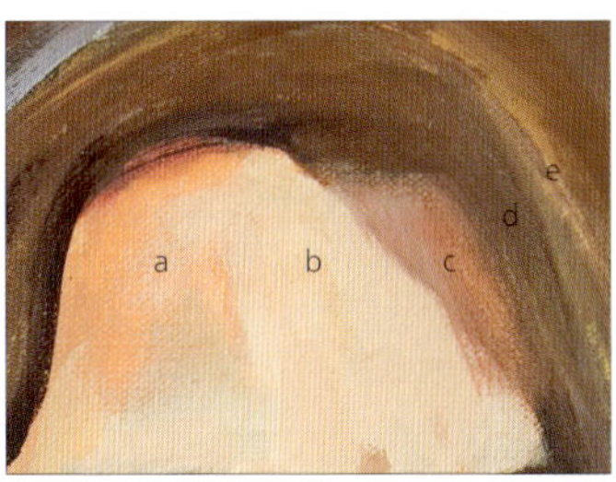

The background has a warm, dark grey (a) and a cooler, lighter colour (b), to contrast with the warm dark of the hair (c). The contrast helps focus the attention on the woman's face.

The jaw and neck are painted in two tones – a mid/light (a/c) and a dark (b). The mid-lights and dark tones are composed of green and brown/red contrasts to create a sense of volume.

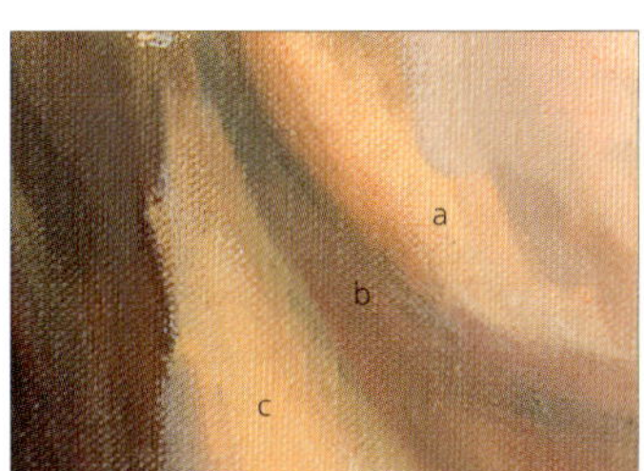

The side plane of the nose is a warm dark (a) composed of two hues. The profile of the nose is a cool, bright light (b). The whiteness of the light suggests natural daylight.

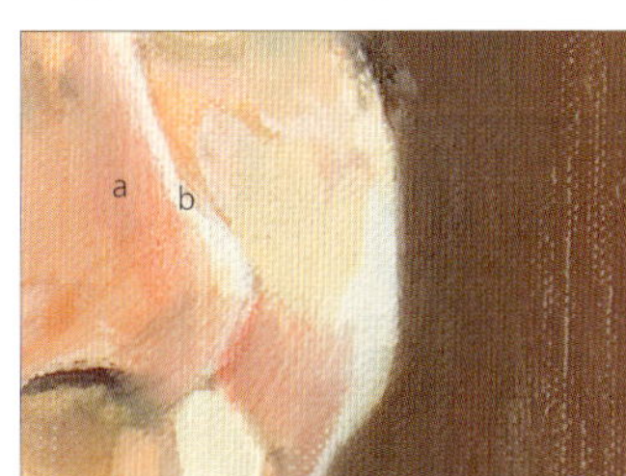

Assessing colours

When you're drawing or painting flesh, be it a portrait or a nude, you need to take into account two things: the actual colour of your model's skin and the effect of the light and surrounding colours on the model's skin. No two portrait situations are alike, so it's important that you make your observations with each model as carefully and as sympathetically as you can.

Beginners are often surprised to see how many colours artists discern (greens, blues, purples) in skin tones. It's impossible to be dogmatic about this, as it all depends on the particular lighting situation and the model, but often it's the interplay of warm and cool colours that makes a portrait really sparkle – so try using warm darks if you've got cool lights/mid tones – and vice versa.

Colour temperature

You also need to think about the relative warmth or coolness of colours. Colour temperature is important because of the way that warm colours appear to advance in a painting, while cool ones appear to recede. So in a portrait, areas that jut forwards, such as the nose, cheekbones and chin, have a contrast of warm and cool lights and mid tones. Highlights can be either warm or cool depending on the light source and the colour of the person's skin. You should have a warm and a cool version of each of the three primary colours – red, yellow and blue – in your palette, as this enables you to mix both warm and cool colours. Lemon yellow, for example, is cooler than cadmium yellow, while ultramarine blue is warmer than cerulean blue – so if you want to mix a cool green, mix it from a cool blue and yellow.

Basic palette plus colour mixes ▶
The palette for the opposite portrait is virtually identical to the one on page 56, with cadmium scarlet instead of the chrome green deep. Each colour has been modified by combining it with one or more colours from the same basic palette – but note how different some of the colours look on the coloured ground in the portrait.

Key

CS	Cadmium scarlet
TV	Terre verte
BU	Burnt umber
AC	Alizarin crimson
VR	Venetian red
YO	Yellow ochre
LY	Lemon yellow
U	Ultramarine
W	Titanium white

Dark skin, painted in oils ▼

This painting was also done on a toned ground; crimson was applied both thinly and thickly to create two different tones in the background. The thin ground colour on the right can also be seen as a mid tone in the face, giving the painting a liveliness that it might lack if the mid tones were painted in with more opaque colours. The basic skin tones are various mixtures of lots of yellow ochre, burnt umber and Venetian red with additions of white. The basic hair colour is a mixture of terre verte, ultramarine, burnt umber and crimson. Both warm and cool highlights can be seen, the warm highlight being a mixture of lemon yellow and white and the cool one a mixture of ultramarine with a hint of white.

The forehead is in two planes – (a–b) and (c–d). (ab) has a range of cooler, light tones and (cd) a range of warmer mid and dark tones. The light tones are made from lemon yellow, white and a violet mixture. The warmer tones are a mixture of yellow ochre, alizarin crimson and burnt umber.

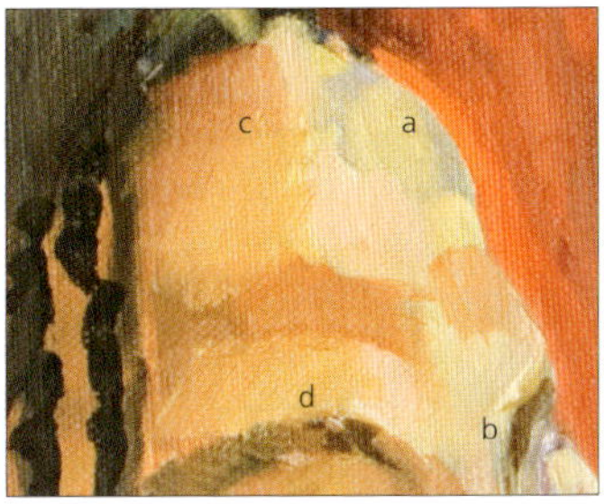

The end of the nose (a) has lights from pink, light blue, light green and lemon yellow and white. The objective was to have warm and cool lights next to each other. The cheek is a warm light (b) over a cooler green. A warm yellow ochre in the upper lip (c) overlaps the dark in the nostril.

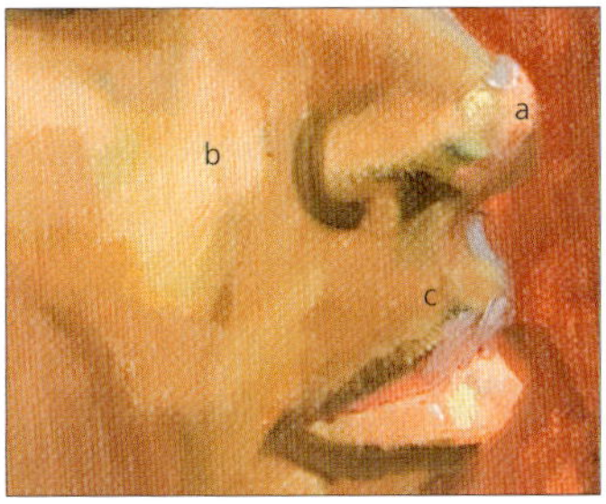

Lemon yellow and white highlights (a) contrast with the mid tones at the end of the nose, which are composed of violet and Venetian red mixtures.
The same highlight appears in the cheek (b), in contrast to a warm mid tone (yellow ochre) and a warm dark (Venetian red). Similar but slightly more subdued colours appear in the light side of the upper lip (c), with a warmer, darker Venetian red mixture on the opposite, darker side (d). Again, similar mixtures appear in the chin (e). The lips are a range of colours derived from alizarin crimson, with white and blue added to make light cooler violets mixed with ochre in the top lip. The bottom lip (f) is neat cadmium scarlet in the mid tone, with white for the lighter tone to show the fullness of the shape.

Live models or photographs?

At some point, the question will arise of whether or not it is acceptable to work from a photograph or whether you should always work from life. There's no doubt that spending time with your model will enable you to pick up on all those quintessential little quirks and mannerisms – that sparkle in the eye, a tilt of the head or a particular stance – that make each one of us so individual. It also forces you to be aware of the fact that your model is a living, breathing person whose pose and expression will inevitably change as the sitting goes on; drawings and paintings made from photographs sometimes lack that sense of life, no matter how accurately observed the individual features are.

Sometimes, however, there really is no alternative: a photograph can capture a fleeting moment that you simply could not recreate in any other way – a memory of a special holiday, for example, or a one-off event such as a family celebration. And for beginners, working with a live model for the first time can be quite intimidating. So never feel you have to apologize for working from photos; it's a great way of getting to grips with things like measuring and creating a sense of light and shade. If you have the chance, however, do try to get some life-drawing experience. There are lots of good and inexpensive evening classes that provide the perfect opportunity to work in a professional atmosphere under the guidance of an experienced tutor. Alternatively, get together with a group of like-minded friends and share the cost of hiring a model – or ask family members and friends if they'd be willing to pose for you. For quick sketches, especially when you're a complete beginner, you might also like to try drawing and painting yourself, by setting up a mirror near your easel or work table.

If you hire a model yourself, there are some things you need to remember. Understandably, many models will be wary of posing for total strangers outside an art-school environment, particularly if you're asking them to pose in the nude. Make sure you tell them in advance exactly what the session will entail, how long it will last, say how many people will be involved and agree a fee. If they don't know you, be prepared to provide references. If you want to hire a model privately, it's a good idea to contact one that you've already met in an official life-drawing class – then the model knows that you're a *bona fide* art student and you know that they've got useful life-modelling experience.

It's also very important to consider your model's comfort during the session. Check that they can hold the pose you're asking them to adopt comfortably, and establish before you start how long they will have to hold that pose; even experienced models will probably need to stretch their legs after half an hour or so, and dynamic, twisting poses can only be held for a few minutes. If they're posing nude, make sure the room is warm and that they have somewhere private to change and undress. Give them a general indication of the pose that you want – for example, a standing pose with the upper body twisted – and then let them move around and settle into a pose that feels natural and comfortable to them. Experienced models will probably come up with their own suggestions, so take advantage of this; the results will be better than if you simply dictate what you want.

Before you start painting, however, take time to really look at the pose. Ask yourself if the background complements or distracts; even a minor adjustment to the way a piece of fabric drapes can make a big difference to your composition. Think about the overall shape of the composition: are there strong lines in the pose that will help to lead the viewer's eye around the picture? Look at the negative spaces in the pose – for example, would changing the angle of the arms allow more of the striped throw to show through, creating an interesting splash of colour in the centre of the picture?

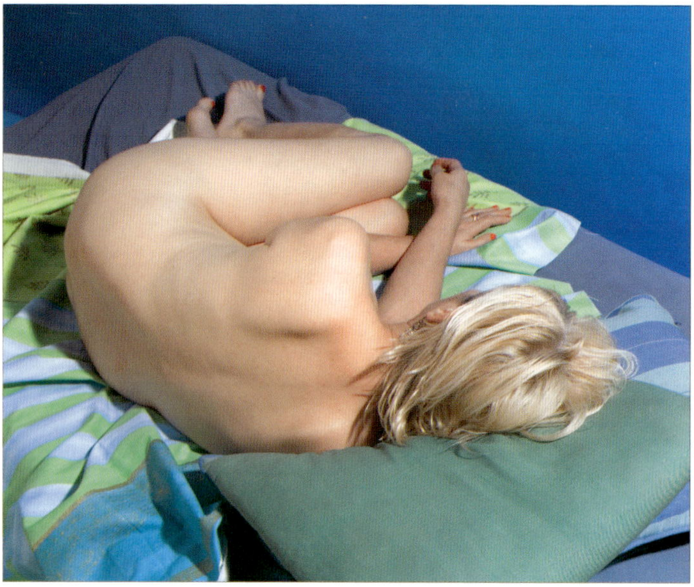

Reclining pose ◄
Once the model has settled into position, a reclining pose is comfortable and easy to hold for a relatively long period of time.

Difficult pose ►
This is a difficult stance for a model to hold, so remember that your model will probably need to break the pose and stretch his muscles; put masking tape on the floor around his feet, so that he can get back into the same position. It would be worth taking some photographs to refer to after the live drawing session, but it is best to do as much work as possible with the model, as it gives you a better idea of muscular and skeletal positions.

Action pose ▲
In an action pose such as this, you only have time to make a few very quick reference sketches, so working from a photo is really your best option – although it helps if you've spent time in situ, observing how the subject moves and which muscles come into play.

Animated subjects ►
Young children are too lively and energetic to sit still for long and even an experienced adult model could not hold an animated smile like this without it looking forced and stilted. This is another situation where it is easier to work from a photograph. Take lots of reference photos so you can identify subtle changes in expression and then select the one(s) that seem most representative of your subjects.

Composition

In its simplest terms, 'composition' is the way you arrange the different elements of your drawing or painting within the picture space. Before you can do that, however, you have to decide on the picture space itself – the size and proportions of your paper or canvas.

Many artists opt for a format in which the ratio of the short side of the canvas to the longer side is 1 : 1.6 – the so-called 'golden rectangle', which evolved as an artistic ideal during the Renaissance. The golden rectangle is a safe bet, as it works horizontally and vertically, so suits many different subjects, but it is by no means the only option. A lot depends on your subject matter and on the effect and mood you want to create. Look at other artists' work and, if you see an unusual format, think about why the artist might have chosen it. An artist might, for example, choose a long, thin panoramic format for a landscape painting to emphasize the breadth of the landscape, or a square format for a portrait in order to fill the canvas with a dramatic painting of just the sitter's head.

Arranging elements within the picture space

Over the centuries, artists have devised various ways of positioning the main pictorial elements on an invisible grid around specific positions within the picture space. One of the simplest is splitting the picture area into three, both horizontally and vertically, which gives a grid of nine sections with lines crossing at four points. The theory is that positioning major elements of the composition near these lines or their intersections ('on the third') will give a pleasing image.

It is also important to lead the viewer's eye towards the picture's main centre of interest. You can do this by introducing lines or curves, real or implied, into the composition. A road leading up to your main subject is an example of a real line; an implied line might be a composition in which the artist has arranged throws or cushions in a curving line that leads the viewer's eye through to the subject, a reclining figure on a sofa.

You can also imply geometric shapes within the composition to lead the viewer's eye around the picture. You might, for example, ask your sitter to hold a book in one hand. If you then take an imaginary line from this point to the crook of the model's other arm, and then up to the head, the three points joined together form a triangle: this leads the viewer's eye around the portrait, with the apex of the triangle – the sitter's head – being the focal and therefore the most important point.

Portraits and figure studies bring their own special compositional requirements. A central placing generally looks stiff and unnatural, as does a direct, face-on approach. Heads in portraits are usually placed off centre, with the sitter viewed from a three-quarter angle. More space is often left on the side towards which the sitter is looking. You also need to think about how much space to leave above the head. Too much and the head can appear pushed down; too little and it will seem cramped.

These are just a few of the compositional devices that have evolved over the years. The best way to learn about composition is to study other artists' work and try to work out how they have directed your eye towards the focal point of the image. You will gradually find that you can compose a picture instinctively – but if you're relatively new to painting, it really is worth taking the time to think about it, and even try sketching out different options, before you commit yourself and mark the canvas or paper.

Triangular composition ◄
In this family group by Ian Sidaway, the figures form a rough triangle that holds the group together visually and focuses attention firmly on them rather than on any background elements. There is also an inverted triangle below this, running across the painting between the heads of the two children and down to the dog. This helps to lead the viewer's eye around the painting. When you're arranging a group with some figures seated and some standing, make sure that there isn't too much of a disparity in height. Here the father is bending over slightly so that he's closer in height to the rest of the family; this also increases the sense of intimacy between him and the other family members.

Diagonal lines and props ▶
In the lovely *Interior with Jacqueline*, which is both a portrait and a visual essay on light, David Curtis has used the diagonal lines of the bureau to direct the viewer's eye to the subject and the work that she is concentrating upon. The gentle curve of the model's back echoes and balances the diagonal line of the bureau on the left and helps to draw the viewer's eye to the focal point of the image – the sitter's face and expression. Her right arm also provides a partial frame for her face, again helping to direct our eyes to the focal point.

When you intend to paint the whole figure rather than just a head and shoulders, you must consider what other elements to include and whether props will help to enhance your description of the sitter. If you paint the subject in their own home, you can show them in familiar surroundings and with personal possessions. Particular props are often used in portraiture to help describe the character and interests of the sitter. A writer or someone fond of reading might be shown with a selection of favourite books, or a musician with his or her instrument. Try to convey something of the atmosphere around your sitter.

Sweeping curves ▶
In this portrait by Paul Bartlett, the viewer's eye is led around the picture in a circular fashion, starting from the focal point – the head, which is positioned roughly 'on the third' – down to the writing hand and back to the head again. The sweeping curves of the figure, chair and writing pad are balanced by the table and the dark upright of the lamp.

Light and shade

Light is a critical part of portraiture and figure painting: it is the contrast between light and shade, as the different planes of the head or body turn away from the light and into shadow, that enables artists to create a three-dimensional impression in their work. The four aspects of light that you need to consider are direction, quality (or intensity), colour and shadow.

Direction of light

First of all, think about where you are going to position your subject in relation to the light source. For beginners, the best direction is when the light is coming from just in front of and to one side of your subject – a set-up known as 'three-quarter lighting'. One side of your subject will be brightly lit, while the opposite side will be in shadow, making it much easier to distinguish the relative lights, darks and half tones. If the light is directly in front of your subject, it tends to 'flatten' the subject, making it harder to see the different planes and create that all-important sense of modelling. If the light is behind your subject it will create a 'halo' effect, again making it harder to see the different planes. This is known as contre-jour lighting and is often used to good effect to create soft, romantic-looking images, so may be one of the many techniques you could work towards after you have become comfortable with working with three-quarter lighting.

Backlighting ►
This technique can create lovely effects, silhouetting the figure, softening the colours and reducing the tonal contrasts. In this charming portrait of a mother and child, Geoff Marsters has exploited this kind of lighting to create a gentle and meditative mood that is entirely in keeping with the subject.

Quality of light

Light, both natural and artificial, varies considerably in quality or intensity. On a cloudy day, natural light may be very soft and diffused, whereas on a sunny summer's day it may be very bright and contrasty. Artificial light, too, can be used to cast a strong beam on to one specific place (think of a theatre spotlight), or diffused and spread over a wider area by being shone through a translucent material such as paper or fabric.

The time of day has an effect, too. Early in the morning and late in the afternoon, when the sun is relatively low in the sky, the light is at an oblique angle, which throws things into relief and creates good modelling; at midday, on the other hand, the sun is almost directly overhead, which tends to make things look flatter.

Midday light ◄
In Ian Sidaway's delightful portrait of a little girl looking at her reflection in a pool, the midday light is harsh and intense, bleaching out much of the detail on the child's hair and skin. The short shadow and still, unrippled water add to the sense of a sultry, hot noon. The darkening tones of grey on the stone surround of the pool give the image a sense of depth, while the warmth of the skin tones in the upper half of the image is balanced in the lower half by the rich, orangey-red of the goldfish, which contrasts with the cool blue dress.

Colour of light

Different kinds of light have distinct colour casts. Late afternoon sunlight, for example, often has a rich, warm glow, while fluorescent light has a pink or yellow tinge. Needless to say, these colour casts affect the colour of the objects that the light is illuminating.

Most of the time colour casts do not matter too much, as our eyes automatically adjust. It can, however, become a problem if you begin a painting in natural light and then, as the day progresses, turn on the artificial room lights to complete your work. If you've been using, say, cadmium yellow for highlights, those same highlights may appear much cooler under electric light, causing you to switch to the more acidic-looking lemon yellow. When you view your work in daylight again, the discrepancies will immediately become apparent. So be aware that this is a potential problem and try to keep the same kind of lighting throughout, even though this may mean that you need several painting sessions to complete your work.

Shadows

In addition to helping you create a three-dimensional impression, shadows can form an integral part of a painting in their own right and add a sense of drama to your work. Think, for example, of horror films, in which the shadow of the monster looms large on a wall before we ever see it in the flesh.

At the other end of the spectrum, dappled light playing on a figure can create constantly fluctuating shadows that suggest a soft, romantic mood. Even something as simple as the glazing bars on a window can cast shadows inside a room, which you can exploit as a compositional device. So although they're insubstantial, shadows are an important way of adding interest to your drawings and paintings.

Remember, however, that natural light is constantly changing and so shadows can change position, or even fade away completely, during the course of a painting session. It's a good idea to block them in, however lightly, at the start – or at least take a few photos to use as reference.

Shadow play ▼
The strong shadows cast on the wall behind the model add drama to this deceptively simple-looking, almost monochromatic portrait by Ian Sidaway.

Backgrounds and props

Unless you're simply making a quick sketch, it is very rare indeed for there to be no background in a portrait or figure study – so it's worth thinking about what kind of background to choose. The background can be as important a part of the composition as the figure or portrait itself, and should be considered right from the start and not merely put in as an afterthought.

Often, the background is there simply to place the focus on the person who is being painted. It provides a contrast in colour or tone, against which the model or sitter can stand out – perhaps a dark colour behind a well-lit person. If you're new to figure drawing and portraiture, this is a good way to start as it allows you to concentrate all your efforts and energy on capturing a good likeness and the personality of your sitter.

You also need to think a bit about the texture of the background. A flat wash of colour can be uninteresting to look at, so look for things like a brick wall, textured stonework or cloths that can be draped to create interesting folds and some sense of light and shade in the painting. It's worth collecting a few drapes in different colours and patterns that you can quickly hang up. Remnants from fabric shops and old sheets are inexpensive options.

Even though they may seem relatively insignificant, background elements with strong vertical or horizontal lines, such as doors and windows, are useful from two points of view. First, they provide you with clear and clean lines that you can use as a guide to the placement and angle of other features. Second, they can be used as a compositional device to frame, contain or even direct the viewer's eye towards the subject.

As you gain more confidence and experience, you can make the backgrounds to your paintings more elaborate. You can use them to convey a sense of who the sitter is – the place that he or she holds in society or his or her interests and personality, for example – by incorporating objects of personal significance or a particular landscape or interior that relates to the subject. Look for relatively small, simply shaped props such as books or musical instruments that your sitter can hold: they can tell the viewer something about the subject. As a bonus, they give nervous and fidgety sitters something to do with their hands.

If you're painting a whole figure, it usually needs to be put into a believable context, so some of the room should be included. Make sure, however, that the background and props do not dominate: always keep the background more subdued than the figure, both in terms of colour and the way that you treat it. Cool colours will accentuate the warmth of a model's skin, while bright colours and patterns will detract from it.

Minimal props ◄
In a head-and-shoulders portrait, the background is often deliberately left vague and undefined in order to focus attention on the face. Here the artist chose to include the sitter's feather boa as a prop, both to 'frame' her face and also to convey something of her exuberant personality.

If the model is brightly lit, then a dark background will act as a foil; if your model is dark-skinned or wearing dark clothing, then a pale background may be more appropriate.

On the subject of clothing, make sure it reflects the sitter's character and their personality. Bright and lively, subdued and sombre – the choice is completely subjective, but clothing can play an important role in establishing the mood of a portrait. As with backgrounds, however, it is generally best to avoid clothing with very dominant patterns so as not to draw attention away from the sitter.

Put more detail into the figure than into the background or any props. Remember that you can use some artistic licence: if something such as a patterned wallpaper or carpet detracts from your subject, then paint it loosely and broadly; you can even choose to omit it altogether.

When you're planning a drawing or painting, think about the proportion of the picture space that is going to be occupied by the background. If it is too small, there is not enough to provide additional information about the sitter; if it is too big, the viewer's attention is drawn away from the main subject.

The figure in context ▲
If you are painting a portrait, the face or figure will be the main centre of attention, with other elements such as furniture playing a subsidiary role, but in Sally Strand's *Passing Quietly*, the figures are fully integrated into the interior of the room. The real subject of the painting is light and colour, and the people have been treated almost as inanimate objects, echoing the still life on the counter and the chair in the corner. Placing them in the background enhances this feeling.

Minimizing the background ◄
It is vital that the background does not dominate, even while it is an important part of the picture. Here, the artist simplified the studio setting, contents of the window sill and the objects outside the window behind the sitter so that they provide visual interest without overpowering the subject. Note the good use of colour – the yellow and white really frame the sitter's head and create a lovely sense of light flooding into the room, and contrast well with the sitter's dark clothing.

Character and mood

Placing the flapping bird's wings so close to the edge of the frame enhances the sense of movement.

The use of complementary colours – here, red and green – is a good way of imparting a sense of vibrant energy to a painting.

The expression is one of sheer delight.

Exuberance ◄
In this painting by Ian Sidaway, the youthful exuberance of this little girl is evident from both her expression and from the energetic portrayal of the birds' flapping wings as they flutter upwards. The complementary colours – the red of the girl's sweater against the vivid green of the grass – also give the painting a sense of life and energy.

Capturing your subject's character and mood in a portrait involves bringing together many of the topics explored in the previous pages of this section, and is one of the most difficult and most rewarding challenges in portraiture. Individual features vary considerably from one person to another and of course you have to use all your technical skill as an artist to capture a good likeness. But portraiture involves much more than this: a good portrait should also capture something of the sitter's mood and personality. This will give the portrait meaning – for example, you could be making a statement about a particular time of the sitter's life or capturing an achievement or element of their personality that you (or the person commissioning the portrait) particularly admire.

Facial expressions, gestures and stance all play an important part in revealing a person's mood and, like individual facial features, these are things that you can capture through keen observation. Spend as much time as possible talking to your sitter and getting to know their expressions before you mark your paper. Laughter, frowns, open-eyed amazement – the muscle movements required to form these expressions all affect the surface form of the face. If your model is smiling, for example, the cheek muscles will pull the mouth wide; they also push up the lower eyelids, narrowing and sometimes completely closing the eyes. In a frown, on the other hand, the brows are pulled down, covering the upper eyelids and allowing the lower lids to drop. Look, too, at the teeth: generally we see much more of the upper teeth than the lower in a laughing expression or smile. In daily life we are very adept at detecting even slight muscular movements and reading the thoughts behind the resultant facial expressions. Combine these expressions with gestures – a shrug of the shoulders, upturned palms – and you can tell a lot about somebody's mood and temperament. Translating this into your artwork takes practice and patience but is one of the keys to successful portraiture.

Beyond this, you also need to make a series of aesthetic decisions. Some of these decisions are to do with composition – in other words, where you decide to place your subject in the picture space. In a conventional head-and-shoulders portrait, the figure is normally placed slightly off centre, with more space in front of them than behind; this creates a feeling of calm. If you feel a more confrontational mood is appropriate, however, you might choose a square format and a head-on view of the face, and place the head right in the centre of the picture space. Similarly, a profile view with the sitter's nose very close to the edge of the frame creates tension in the portrait.

You also need to think about what else to include in the portrait. Your choice of background will go some way to determining the mood of the portrait – so do you want a calm, pale background in a single colour or a lively, busy pattern? If you're painting a figure in a room setting, the items that you include can speak volumes about the sitter's interests and personality. Many great artists have taken this further, to include props or decor that are symbolic – think of the heraldic devices often present in portraits of aristocratic figures, for example. Every item included in the picture space is important in some way. While you may not be interested in symbolism, it is worth being selective about the props and background as they will affect the way your portrait is interpreted.

The way you light your subject affects the mood of the portrait. For a romantic portrait of a young girl, you might choose soft, diffused lighting or even position your sitter with window light coming from directly behind her, so that the colours are muted and detail is subdued. Harsh, strongly directional light can accentuate details such as wrinkles and expression lines in the face, which can work for some dynamic, 'action' or character portraits but may be too unflattering or stark for other subjects.

Finally, there are decisions to be made about your colour palette and the way you apply the paint. You might think that you just paint the colours that you see, but colour can be critical in evoking a mood so choose the spectrum carefully. Bright, hot shades generally create a lively mood, whereas sombre, muted shades give the opposite effect. Pick up on the colours that your sitter is wearing and use them elsewhere in the painting to reflect their mood. Of course, you can change the colours of the clothing to suit the mood of your portrait, if you wish.

Your brush and pencil strokes, too, can affect the atmosphere of the drawing or painting. Lively, vigorous strokes and thick, impasto work can create a feeling of energy, while soft washes, in which the brushstrokes are not really visible, can evoke a mood of calm. Generally, getting to know your sitter's personality will help you to decide the colours, techniques and strokes that will suit your portrait best and create an appropriate mood.

Sombre mood ▼

Portraiture involves more than simply achieving a likeness through correct observation of the shapes of noses, eyes and mouths. The best portraits give a feeling of atmosphere and express something of the sitter's character. In Karen Raney's *David* a sense of the sitter's melancholy and introspection is conveyed through the sombre colours of the clothing and background, and heavy, downward-sweeping brushmarks, as well as by the sitter's intense, yet inward-looking, gaze. The sitter seems to make direct eye contact with the observer, which is an important method by which a painting 'draws in' the viewer and encourages them to ask questions about the sitter's mood, the meaning of the painting, and about the feelings the artist wanted to evoke. Unlike the portrait on the opposite page, this painting evokes feelings of discomfort and curiosity.

Long, downward-dragging brushstrokes and the cool, muted colour of the background enhance the sense of melancholy.

The subdued expression and the direct, almost challenging, gaze say much about the sitter's mood.

The dark, blue-grey clothing matches the sitter's sombre mood.

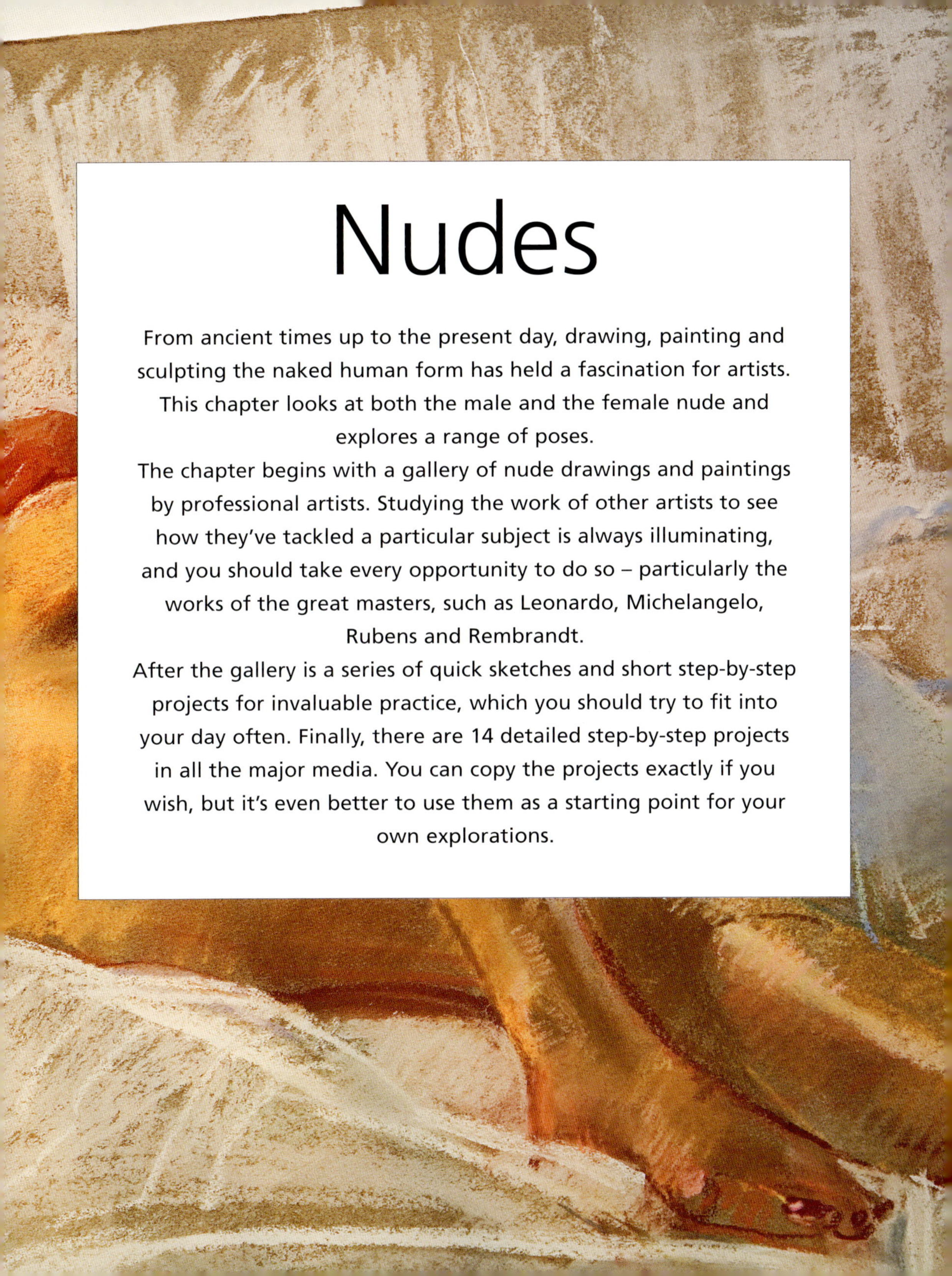

Nudes

From ancient times up to the present day, drawing, painting and sculpting the naked human form has held a fascination for artists. This chapter looks at both the male and the female nude and explores a range of poses.

The chapter begins with a gallery of nude drawings and paintings by professional artists. Studying the work of other artists to see how they've tackled a particular subject is always illuminating, and you should take every opportunity to do so – particularly the works of the great masters, such as Leonardo, Michelangelo, Rubens and Rembrandt.

After the gallery is a series of quick sketches and short step-by-step projects for invaluable practice, which you should try to fit into your day often. Finally, there are 14 detailed step-by-step projects in all the major media. You can copy the projects exactly if you wish, but it's even better to use them as a starting point for your own explorations.

Gallery

This section displays a range of nudes in different media and styles, from rapid brush-and-wash drawings made in a matter of minutes, which capture the essence of the pose with a few carefully placed strokes, to detailed paintings that explore the intricacies and subtleties of the human form in all its glory. Studying other artists' work is always a revealing exercise, so examine them carefully and try to analyze what the artist did. Look at the use of light and shade to create rounded, three-dimensional forms. Try to work out whether colours are warm or cool, and what effect this has. Think about the techniques that the artist has employed and consider what aspects you might be able to apply in your own work. Going beyond the technical aspects of drawing and painting, think about things like composition, lighting, and props, and how they contribute to the work as a whole. Everyone's taste differs and you will find your own favourites in this gallery, but even paintings that do not appeal to you can turn out to be surprisingly informative. The more you look at other people's work, the more you will learn – and the more you will be able to apply those lessons to your own work.

Composing with shapes ▶
In his pastel drawing, *Elly*, David Cuthbert has made an exciting composition by reducing detail to a minimum and concentrating on the interplay of shapes – the curves of the limbs counterpointing the more geometric shapes of the clothing and chair.

Muscle and bone structure ◀
The appeal of Edward Frost's *Life Study of the Female Figure* lies in the lovely, sinuous curves of the body. The underlying musculature and bone structure can be clearly seen and the subtle tonal transitions across the form have been painstakingly rendered. Note the cast shadows across the lower back and under the buttocks: these add interest to the composition and enhance the three-dimensional feel. The composition, with the figure cutting through the picture space from bottom left to top right, is unusual but adds a strong, dynamic element to an otherwise calm, static pose.

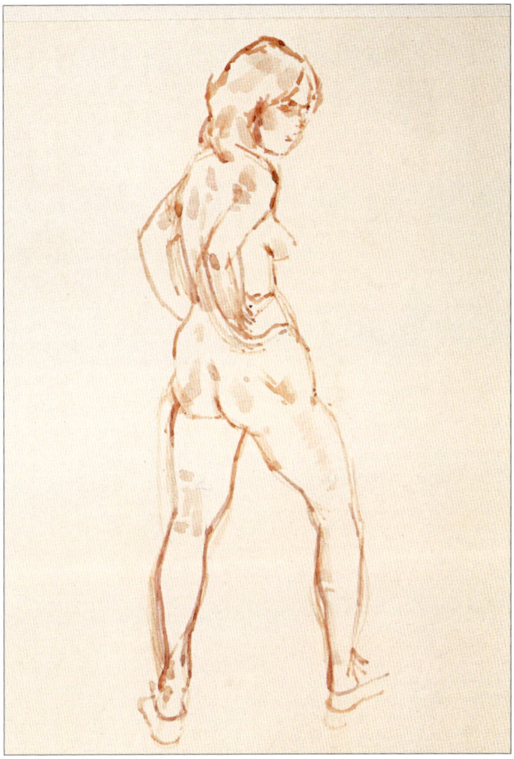

The standing figure ▲

In drawing or painting the human figure, it is vital to analyze the pose and to understand how the weight is distributed and how the whole body is affected by any movement. In these brush-and-wash drawings, James Horton captures beautifully both the swing of the body, and also its three-dimensional quality of mass and weight. Although these are intended as nothing more than quick sketches, note how effectively the artists has combined bold, linear marks (made using the tip of the brush as a drawing implement) with deftly placed washes in varying dilutions of ink to create modelling on the figure.

Rounded forms ▶

This simple pencil drawing by Elisabeth Harden concentrates on the rounded nature of the female form. The relaxed pose of the model and raised left leg are depicted in a flowing outline, with no sharp angles used at all. Note how fluently the artist has used the pencil here: always try to keep the pencil moving as you search out the forms in a drawing like this, so that you build up a momentum and a degree of fluidity in your lines and can make adjustments as necessary.

▶

Muscles visible beneath the skin ▲

The impressive thing about this pencil sketch, *Standing Figure* by Vincent Milne, is the way that the artist has used tone to convey how the muscles affect the surface form of the body. Note how strong linear strokes, hatching and smudging have all been used to good effect to create tones of different densities.

Light and shadow for modelling ◄

In *Standing Male Nude* by William Etty, the cast shadows show the relief in the anatomy of the model. A deeper space is suggested beyond the model in the use of roughly defined shapes of a darker tone, which acts as a backdrop in contrast to the precise definition of volume in the model's form.

Etty's skill with oils explores all the major muscle groups in the figure as the model flexes his left leg, reaches up and pulls back his right arm creating a twist on the torso. His left raised arm defines the centre of the composition and a series of diagonals to the right creates structure and balance within the rectangle – the right hand rests on a horizontal, defining a square – a clever device to create stability.

Brush-and-ink ▼

Both these drawings by Hazel Harrison were done in under ten minutes, with slightly diluted brown ink and a Chinese brush. The method is excellent for quick figure drawings and movement studies.

Drawing light ▲

Forms are described by the way in which the light falls on them, so in life drawing or portraiture it helps to have a fairly strong source of illumination. In Gerry Baptist's simple but powerful charcoal drawing, the light comes from one side, slightly behind the model, making a lovely pale shape across the shoulders and down the hip and leg. Of course, we only read the white paper as being a highlight area because of the contrasting darks nearby. Here, the shadows have been created by wiping the side of the charcoal stick across the paper, applying only minimal pressure for the mid tones and much more pressure for the really dark areas. The artist has then softened these dark areas by smudging the marks.

▶

Dramatic light ▶
Maureen Jordan has called her painting *In the Spotlight* and, as the title implies, the main subject is light rather than the figure itself, which is treated as a bold, broad generalization. She has applied the pastel thickly, working on textured watercolour paper, which allows a considerable build-up of pigment.

Directional strokes ▼
A classic combination of line and side strokes can be seen in this lively figure study, *Nude against Pink* by Maureen Jordan. Note how the artist has used the pastel sticks in a descriptive way, following the directions of the shapes and forms.

Painting flesh tones ▶
In *Seated Nude* Robert Maxwell Wood has chosen the paper wisely; it is almost the same colour as the mid tone of the model's flesh, which means he can allow the paper to show in the final painting and create a sense of lightness and airiness that could not be achieved by covering the entire paper with pastel pigment. This use of a coloured ground is a traditional technique in pastel and oil painting. Wood has used blending methods in places, but has avoided overdoing this, as it can make the image appear bland. Instead he has contrasted blends with crisp diagonal hatching and fine outlines made with the tip of the pastel to describe the fall of light on the head, neck and arms.

Vignetting technique ▲

James Horton has not attempted to treat the background or foreground in detail, concentrating instead on the rich, golden colours of the body in *Reclining Nude*. This vignetting method, in which the focal point of the picture is emphasized by allowing the surrounding colours to merge gently into the toned paper, is a traditional pastel-drawing technique. The method is also often used in photography, where the centre of a composition will be brightly lit or in clear focus, and the outer detail fading into dark or slightly out of focus.

Perspective and foreshortening ►
Vincent Milne's *Reclining Nude* is a simple but effective study in drawing the figure in perspective. Note, for example, how tiny the feet appear compared with the hands. The model's legs are raised, adding a vertical element to the composition and allowing the artist to incorporate strong shading on the side of the legs that is furthest away from the light. Both these things turn an otherwise straightforward technical exercise into something that is visually much more interesting. Although the artist used the same charcoal stick throughout the drawing, note how varied the marks are: fine linear detail in the hands and feet, broad areas of mid and dark tone put in using the side of the stick, and dense, heavy shadows that have been vigorously scribbled in. Note, too, how blocking in the background behind the model's feet has the effect of both creating a context for the scene and focusing our attention on the figure.

Mood and tension ◄
In Harold Gilman's *Nude on a Bed* the direct gaze is almost confrontational in mood and the pose, in which the model is hunched up hugging her knees, also contributes to a feeling of tension. The figure forms a rough triangle within the picture space, the base of the triangle being the diagonal line of the blankets that runs upwards from the bottom right corner. The patterned wallpaper in the background might well be overpowering had the artist not left space to the right of the model's head.

Quick sketches

Making a series of quick sketches – say, up to 10–15 minutes each – is a great way to start a life-drawing session. Think of the process as a series of loosening-up exercises, in much the same way as you would start a session in the gym with warm-up exercises. Try to work on a large scale, filling the paper with a single sketch and moving your whole arm rather than just your fingers. This will help to free up your hand and wrist, so that you can use your pencil or brush with bold, confident strokes; if you work on too small a scale, the likelihood is that you will tighten up and lose spontaneity.

Look at the angles of the hips and shoulders to assess the balance of the pose and, even though you're working quickly, remember to measure features in relation to others and look at how features interrelate. Make use of inverted triangles to check the alignment and positioning. Put in any light guide marks that you can. The process will encourage you to really look at your subject and assess the essentials of a pose. An added bonus is that the model does not have to pose for long.

Naturally, some media are better for quick sketches than others. Soft pastels and charcoal are wonderful, as you can use the side of the sticks for broad sweeps of colour and the tips for finer detail. Pencils and pen and ink are slower, as you have to use hatching to create mid and dark tones – but you could try diluting ink and applying it with a brush instead. If you've only got a few minutes, there simply isn't time to lay down delicate watercolour or acrylic washes and allow each one to dry before you move on to the next so, rather than trying to introduce a lot of colour, opt for tonal studies. Pre-mix a range of tones from one colour so that you can quickly put in the light, mid and dark tones. You can use very dilute oil paints in the same way. Tonal studies are a useful exercise in their own right, as they force you to think about light and shade and how to render a three-dimensional form on the flat surface of the paper or canvas.

Charcoal pencil, 3–4 minutes ▼
This sketch was made very quickly, as an exercise in seeing the figure as a series of geometric forms. The torso is basically a box shape with the front and one side plane clearly visible, while the model's left leg is made up of two interlocking cylinders. A curved line over the belly helps to imply its rounded shape. Faint construction lines indicate how the artist has checked the relative positions and angles of different features: the right nipple is almost directly above the navel, the left knee aligns with the tip of the right hip and the right shoulder slopes down at the same angle, parallel.

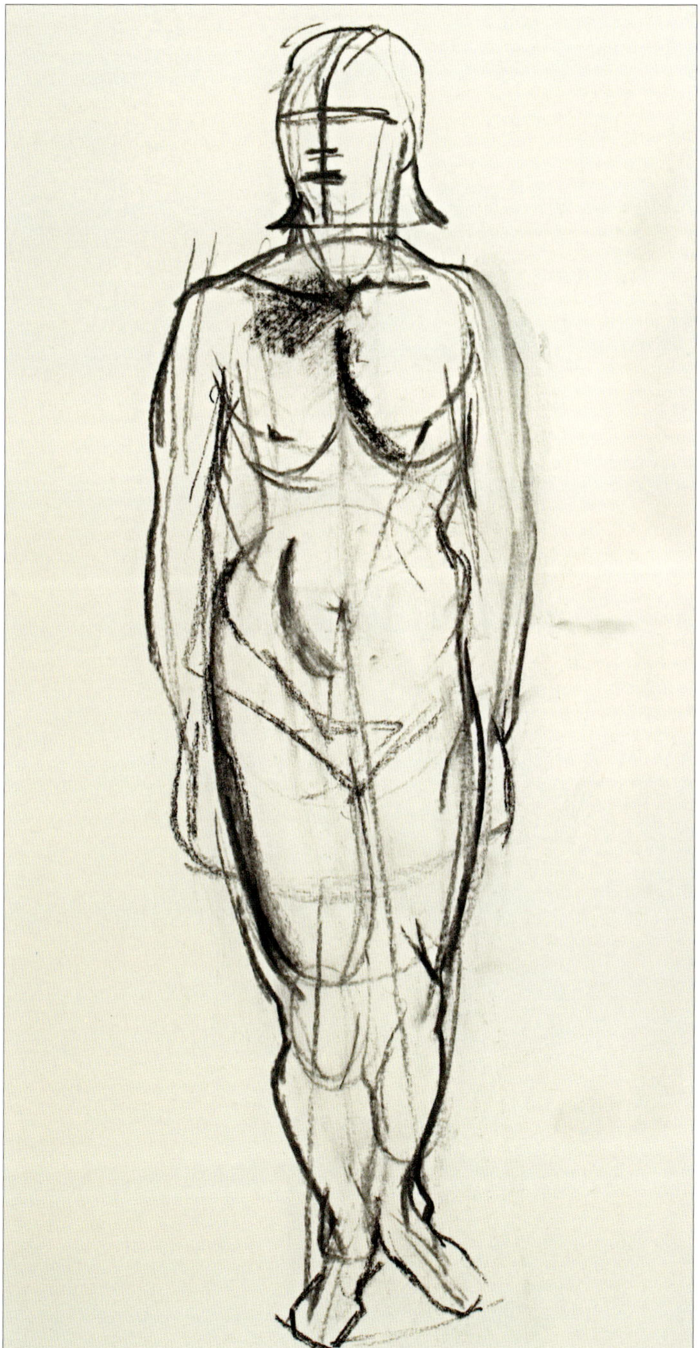

Charcoal pencil, approx. 5 minutes ◀
This is a very simple pose with the model standing almost square on to the artist's viewpoint. It does not make for a dynamic composition, but it is a good starting point if you're new to drawing the figure as it will give you practice in measuring and placing the limbs and other features correctly. Note how the artist has put in faint construction lines as a guide: a line through the central axis of the face establishes that the model's head is turned slightly to her right, while the nipples and navel form an inverted triangle. Even in a really quick sketch you can make the figure look rounded by using faint, curving lines within the form as well as contour lines around it.

Charcoal and white chalk, approx. 10 minutes ▼
Here you can see a faint diagonal line running up through the model's right leg right up to the base of the neck. This is a dynamic angle that gives the pose a sense of energy. The figure was drawn as a series of interlocking boxes, using the tip of a charcoal stick. Using the side of the stick, tone was then added to the figure and background and smudged with the fingertips. The highlights on the figure were put in with white chalk; lifting off charcoal using a torchon achieves the same result, but perhaps not so bright.

▶

Pen and ink, brush and ink, approx. 5 minutes ▲
The outline of the figure was made using a dip pen and ink, which gives a slightly irregular quality of line that is very appealing. Dilute sepia ink was then brushed on for the shaded areas of the body – a quick-and-easy way of implying the direction and intensity of the light and of making the figure look three-dimensional.

Charcoal and white chalk on toned ground, approx. 5 minutes ▶
Here, the artist has used both linear marks and the negative space around the figure to define her outline. The raised arm, the tilt of the shoulders, the inner edge of the left leg and the outline of the right hip and buttocks are in fine charcoal stick. The shaded left-hand side of the body was blocked in with the side of the stick, then chalk was added around the edge, using the space outside the body to delineate the figure and differentiate it from the background. Chalk was also used for the highlights on the figure, telling us which direction the light is coming from. The lines of the skirting board and dado rail imply the room setting, albeit in the most minimal way, and establish the plane of the floor.

Brush and ink, 3–4 minutes ▲
For these two brush-and-ink sketches, the model was asked to adopt an 'action' stance, as if taking part in a fencing duel. With both arms and legs outstretched, these are not poses that can be held for long, but they are a useful means of studying the body in positions that are slightly out of the ordinary. In both sketches, the artist concentrated on establishing the geometric shapes of the limbs first, then added a little tone – as a light wash in the sketch on the right, and as hatching in the sketch on the left – to imply light and shade and introduce a subtle hint of modelling.

Pastel pencil, 3–4 minutes ▶
Here, the artist has put in a faint vertical line to check what aligns with what: you can see that the tip of the nose, the tip of the breast, the stomach and the tip of the right foot all touch this line, which helps establish the balance of the pose. Even with minimal shading, there is a sense that the figure is three-dimensional.

Half-hour pastel pencil sketch

If you're new to life drawing, you may be surprised at how tiring concentration and careful measuring can be! Work in relatively short bursts to begin with and remember to allow frequent breaks for you and your model. The sketch on these two pages took no more than about half an hour – but much detail has been captured in that short time.

This is a practice exercise in quickly grasping the essentials of the pose. Concentrate on careful measuring and assessing how each part of the body relates to the rest. A plain, undistracting background is ideal.

This is also an exercise in using tone for a three-dimensional impression. Only two pastel pencils were used, but by looking carefully at the relative lights and darks, the artist has created a convincing study in which the fullness of the model's body is apparent.

Materials

- *Pastel pencils: yellow ochre, burnt umber*
- *Pastel paper*

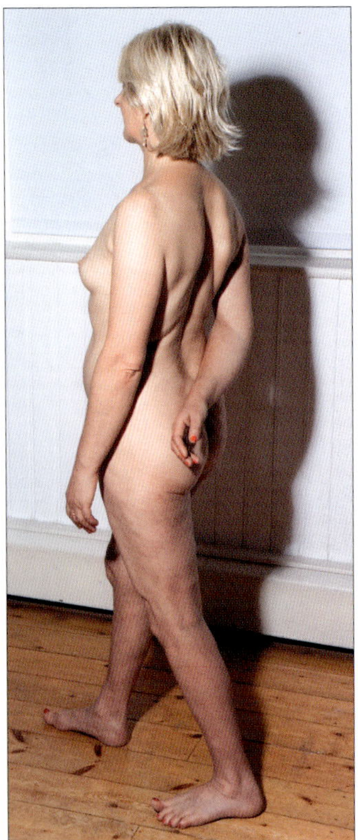

The pose

The model was asked to pose with more of her weight on one foot, with her shoulder blades thrust back to emphasize the curve of her spine. A strong light positioned to the left and slightly behind the model helps to accentuate this. Placing the right arm behind the back creates a more interesting shape than simply letting it hang by her side.

1 Using a yellow ochre pastel pencil, begin to establish the main lines of the pose. Look for strong lines that you can use as a guide to checking the position and size of different parts of the body. The line of the shoulders in relation to the hips, the hollow of the spine and the negative space between the model's right arm and torso are good checkpoints.

Tip: You may find you have more control over the pencil and can create more flowing lines if you hold it with your hand over the pencil, as in the photograph, rather than with your hand under the pencil as when writing.

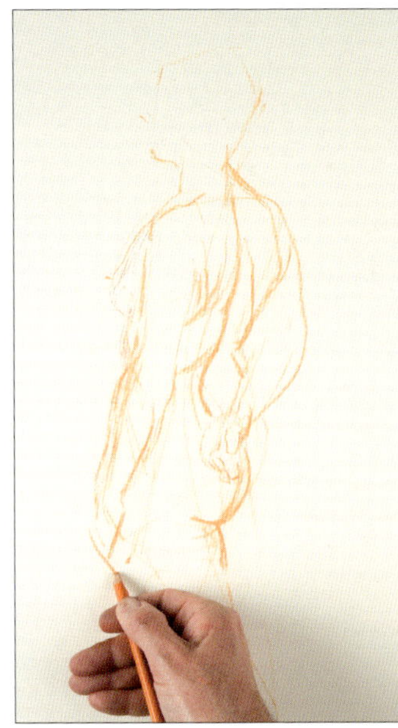

2 Continue mapping out the pose, using contour rather than tone at this stage. Remember to look for geometric shapes that imply the three-dimensional form of the body – the cylinder of the legs and the box shape of the head, for example. Refine the shape of the arms, remembering to look for the different planes. Put in some of the contour lines that describe the creases in the skin – under the shoulders and at the point where the model's right arm bends at the elbow, for example. Restrict yourself to those lines that are structurally important, otherwise you'll lose the spontaneity of the drawing in a welter of detail. Remember you can use the lines to check the placements of other features.

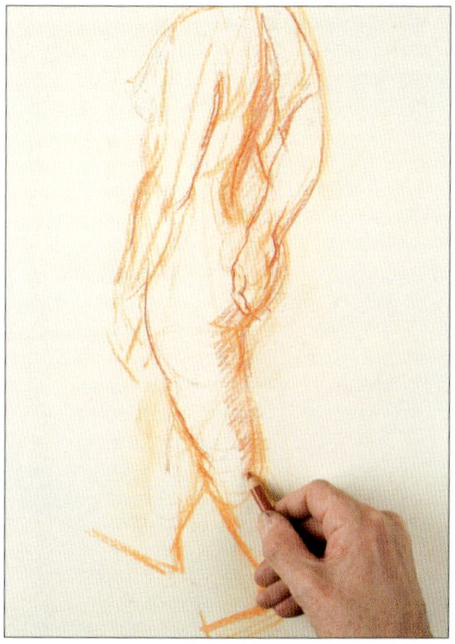

3 Once you're happy with the placement of the different parts, you can begin to make the figure look more three-dimensional. Using a warmer burnt umber, begin to hatch in some of the darker tones on the back as well as along the shaded part of the left leg.

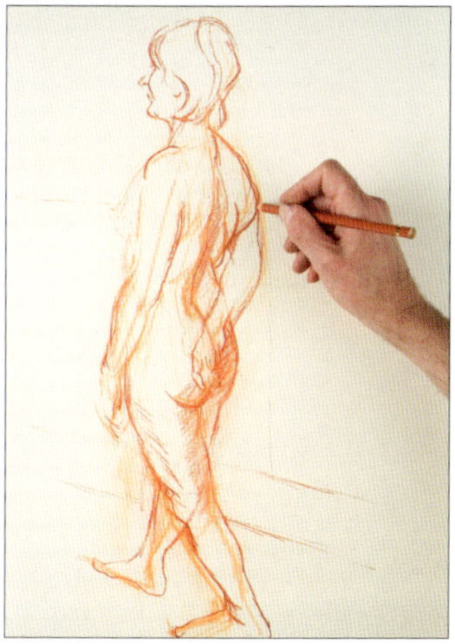

4 Put in some detail of the head – a simple indication of the features is sufficient. Put in the lines of the skirting board and dado rail; now check the perspective of the pose and that the feet are positioned correctly. Reinforce the outline of the left shoulder.

The finished sketch

Careful measuring, constantly checking each part of the body in relation to the rest, is one of the keys to success in figure drawing and painting; taking the time to assess tones so that you can make the figure appear three-dimensional is another. This sketch succeeds on both counts. Note also how the white of the paper stands for the lightest tones in the study – the background, the highlights on the figure, and the model's light-coloured hair, with only a few strands implying the direction of hair growth and the way the hair follows the shape of the cranium.

Half-hour charcoal sketch

Charcoal is a wonderful medium for quick sketches, as it can create both fine, strong linear marks and broad areas of shading. Leave the white of the paper for the brightest highlights.

The purpose of this sketch is to practise looking for balance lines within a pose. Look for any lines that you can draw in lightly between features to use as a guide. Drop lines (real or imaginary) down from the base of the skull or the lobe of the ear and see what other features intersect those lines. Look at where the front of the knee sits in relation to the back of the heel. (In this pose, the knee of the right leg is almost directly above the back of the heel.) Look at the relative angles of the hips and shoulder blades: is one higher or are they parallel to one another?

Remember that drawing any subject is a gradual process of refinement so don't fall into the trap of trying to be too detailed to begin with. Start with tentative marks and lines, then gradually build up the structures through a combination of contour lines and tone.

Materials

- *Good-quality drawing paper*
- *Thin charcoal stick*
- *Kneaded eraser*

The pose

Here, much of the model's weight is on his right foot, but he is also using the pole for support, so the 'balance line' falls some way between the feet rather than being entirely over the right foot. Placing his left hand on his hip thrusts his shoulder backwards and provides some tension and definition in the muscles of both the arms and the upper back. You can also use the negative space between the left arm and torso as a compositional aid.

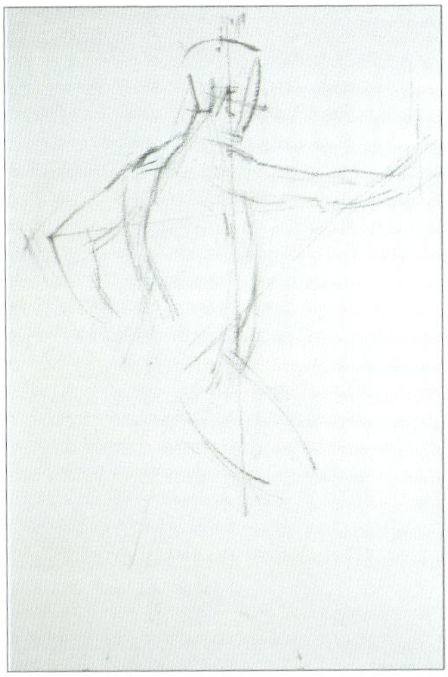

1 Using a thin stick of charcoal, begin putting in tentative lines to establish the pose. Look for any lines and angles that you can use as a guide. Here, the artist has dropped a plumb line down from the ear to the ground: note how it intersects the top of the right thigh. He has also drawn in a sloping line across the upper back from elbow to elbow.

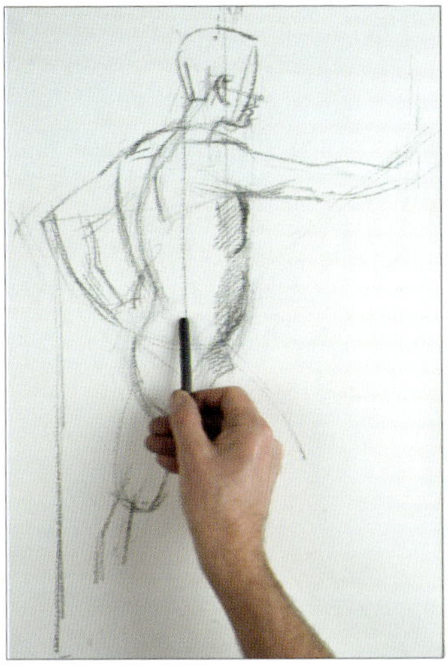

2 Continue mapping out the pose, then begin to strengthen your charcoal lines and also to block in some of the darkest areas of shade. Keep measuring and checking throughout. Here, the artist is drawing a plumb line, as he has noticed that the base of the right buttock is directly in line with the base of the skull.

3 As you work, look at how shadows can help you create a sense of form. On the model's upper right arm, for example, there is a series of parallel shadows that reveals the muscles under the skin. Continue the shading down from the torso on to the inner edge of the model's left leg. Put in the feet and then the curve of the left buttock.

4 (Left) Continue shading, using the tip of the stick very lightly to create light hatching on the side of the face and the side of the stick for broader, darker areas of tone on the top of the right thigh and the cast shadow on the floor. Use the tip of the stick for strong, linear marks such as the edges of the legs and outline of the buttocks.

5 (Right) Lightly shade the background. This serves two purposes. First, you can use the negative shape around the figure to define it more precisely by shading right up to the edge of the figure and using this to check the outline is correct. Second, the shading allows the figure to stand out from the background.

6 Charcoal is a very powdery medium and it's very easy to get smudges where you don't want them. Use a kneaded eraser to clean off any dirty marks and create crisp, bright highlights.

The finished sketch
You may be surprised at how many different tones the artist has created from a single stick of charcoal, simply by varying the amount of pressure, smudging and lifting off pigment to create the light-to-mid tones. The tension in the model's muscles is evident in the bold, linear marks of this sketch.

Watercolour and pastel pencil study

This two-hour project combines the linear quality of pastel pencils with soft watercolour washes. Watercolour is a slower medium to work in as, unless you are working wet into wet, you need to allow time for each layer to dry before you apply the next. Although this is not a highly resolved painting, it is nonetheless a little more elaborate than those on the previous pages. A straightforward set-up such as this offers you the chance to place the figure in a recognizable context without having to worry about props.

A reclining pose is easy for the model to hold, which in turn makes life a lot easier for you as the artist: there is less chance of the model accidentally shifting position and thereby forcing you to make adjustments to your basic underdrawing.

The sketch shown here took approximately two hours but you could, of course, spend more time on it and put more detail into both the figure and the surroundings. However, take great care not to overwork the painting or you may be in danger of losing the freshness and spontaneity of those lovely watercolour washes.

Materials

- *HP watercolour paper*
- *Pastel pencils: red, Naples yellow, burnt umber, raw sienna, lemon yellow, cerulean blue*
- *Watercolour paints: ultramarine blue, burnt umber, cadmium yellow, yellow ochre, cadmium red, cerulean blue, Venetian red*
- *Brushes: large mop, medium round*
- *Kitchen paper*

The pose

The way the model bent her legs provided an interesting composition as it threw the lower part of her legs into shadow. A lamp placed to the left of the sofa provides some directional lighting and casts shadows from the figure on to the sofa. The cushion under the head provides a splash of red that warms up the whole painting and counterbalances the blue throws.

1 Using a red pastel pencil, begin mapping out the pose. Don't try to put in any detail at this stage – just concentrate on measuring carefully so that you place the features correctly. Here you can see how the artist has used a combination of geometric shapes and faint guidelines, such as the central line through the torso and an inverted triangle between the nipples and navel.

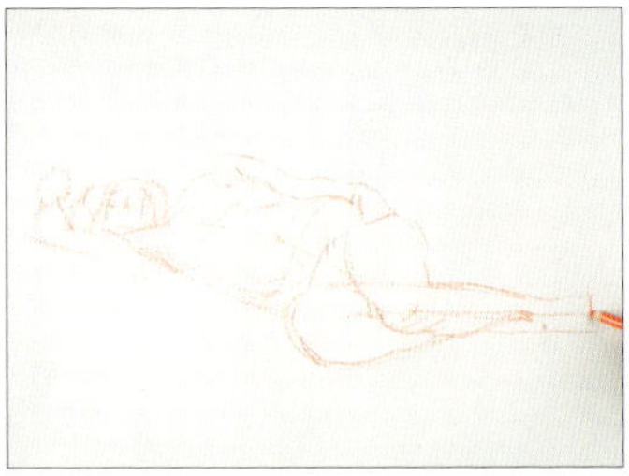

2 Continue until your underdrawing is complete and you are confident that everything is in the right place. It's very easy to get the proportions wrong if you do not take careful, objective measurements. Because the pose is foreshortened, the right knee appears to be considerably larger than the head, so take your time and keep measuring and checking as you work.

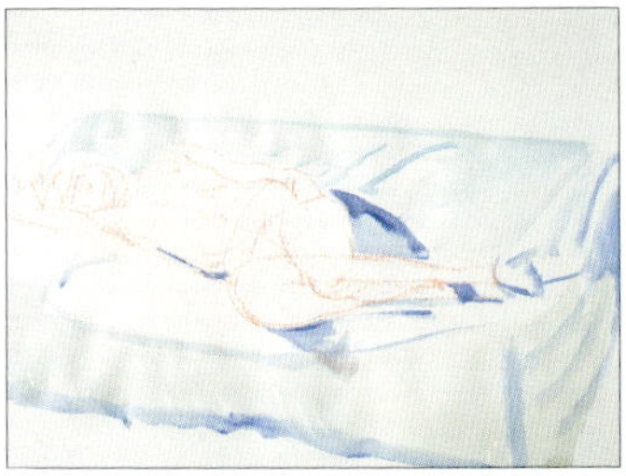

3 Now move on to the watercolour stage. It's often helpful to define the figure by putting the negative shapes around it. Using a large mop brush, wash very dilute ultramarine blue over the sofa, carefully avoiding the figure. Put in the folds and the deepest shadows in the bright blue fabric. To paint in the grey throw along the front edge of the sofa, mix a greenish grey from ultramarine blue, burnt umber and cadmium yellow. Allow to dry.

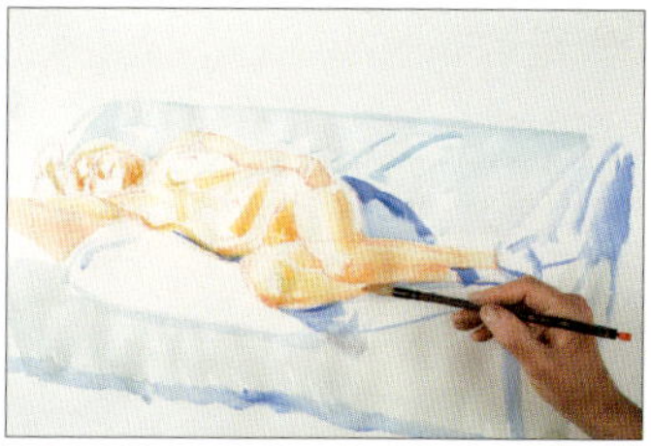

4 Mix a very dilute wash of yellow ochre with a touch of cadmium yellow and, using a medium round brush, put in the mid tones on the body. Paint the shadow areas under the chin and breasts and the underside of the right arm and leg with a cool mix of cadmium yellow and ultramarine. For the warmer skin tones, drop on dilute cadmium red and allow it to spread, wet into wet. Paint the red cushion in the same colour.

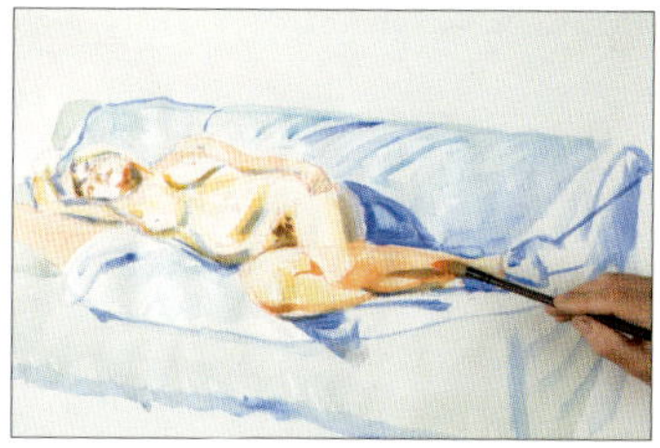

5 Strengthen the colour of the blue throws by brushing on cerulean blue (for the lighter areas) and the greenish grey mixture from Step 3 (for the shadows), as appropriate. For the shaded areas on and between the legs, add Venetian red to the yellow ochre and cadmium yellow mix. Add a little ultramarine to the mix to make a greyish purple and touch in the facial details – the eyebrows, pupils, nostrils and the shadow under the chin.

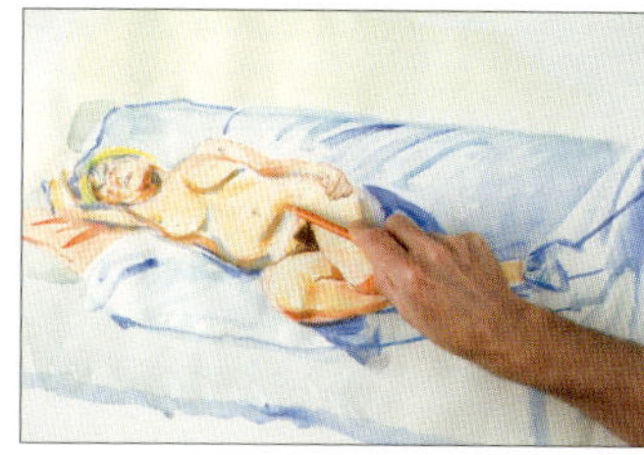

6 Darken the mid tones on the skin and cushion with dilute cadmium red. Brush a very dilute wash of lemon yellow over the area above the sofa. Using pastel pencils, loosely scribble Naples yellow over the body. Put in the pubic hair in burnt umber and go over the mid tones with a raw sienna. Use a lemon yellow pencil for the hair, with cerulean blue for the shadows.

The finished painting

Although this is a relatively quick study, the different planes and curves of the body have been skilfully observed and painted. The cast shadows enhance the sense of light and shade. The background is minimal but it sets the figure in context, while the folds and creases in the fabric throw and cushion add visual interest to the scene.

Brush-and-ink sketch

This project uses Chinese wash painting brushes, which are similar to those used for calligraphy, and a standard black waterproof ink, diluted to varying degrees to create a range of tones. Chinese wash painting brushes are inexpensive and readily available from art and craft suppliers. They hold a lot of ink, so you don't need to keep stopping to reload the brush, and the tip comes to a fine point so you can vary the width of the line with ease. Like watercolour brushes, the hairs are very flexible, making it easy to alter the direction of the line you are making; you can round corners smoothly in situations where you might falter with a pen or pencil. Obviously, if you make a mistake in ink, it is much harder to erase than a pencil mark. For this reason it is always a good idea to map out the main lines of your subject first – either by making a very light pencil underdrawing or, as here, by making your underdrawing in very dilute ink.

When you're setting up the pose, remember to look at the negative spaces around the figure as well as at the lines of the figure itself, as the spaces play an important part in the balance of the composition as a whole. This is particularly important in a deceptively simple composition such as this one, where there are no other elements to consider, not even a background colour or pattern.

In this sketch the artist has composed the picture so that the model's right hand is almost touching the edge of the paper. This gives a more dynamic feel than placing the figure centrally, and enhances the great sense of movement in the pose.

Materials

- *Watercolour paper*
- *Selection of Chinese brushes*
- *Black Indian ink*

The pose
This is a dynamic, tense pose reminiscent of a classical statue of an athlete throwing a discus. Note how the negative spaces around the figure contribute to the composition.

1 Using very dilute black ink and a Chinese brush, establish the basic pose. Remember to think of the body as a series of geometric shapes and to look at the negative spaces around the figure (the space between the legs, or between the left arm and torso, for example) as well as at the outline of the figure itself.

2 Using a slightly darker tone of ink, begin to put in some of the shadow areas – on the underside of the right arm, for example. You do not want this to be an entirely linear brush drawing, so try to make a conscious effort to alternate between putting in the contour of the figure and using tone to build up the form.

Assessment time

The initial underdrawing is now complete. The lines of the pose have been established and a little shading on the underside of the right arm and on the left thigh has begun the process of conveying the form of the figure. You may need to make adjustments at this stage, but once you're happy with the underdrawing, you can move on to using a stronger dilution of ink, reinforcing and adding to the lines and tones that you have already put down.

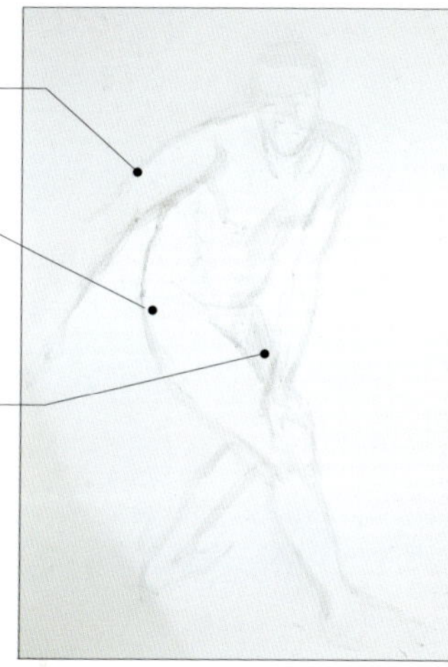

Note how the contour lines around the body are slightly broken: this adds to the sense of movement and energy.

Note how the body and legs form a sweeping S-shaped curve that holds this very simple composition together.

With just a small amount of light tone, the figure is already beginning to look three-dimensional.

3 Using the tip of the brush and undiluted black ink straight from the bottle, touch in the eyes, eyebrows and hair. Use short, spiky brushstrokes to capture the texture of the hair. Dilute the ink very slightly and put in the shadows on the left shoulder under the collarbone and on the shaded side of the left arm. Because the underpainting is still slightly damp, you can simply drop the stronger ink on to the initial lines and allow it to flow naturally; this creates a slightly fuzzy line that is very appealing.

Tips:

- Vary how you hold the brush depending on the kind of mark you want to make: for more control, hold it near the tip; for broad, sweeping marks hold it further down the shaft of the brush.
- If the ink is too strong, dip a clean brush in water and carefully lift off the ink. Wipe the brush on absorbent tissue paper and repeat as necessary.
- You can make an incredibly wide variety of marks with a brush, depending on the type you use, how you hold it and the amount of pressure you apply, so it is worth making some 'doodles' to explore the possibilities.
- Oriental artists and calligraphers have evolved many different hand positions; sometimes they work with the brush vertical and held loosely near the top of the handle rather than gripped firmly at the ferrule.

4 Using undiluted ink, reinforce the lines of the pose. Note how the width of the brush strokes varies, which gives a lovely, flowing line; exploit the natural qualities of the brushes to create this effect. Using slightly dilute ink, carefully apply more tone to the shaded side of the model's face.

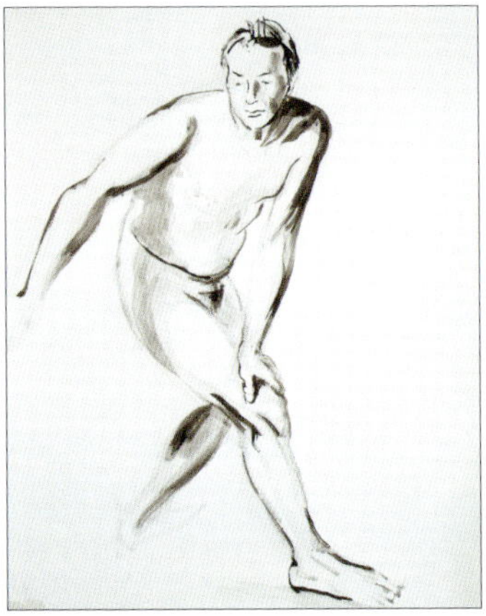

5 Continue alternating between contour lines and mid tones to reinforce the lines of the pose and create a sense of form. It's a good idea to have at least two brushes at hand – one for undiluted ink straight from the bottle and another for lighter tones.

6 Using dilute ink, roughly scumble in the cast shadow on the floor. Although this is barely visible in real life, it is perfectly acceptable to over-emphasize shadows in a monochrome painting like this for dramatic effect. The rough brushstrokes remain visible on the paper and enhance the energy of the pose.

7 Using the tip of the brush and undiluted ink again, define the shape of the feet and apply more detail to the facial features. Use varying dilutions of ink to put in the shading around the eyes and on the side of the nose, the neck muscles, the relatively pale shading on the torso, and the much darker tone on the outer edge of the left arm. This shading is what will make the figure look rounded and three-dimensional, so take the time to assess the relative tones carefully.

Tip: It's important to keep alternating between neat and diluted inks so that you build up the tonal differences gradually. If you put in the darkest details all in one go, you may make them too dark – and once you've done that, there's no going back.

The finished painting

The artist has combined linear 'brush drawing' with dilute washes of tone to create a deceptively simple-looking sketch. Note how many different tones he has managed to create from just one ink, and how he has emphasized the cast shadow on the floor – which is only just visible in real life – to balance the composition and add more drama to a very simple, quick sketch. In a sketch as simple as this, the negative spaces are as important as the positives. They balance the composition and create interesting shapes within it that help to draw the viewer's eye around the picture. The cast shadow on the floor has been exaggerated for dramatic effect. Its strong diagonal line counterbalances the line of the figure. It also helps to anchor the figure and prevent it from looking as if it is simply floating in thin air.

Dilute washes of ink create soft-edged areas of mid tone.

Chinese brushes come to a fine tip and are capable of producing surprisingly fine detail, where required.

For strong, linear marks and deep shadows, the ink can be used undiluted, dipping the brush straight into the bottle.

Male nude in pencil

The aim of this project is to practise using shading techniques to create modelling, and convey the three-dimensional form of the body.

Before you put pencil to paper, take time to really look at your subject and assess where the lightest and darkest areas are, as this is what will create the impression of three dimensions. In the pose shown here, for example, look at the model's right arm: there's a bright area on the left-hand side of the arm, where the light strikes it, then the light gradually falls off towards the right-hand side as the arm curves away from the light. This means that your shading has to be equally gradual, with no hard-edged transition between one tone and the next.

With graphite pencils, you can create different tones simply by varying the amount of pressure you apply. You can also create darker areas of tone by drawing your hatching lines closer together – and lighter ones by spacing them further apart.

You also need to think about the direction of the hatching lines that you make. If all your hatching and cross-hatching lines run in the same direction, your drawing will take on a rather mechanical feel. Varying the direction of the hatching lines will help to give life to your drawing.

It's a good idea to make your hatching marks follow the shape of the form that they're describing. If you're drawing a rounded shape such as a buttock or breast, for example, make your hatching lines curved. Follow the shape of the form that you're drawing with both your eye and your hand and use the pencil to 'caress' the shape as you draw.

Finally, remember to allow the white of the paper to stand for the very brightest highlights. This will give life and sparkle to your drawings.

Materials

- *Good-quality drawing paper*
- *2B pencil*
- *Kneaded eraser (optional)*

The pose

Position your model in front of a plain-coloured wall or backcloth. Place a light to one side, as side lighting gives good modelling and shows up the muscles, shoulder blades and the line of the spine. (You don't need specialist lighting: a standard lamp will do.) Here, the model's shoulders are thrust back, making the shoulder blades and muscles of the upper back appear more prominent.

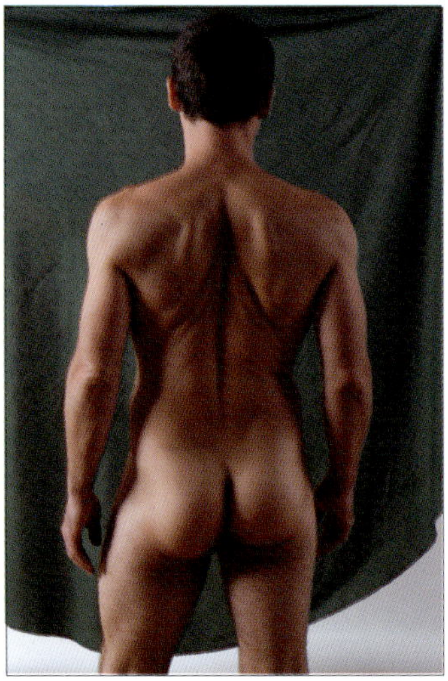

Tones

The artist used only one grade of pencil throughout this drawing – a 2B – simply varying the pressure to create different tones. It's better to do this than to keep switching from one pencil to another, as it allows you to maintain the flow of the drawing and also to improve your ability to manipulate the pencil to create different effects.

1 Using a 2B pencil, very lightly map out the underlying geometric shapes, beginning with the 'egg' shape of the head and the cylinder of the neck. Look, too, for the angle of the shoulders in relation to the neck; here, the shoulders are at slightly different angles as one is a little higher than the other. In this sketch, the artist deliberately made his initial marks darker than normal, in order to let you see the process of searching out the forms. Make your own initial marks so light that they're barely there – just enough to show up on the paper and give you a starting point.

Tip: When you are looking at lines such as the angle of the shoulders, try mentally superimposing the hands of a clock on your subject and then working out what number the hands are pointing to. Here, for example, the model's left shoulder slopes down at between 9 and 8 o'clock from the vertical 'cylinder' of the neck, while the line of his right shoulder is very slightly lower, at between 4 and 5 o'clock.

2 Now put in the line of the central spine: it isn't a totally straight vertical line, but is angled very slightly to the right. When you've established this, you can begin to put in the line of the shoulder blades: they are at roughly 4 o'clock and 8 o'clock respectively.

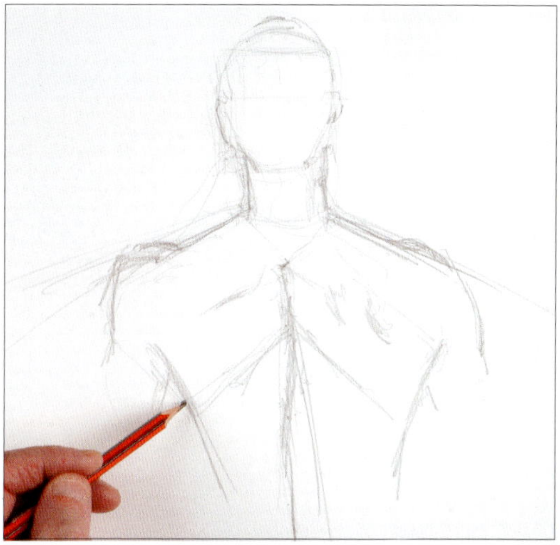

3 Establish the line of the torso and the arms, noting where the arms are positioned in relation to the shoulder blades. Remember to look at the negative shapes (such as the space between the arms and the torso) as well as at the positives. Note, too, how the line of the torso slants in, toward the hips.

Assessment time

The basic structure has been mapped out. The next stage is to begin putting in some shading and refine the basic blocks in order to make the figure look more rounded and three-dimensional.

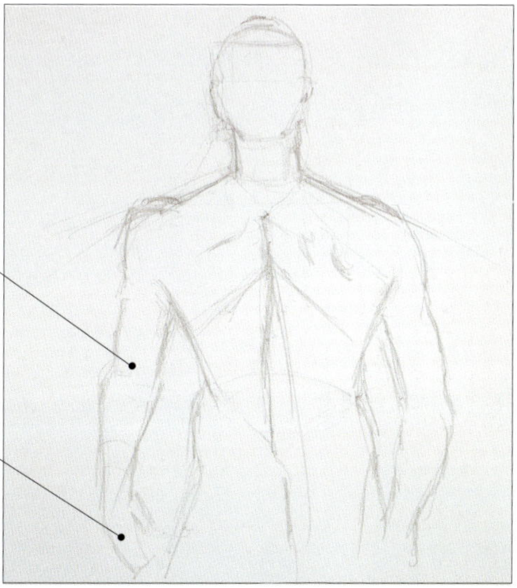

Faint, curved pencil lines around the elbow area indicate where the arm bends.

At this stage the hands are nothing more than simple geometric blocks.

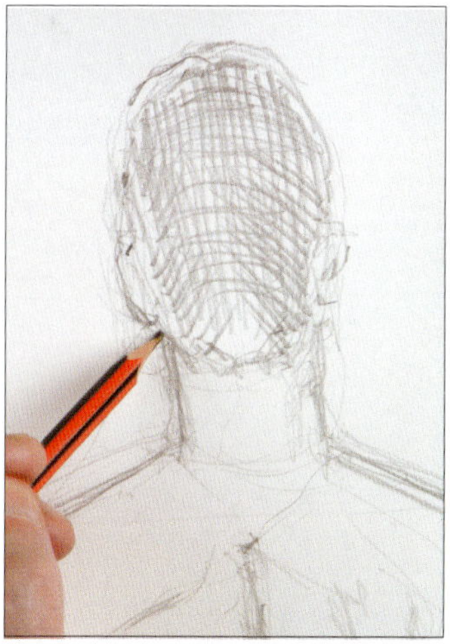

4 Loosely indicate the shape of the ears. You can also start to put in some tone on the hair, using some simple cross hatching. Your hatching lines should follow both the direction of hair growth and the contour of the form it's describing – so here the lines are slightly curved to echo the contour of the skull.

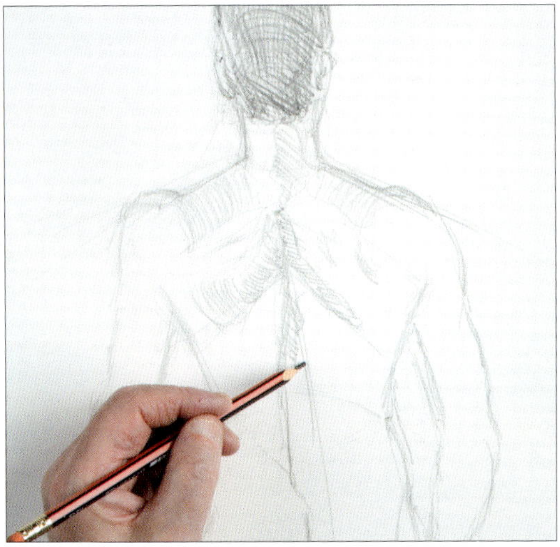

5 Begin to develop the shadow lines on the right-hand side of the neck, and lightly hatch along the spine to indicate the areas of muscle and bone under the skin, curving the hatching lines to follow the form. Since the shoulders are pushed back so that the shoulder blades protrude, there are very noticeable shadows underneath them.

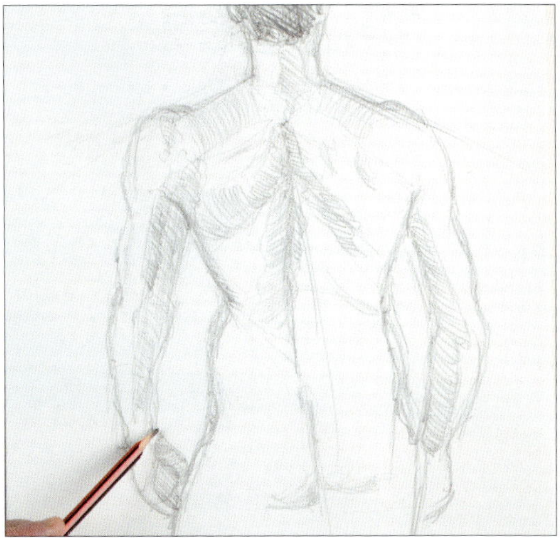

6 Carry on working down the back and the undersides of the arms, gradually developing the shading. You may find it helps to sketch in a light line indicating where the deepest area of shade ends; this can be refined later, since the hatching should gradually decrease and fade out as the arm turns towards the light.

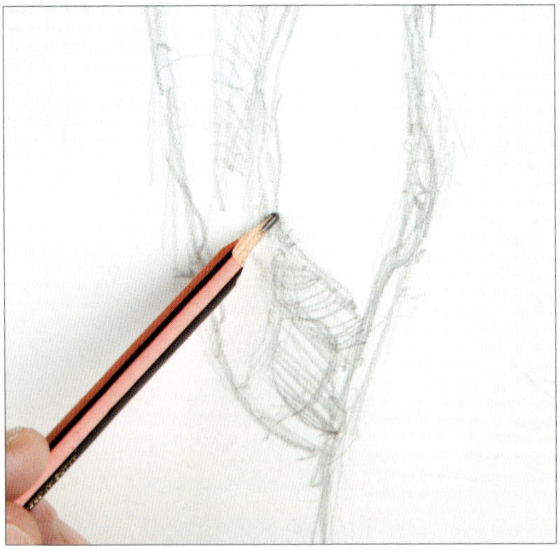

7 Now move on to the hands: you've already established the basic block shape, and now you can begin to refine this, cutting in with the pencil to reveal the planes of the fingers and wrist. Paying close attention to which parts of the hand are in the light and which are in shadow will help you to achieve this.

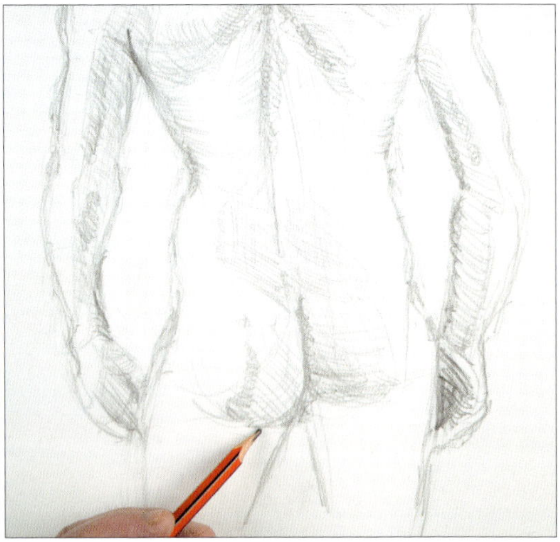

8 Continue shading across the whole drawing where necessary, using straight lines, circular movements and curves to create variety. Now that you've searched out the basic structure, you can gradually increase your pressure on the pencil to achieve the necessary depth of tone in the very dark areas. Make small 'ticks' with the pencil along the darkest edges, such as the underside edge of the right arm.

The finished drawing

Although the same pencil was used throughout this drawing, the artist has created an impressive and subtle range of tones through his careful use of hatching and cross-hatching. The shading follows the contours of the body and helps to imply the shapes of the muscles and bones that lie beneath the surface of the skin.

Note how the hatching in this area comprises a series of diagonal lines that echo the direction of the shoulder blades.

Small, delicate 'ticks' of the pencil are used to convey the darkest tones along the very edge of the arm.

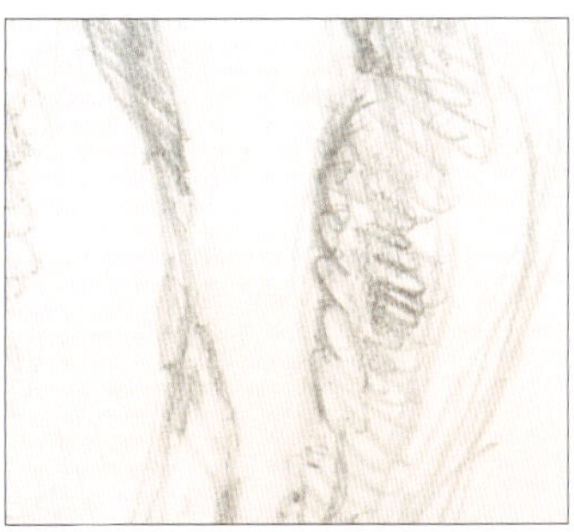

The white of the paper stands for the most brightly lit areas and helps to give sparkle to the drawing.

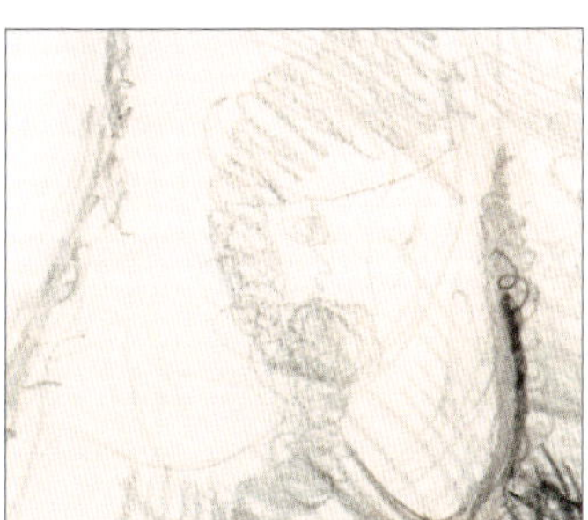

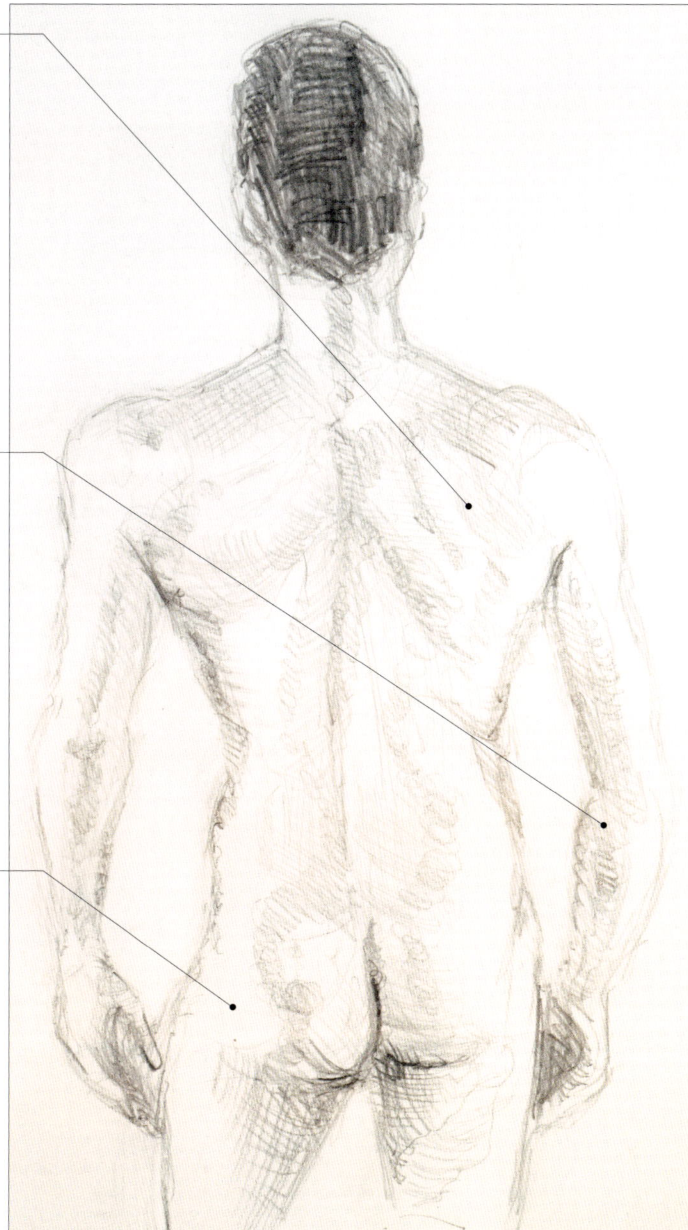

Female figure in soft pastel

In addition to looking at the curves of the spine and the musculature of the body, this project gives you the chance to practise assessing skin tones. At first glance it might look as if the model's skin is very even in colour, but there are actually lots of different tones. This is due to the way light falls on the figure. When light hits a raised area such as the collar or shoulder bone, a shadow is formed on the opposite side, which is not in the light. The shadow area is darker in tone – it is these differences in tone that create the impression of a three-dimensional figure. Being able to assess tones accurately is the key to the success of your artwork.

Pastel drawings are often done on coloured paper, just as oil and acrylic paintings are often done on a toned ground. This enables you to start from a mid tone and work back to the darkest tones and up to the highlights. And as all these media are opaque, if you want to make adjustments later, you can apply a light colour on top of a dark one – something that is impossible in a transparent medium such as watercolour. It's also a good idea to allow some of the original paper colour to show through as a mid tone in the finished drawing, as this gives a more lively feel to the work.

Pastel papers come in a wide range of colours, from pale biscuit colours to deep, dark greens and reds. When choosing which colour of paper to use, look at the range of mid tones present in your subject; here, the mid tones of the model's skin are a rich, terracotta colour, which is almost identical to the paper colour that the artist selected.

When drawing skin in soft pastel, you can finger blend your marks to create a smooth skin texture – but take care not to lose the linear quality completely.

Materials

- *Terracotta-coloured pastel paper*
- *Soft pastels: mid brown, white, dark brown, pale blue, pale mauve, khaki brown, burnt umber*
- *Pencils: charcoal or black pastel*
- *Kneaded eraser*

The pose

This is a very simple pose, but the curving shapes are very appealing. Asking the model to turn her head to the left, so that her face can be seen in profile, prevents the picture from becoming too abstract and impersonal.

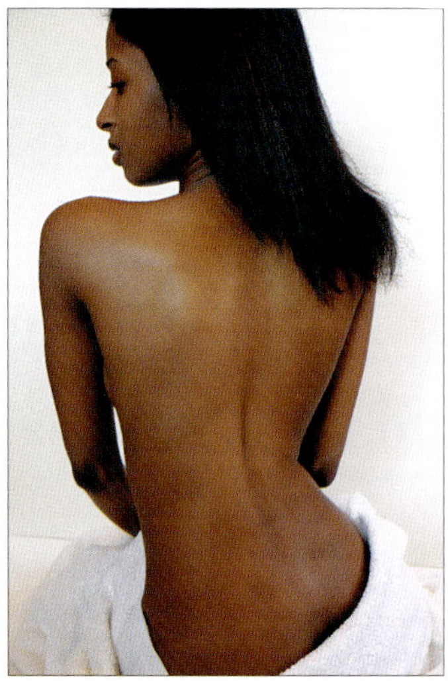

1 Working on terracotta-coloured pastel paper with a mid-brown soft pastel, sketch out the basic shape of the pose. Take careful measurements to ensure you get the proportions right. Look, in particular, for the line of the spinal column and the angle of the hips and shoulders.

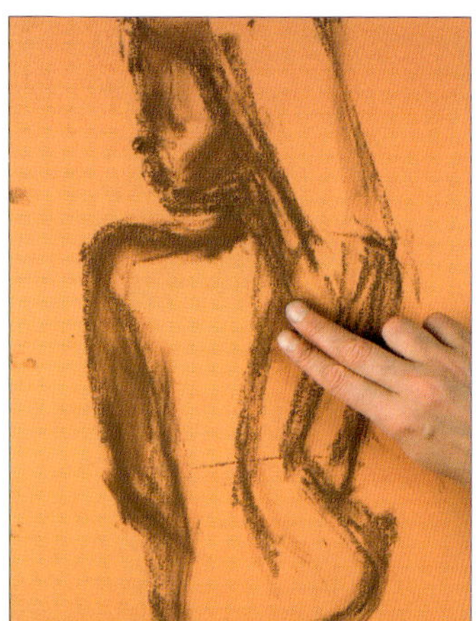

2 Establish the position of the eyes, nose and mouth. Blend the pastel marks on the paper with your fingers so that you begin to build up form and tone without adding too much pastel.

3 Using the side of a white pastel, begin to block in some of the white background to help define the figure. Use the tip of the pastel to put in some of the deep, sharp creases in the towel.

4 Using a darker brown pastel, put in some tones for the shadows under the chin, on the undersides of the arms and around the top of the towel. Use both the side and the tip of the pastel, depending on the kind of mark you need. Put some darker tones into the hair, following the direction of growth.

5 Stroke on some white highlights across the shoulder blades to begin to develop modelling on the back. Redefine the line of the spine. Then, using your fingertips, apply and blend some dark brown pastel over the muscle area below the shoulder blades (the latissimus dorsi, which wraps around the sides of the trunk) and gently wipe off some of the colour with a kneaded eraser to soften it and avoid the mark being too harsh and obtrusive.

6 Using a dark brown pastel, put in the darkest points of the facial features – the nostrils, mouth, eyebrows and eyelashes. Gently stroke a white pastel across the cheek for the highlight and put in the dark shadow under the cheekbone. Smudge the marks with your fingertips or a torchon, or wipe off colour with a kneaded eraser, if necessary, to soften the colour.

7 Using a white pastel, strengthen the line around the profile and the left shoulder so that the figure really stands out from the background. Because of the creases in the fabric, there are some shaded areas in the towel; lightly hatch them with a pale blue pastel. The blue is modified by the underlying white.

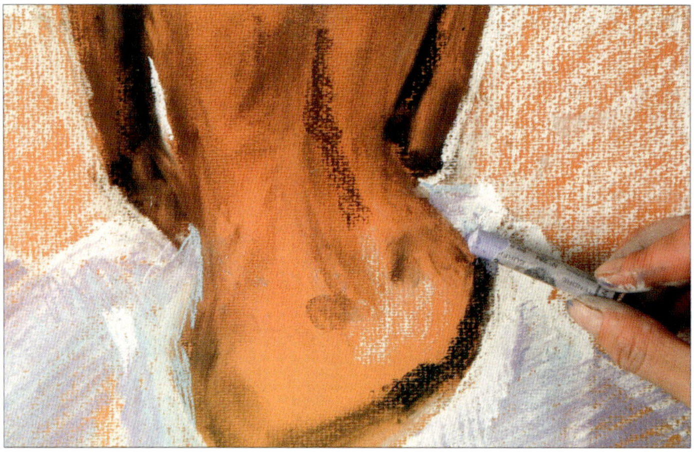

8 Apply pale mauve over the blue, so that you are alternating between cool (blue) and warm (mauve) tones. Alter the direction of your hatching to create variety and texture in your marks.

Tip: Leave some of the underlying tones and the terracotta colour of the paper showing through.

9 Apply more mauve over the left shoulder and the top of the buttocks, where there are some warm shadows. Hatch in the mid tones on the figure, using a khaki brown pastel.

10 Put more dark tones into the hair to build up both tone and texture. Use the same colour to put in the darkest skin tones on the undersides of the arms and between the arms and the torso.

11 For the mid-toned area on the left hip and buttock, use a warm brown or burnt umber. Also apply some burnt umber to the face to help build up the modelling, taking care to observe the light and dark areas very carefully.

Assessment time

Although the contrast between warm and cool colours has created a convincing sense of modelling on the figure, some minor adjustments are still required. The shadow on the left hip is too dark and the pastel marks need to be both lightened in colour and blended a little more. The shadow between the model's body and the top of the towel is also too heavy. But these are relatively minor details that can be fixed by hatching a lighter tone over the existing marks and finger blending the pastel. The biggest change that is required is in the background: at present, there is only a light covering of pastel on the paper. This needs to be intensified and blocked in more strongly. The very slight shadow that the model casts on the wall also needs to be added, to give the picture depth.

The background wall is very patchy in colour and too much of the underlying paper colour shows through.

The shape of the left breast needs to be defined more clearly.

These shadow areas are too dark and heavy.

12 Use a kneaded eraser to wipe off some of the colour and 'draw' in the shape of the left breast. Then apply a little burnt umber to the underside of the left arm, blending the colour with your fingertips, so that the paler-coloured breast stands out more clearly.

13 Using the side of a white pastel, block in the wall in the background. There is also a very faint cast shadow on the background wall to the right of the model. Put this in using the side of a pale blue pastel. It adds a little change of texture and provides a visual link to the cool, blue shadows in the towel.

14 Some areas of the face have become rather too dark. Use a kneaded eraser to pull out a few highlights. With this particular model's coloration, you can take the colour right back to the original paper colour, which is virtually identical to the warm, highlit skin tones.

15 Hatch burnt umber over the left hip and blend the marks with your fingers to lighten the tone and soften the texture of this very dark shadow area. Using a dark brown pastel, strengthen the line between the left arm and the torso and create a little more modelling on the skin of the elbow.

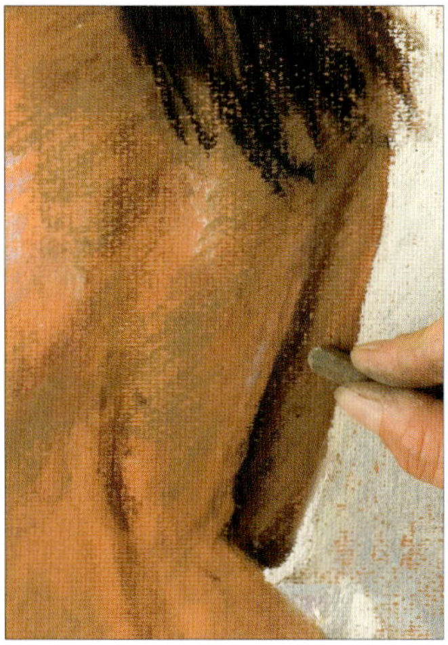

16 Even out the tones on the right arm, using a khaki brown pastel.

17 Use a charcoal or black pastel pencil to put in the fine line of the eyebrow and the nostrils. (Soft pastel sticks are too chunky for fine lines such as this, although you can try breaking one to get a sharp edge.)

Tip: Rest your hand on scrap paper as you work to prevent smudging other areas of your drawing. Keep the hand quite still and move the fingers.

The finished drawing

Through a combination of light hatching and finger blending, the artist has created subtle but effective shifts between light and dark tones, replicating the effect of light and shade on the body and creating a sense of form. With soft media such as pastel, the colour adheres to the raised bits of the paper but does not sit in the 'dips', creating a broken texture that gives the drawing great liveliness. The colour of the paper has also been utilized to good effect. Although the background is simple, it contains enough tonal variation to be visually interesting without detracting from the subject.

Shading and tonal contrasts are used to indicate different planes of the body: the left side is in shadow while the back is more brightly lit.

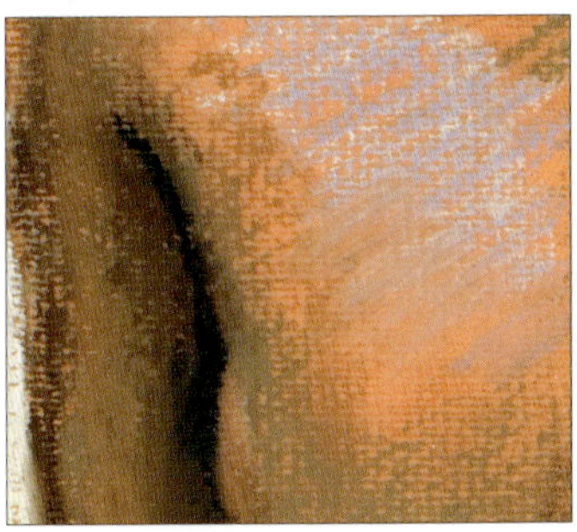

The hair is drawn using strong, broad strokes of black pastel, which conveys its texture and thickness well.

In places, the colour of the paper stands for the mid tones in the model's skin.

A hint of cast shadow on the background breaks up the monotony of the white wall.

Standing female figure in watercolour

Here, the skin tones are built up using wet-into-wet washes of watercolour that blend on the paper to create lively mixes. The most important thing to remember when you're using lots of very wet washes is that you must either use a heavy watercolour paper (300 gsm/140 lb or more) or stretch it beforehand so that it does not cockle.

Many beginners (and even more experienced artists) are scared of making their watercolour washes very wet, as they feel they may not be able to control the paint – but the ability to work wet into wet and allow colours to merge is one of the things that makes watercolour painting so much fun.

The trick is not to dampen any area into which you do not want the paint to spread. There may be times during the painting when you need to step aside for a few minutes to let the paper dry.

It's also important not to use too many colours, or your mixes may start to look dull and muddy. Let the white of the paper shine through in places.

In watercolour, it is always best to work from light to dark to keep the painting clean and the colours true. Apply the light tones first, then the deeper tones and shadows. It takes practice to see the blues and greens in flesh tones, but they are there – particularly in the shadow areas.

If you're new to figure painting, a project such as this is a good one to begin with because the pose and surrroundings are simple. Position your model against a plain-coloured background such as an old sheet (a painted white wall can look too stark). Place a light slightly to one side; this creates shadows on the body and makes it easier to explore the form.

Materials

- *Heavy watercolour paper*
- *Watercolour paints: yellow ochre, ultramarine blue, alizarin crimson, vermilion, cerulean blue*
- *Brushes: medium round*

The pose
Placing the model's left hand on her hip breaks up the vertical line of the body and makes an interesting negative shape within the composition. Her hair frames her face.

1 Mix a dilute wash of cool green from yellow ochre and ultramarine blue. Using a medium round brush, begin putting down the basic shape of the pose. Don't try to put any detail into complicated areas such as the hands and feet; the basic geometric shapes are all that is required at this stage.

2 Continue until you have mapped out the whole figure. As you work, keep checking that you've got the proportions right. Look at how each limb or feature relates to others. In this pose, for example, the right hand is at the base of a diagonal line that runs across the left hip up to the left elbow.

Tip: The beauty of using a very dilute wash for these early stages is that, if you find you've made a mistake, you can simply clean your brush and then brush water over the relevant area to lift off the colour.

3 Mix a dilute wash of a bluish purple from ultramarine blue and alizarin crimson. Apply a light wash over the hair, using flowing brushstrokes that imitate the curls in the hair. Putting in the hair at this stage helps to define the shape of the face. Mix yellow ochre with a tiny bit of ultramarine blue and touch in the shadow under the jaw.

4 Mix yellow ochre with a hint of vermilion for warmth, and put in the shadows on the back, clavicle and under the breasts. Wash very dilute cerulean blue over the background, pulling the brush away so that none seeps on to the figure. The background helps define the figure and makes it easier to see if the shapes are right.

5 Using a redder version of the purple tone that you mixed for the hair in Step 3, apply some tones to the undersides of the arms. This warmer tone balances the cool tones of the early stages of the painting.

6 Continue applying this purple mix to the darkest areas of skin tone – the fingers, the undersides of the arms, and the edges of the buttocks and the hips – putting in more alizarin to create more warmth where necessary. Begin to develop the hair, using a bluer version of the same mix.

7 Add some vermilion to the purple flesh tone used in Step 6 to warm it up and loosely wash this colour over the breast and breast bone. Next, looking at the negative shapes, wash more cerulean blue into the backdrop fabric, putting in stronger lines for some of the main folds in the cloth.

8 Using the very tip of your brush and the dilute purple mix from Step 3, touch in the facial features, taking care to leave the white of the paper to stand for the highlights on the nose and cheeks. Next, begin to darken the hair with thicker, redder versions of the same purple mix.

9 The spine is furthest away from the light source and is hence both darker and cooler in tone. Mix a greenish tone from yellow ochre and ultramarine blue and apply it to the curve of the spine, so that you begin to get some modelling in this area.

10 Using both yellow ochre and the purple skin tone from Step 8, loosely wash colour over the legs, allowing the colours to blend wet into wet on the paper. Note that the back leg is slightly darker in tone, as it is further from the light. Use yellow ochre to begin putting in the floorboards.

11 Using the same purple mixes as before, darken the skin overall to create modelling. Then drop dilute yellow ochre into the skin, wet into wet, so that the colours blend naturally on the paper and create a more golden skin tone.

12 Look for any final shadows that need to be put in – for example, the shadow cast by the left leg on the right – and drop more of the purple mix in where necessary to darken the tones. Apply a pale wash of cerulean blue over the background.

Assessment time

Overall, the skin tones are too pale and there is insufficient modelling to make the pose look properly three-dimensional. Although the most deeply shaded areas, such as the underarm area and the small of the back, are darker in tone than the rest of the body, still greater differentiation between them is needed. In the final stages, take time to assess the skin tones and add extra tone where necessary in order to build up the modelling. Make the paint coverage uneven, otherwise you'll end up with flat colour and no sense of modelling.

Overall, the skin tones are too pale and flat.

More colour in this area would help the model to stand out from the background.

The finished painting

This is an impressionistic painting in which the artist has allowed the paint to do a lot of the work for him, with colours merging wet into wet on the paper to create areas of tone in which several colours can be discerned. As a result, there is a great deal of liveliness in the skin tones; one of the worst mistakes you can make when painting skin tones in watercolour is to make your washes flat and uniform.

For the very brightest highlights, the paper is left unpainted.

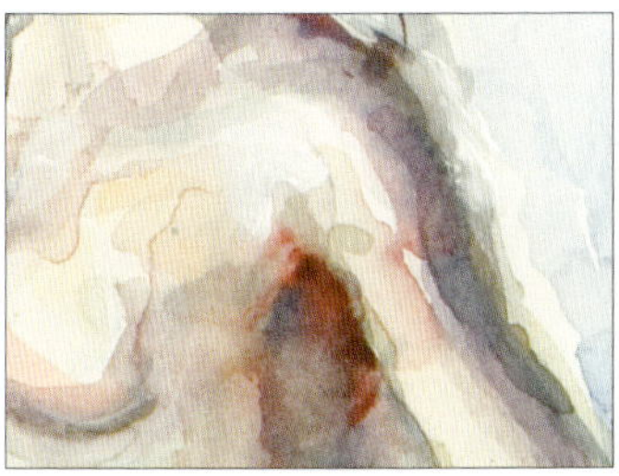

Touches of warm yellow ochre can be discerned in the skin, alongside cooler purple tones in the shadow areas.

Just enough of the background is included to set the figure in context, without distracting from the subject.

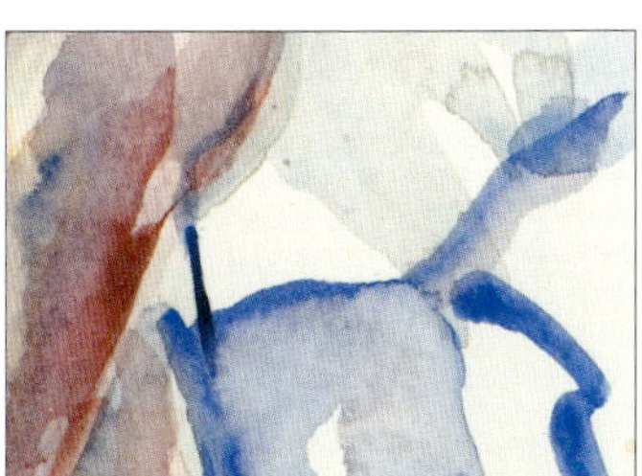

Reclining nude in oils

The reclining nude – more particularly, the reclining female nude – is a classic subject in Western art.

There are a few practicalities to take into account – particularly if you are painting from life. First, make sure your model is comfortable: provide a sofa, blanket or other soft surface for her to lie on and make sure that the room is warm and free of draughts.

For the pose, it is often better to allow the model to settle into a position that feels natural than to tell her what pose to adopt. Although you can obtain interesting and dynamic paintings by directing the model to tense her muscles, such poses are difficult to hold.

This particular pose is easy to hold, even for a long period. The model's weight is evenly distributed along the whole length of her body and she is able to rest her head on her right forearm, cupping her hand around her head for extra support.

The differences in flesh tone need to be very carefully assessed in this project. Certain areas, such as the hands, the soles of the feet and the lower body, tend to be warmer in colour than others, because the blood vessels run closer to the surface of the skin. The upper body, on the other hand, is usually cooler in tone. However, one of the joys of painting in oils is that the paint remains soft and workable for a long time, so you can blend colours on the support as you work to create subtle transitions from one tone to another to show the way the body curves towards or away from the light source.

Materials

- *Stretched canvas*
- *Rag*
- *Oil paints: cadmium orange, brilliant pink, raw sienna, cadmium red, cadmium yellow, brilliant turquoise, titanium white, ultramarine blue, lamp black, vermilion, cerulean blue*
- *Turpentine or white spirit (paint thinner)*
- *Drying linseed oil*
- *Brushes: selection of small and medium rounds, small or medium flat*

The pose

One of the most interesting things about this particular model is the way in which her upper vertebrae and ribs are so clearly defined. The natural curves of her body create clearly defined areas of light and shade, which add interest to the composition. Note the masking tape on the blanket, outlining the model's pose. This enables the model to get back in the same position if she inadvertently moves during the session or has to take a break.

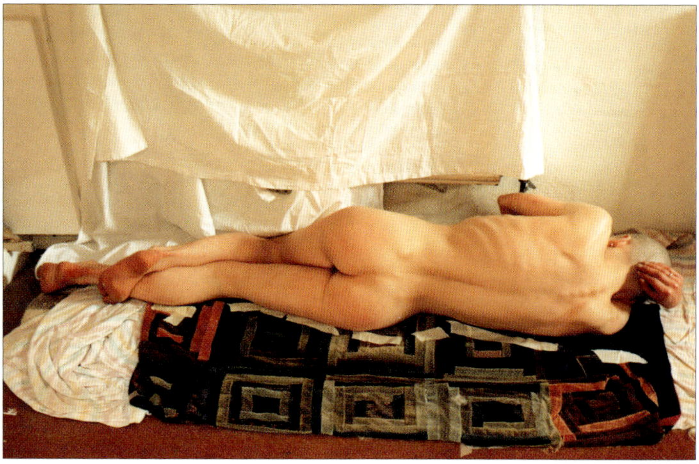

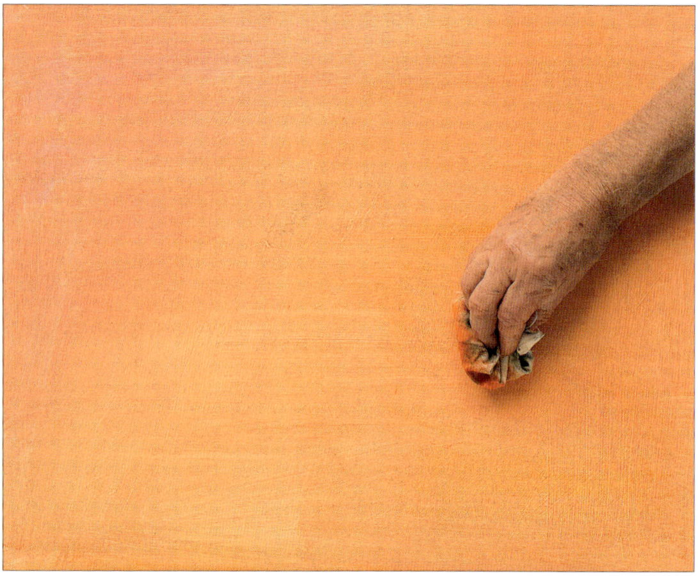

1 With a rag, spread cadmium orange paint evenly over the canvas, changing to brilliant pink in the top left. Leave to dry.

2 Using a medium round brush and raw sienna, 'draw' the edges of the blanket on which the model is lying and the dark shadow under her hips. Delineate the head, upper body and legs in cadmium red. The actual colours are not too important at this stage, as this is merely the underpainting, but warm colours are appropriate to the subject. Mix a range of warm flesh tones from cadmium yellow and cadmium orange and block in the warmest toned areas – the buttocks, the soles of the feet and the curve of the spine. Start putting in the main folds of the background cloth using mixtures of brilliant turquoise and titanium white.

3 Mix titanium white with a little ultramarine blue and block in some of the dark folds in the background cloth. Using a fine brush and cadmium red, loosely draw the head and supporting hand, reinforce the line separating the legs and indicate the angle of the hips.

Tip: It is always important to remember the underlying anatomy of the pose, even when you are painting fleshy parts of the body where the shape of the bones is not visible.

4 Using green (mixed from titanium white, cadmium yellow and ultramarine blue) and a dark grey (mixed from ultramarine blue and raw sienna), start putting in the pattern of the patchwork blanket. Mix a pale blue-green from ultramarine blue and raw sienna and indicate the shadows under the ribs and the shaded part of the back. Note that this mixture is a complementary colour to the first flesh tones: shadow areas often contain a hint of a complementary colour.

5 Mix a pale orange from cadmium red, cadmium yellow and titanium white and begin putting in some of the paler flesh tones. Alternate between all the various flesh tones on your palette, blending them into one another on the support and continually assessing where the light and dark tones fall and whether the colours are warm or cool in temperature. Almost immediately, you will see that the body is starting to look three-dimensional.

6 Continue working on the flesh tones. The highlights and shadows reveal the curves of the body: the backs of the thighs, for example, are in shadow and are therefore darker in tone than the tops of the buttocks, which are angled towards the light. Note the greenish tones on the upper body: the upper body is often noticeably cooler in tone than the lower body, perhaps because the blood vessels in this area are not so near the surface of the skin.

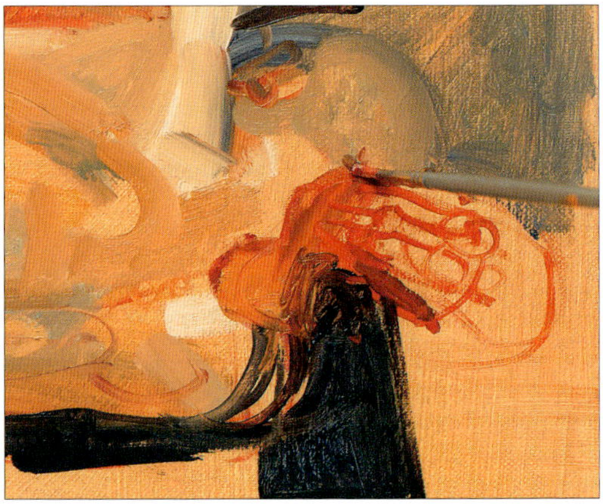

7 Block in the most deeply shaded areas of the white background cloth with a blue-biased mixture of ultramarine blue and titanium white. Use a slightly lighter version of this colour to paint the model's shaved head, allowing some of the ground to show through in parts as the colour of her scalp. Loosely draw the hand and fingers in cadmium red, indicating the joints in the fingers by means of rough circular or elliptical shapes.

Assessment time

Although the areas of warm and cool tone have been established, the figure still looks somewhat flat and one-dimensional. More tonal contrast is needed: spend time working out how you are going to achieve this. Remember to work across the picture as a whole rather than concentrating on one area – otherwise you run the risk of over-emphasizing certain areas and making them too detailed in relation to the rest, thus destroying the balance of the painting. At this stage it would be as important to work up the modelling on the calves and feet as make more progress on the torso.

The broad areas of light and shade have been established – now you can refine this area.

There is not enough tonal contrast for the figure to look truly three-dimensional.

8 The cloth at the model's feet is draped to create interesting folds. Block in its shape loosely in a mixture of ultramarine blue and white, then put dark strokes of a darker grey or brown over the top to indicate the main folds. Begin putting in some of the mid tones in the background cloth, using mixtures of ultramarine blue and white as before.

9 Loosely paint the pattern of the patchwork blanket on which the model is lying, using broad strokes of the appropriate colour. Do not try to be too precise with the pattern: a loose interpretation will suffice. You should, however, note how the lines of the pattern change direction where the blanket is not perfectly flat.

10 Continue working on the blanket, gradually building up and strengthening the colours while keeping them fresh and spontaneous.

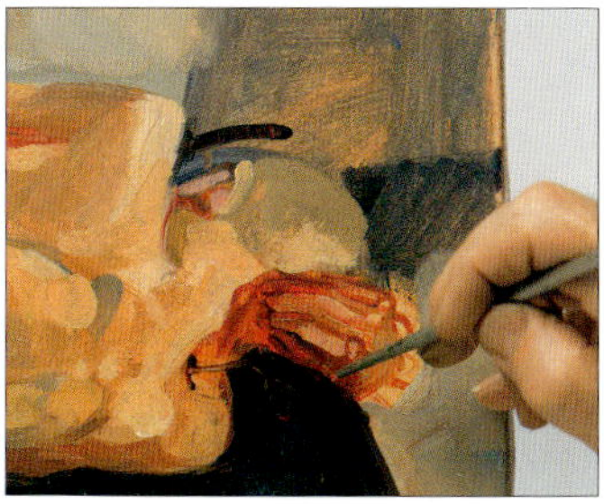

11 Redefine the fingers in cadmium orange and a little brilliant pink.

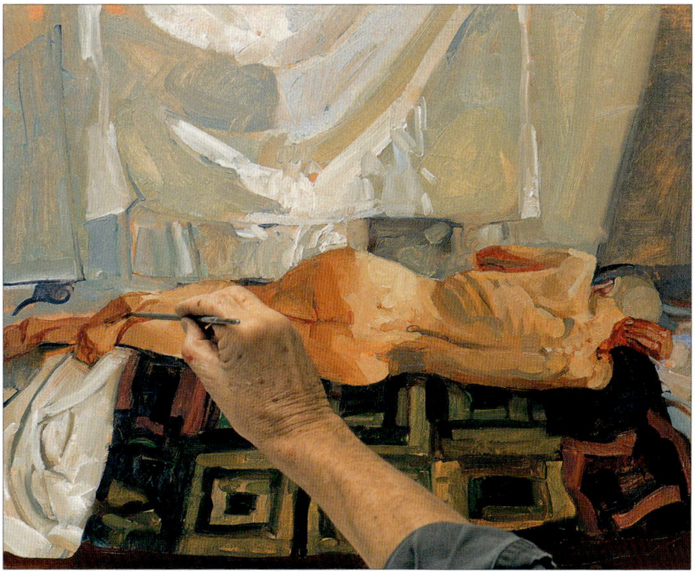

12 Darken the area around the head with a mixture of ultramarine blue, white and a little lamp black, so that the head stands out from the background. Work on the flesh tones, to improve the tonal contrast: the shoulder blade, for example, is lighter than the tones laid down so far, so paint it in a mixture of cadmium orange and white. Use the same colour to define the highlights on the top cervical vertebrae. The soles of the feet are very warm in colour; paint them in a mixture of cadmium red and vermilion.

13 Now turn your attention to the background cloth, reinforcing the dark and mid-toned folds with a mixture of ultramarine blue, white and a tiny amount of cerulean blue – all the time assessing the tones of the cloth in relation to the overall scene rather than looking at it in isolation.

14 Use pure white for the brightest areas of the background cloth, changing to a smaller brush for the finest creases. Note how the folds vary in tone depending on how deep they are: use some mid tones where necessary to convey this.

15 Mix a dark green from ultramarine blue and cadmium yellow and reinforce the dark colours in the blanket. Use the same colour to strengthen the shadow under the model and give a sharp edge to the curve of her body. Brighten the light greens and pinks in the blanket; as the patchwork pattern is made up of straight strips of fabric, you may find that it helps to switch to a small or medium flat brush so that the lines of the pattern are straight and crisp-edged.

16 The triangular-shaped wedge of cloth on the right, just above the model's head, is too light and leads the viewer's eye out of the picture. Mix a mid-toned green and block it in, directing your brushstrokes upwards to avoid accidentally brushing paint on to the model's head.

The finished painting

The figure is positioned almost exactly across the centre of the picture – something that artists are often advised to avoid, but in this instance it adds to the calm, restful mood of the painting. The dark colours and sloping lines of the blanket and the folds in the background cloth all help to direct the viewer's eye towards the nude figure. The background cloth is painted slightly darker in tone than it is in reality: overly stark whites would detract from the figure.

The legs are slightly bent: light and dark flesh tones show how some parts are angled into the light while others are shaded.

Careful assessment of tones is required in order to paint the white backcloth convincingly.

Skin is stretched taut over the ribs and upper vertebrae: subtle shading reveals the shape of the underlying bones.

Male nude in charcoal and soft pastel

This project, made on grey pastel paper, combines charcoal (for the main lines and shading) and a cream-coloured soft pastel (for the highlights). Cream is a more sympathetic colour for the highlights in this drawing than white, which could look extremely stark. The two media are used in the same way.

As the model's position is one that can quite easily be held for a long period, you have plenty of time to map out the essentials of the pose. It might be tempting to start by simply outlining the pose – but if you can imagine the skeleton of the body underneath the skin as you draw, and think of the body as a series of three-dimensional forms, you will undoubtedly find it much easier to get the shapes right.

Materials

- *Grey pastel paper*
- *Thin willow charcoal stick*
- *Kneaded eraser*
- *Soft pastel: pale cream*

The pose

This sofa provides support, making the pose easy to hold for a long time. Even so, it's a good idea to mark the position of the feet and hands with pieces of masking tape, in case the model moves. The back is slightly bent and the stomach is convex, creating interesting shading on the torso. Note the slight foreshortening: the legs are closest to the viewer and so appear slightly larger than they would if the model were standing up.

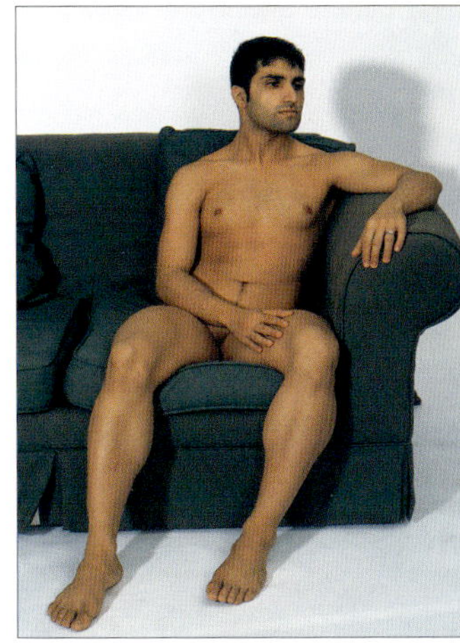

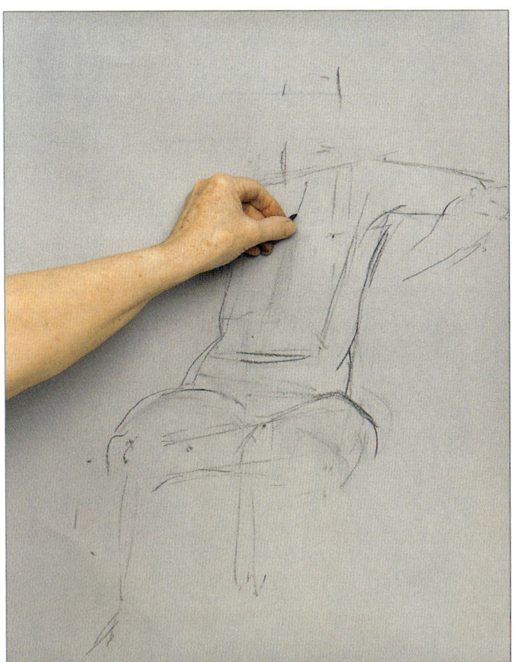

1 Sketch the figure using a thin stick of charcoal, making sure you allow space for the sofa on either side. Measure and mark where each part of the body is positioned in relation to the rest; the face, for example, is in line with the model's left knee. Also look at the slope of the shoulders and at where the elbow is positioned in relation to the chest.

2 Begin searching out the form, making angular marks that establish the three-dimensional shape of the head and torso. Put in faint guidelines running vertically and horizontally through the centre of the face to help you position the facial features. Lightly mark the shape of the sofa – the curve of the arm and the cushion behind the model.

3 Once you've mapped out the basic composition, you can begin to strengthen the lines and put in the facial features in more detail. Draw the eyes, noting how the upper lids fold over the lower ones at the outer corners and how the line of the nose obscures the inner corner of the far eye. Roughly scribble in the hair line. Put in some shading under the chin, on the legs and arms, and on the left of the torso.

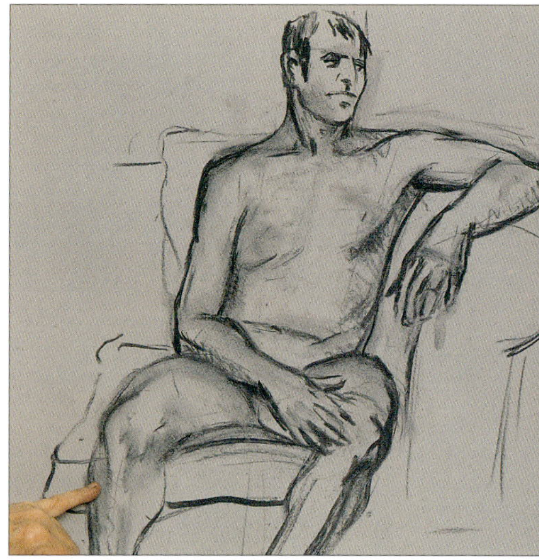

4 Using the tip of the charcoal, draw the muscle that runs diagonally along the side of the neck. This is a very strong, pronounced muscle and putting it in helps to emphasize the tilt of the head. Using the tip of your little finger, smooth out some of the shading on the torso and legs to create more subtle modelling. The figure is already beginning to look more three-dimensional.

5 Loosely scribble over the sofa, so that the figure stands out. Look at the negative shapes – the shape the sofa makes against the body – rather than at the body itself. This makes it easier to see if any adjustments need to be made to the outline of the body. Alter the direction of the hatching lines to make the different planes of the sofa more obvious.

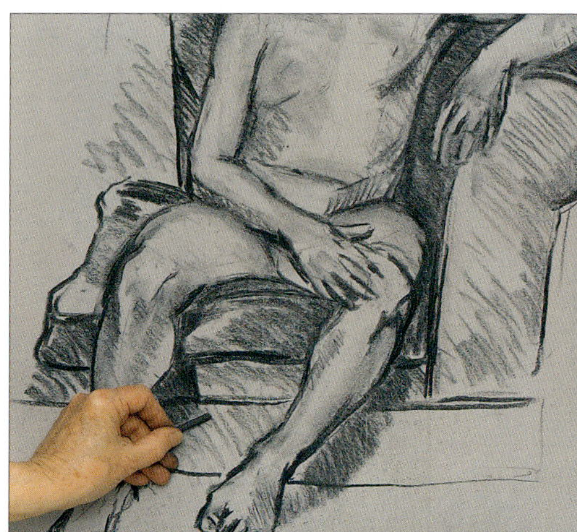

6 Draw the model's left foot. (Try to think of it as a complete unit rather than a series of individual toes.) Shade one side, and indicate the spaces between the toes with very dark marks. Loosely scribble in the shadow cast on the base of the sofa by the model's legs, and hatch the different facets of the cushions.

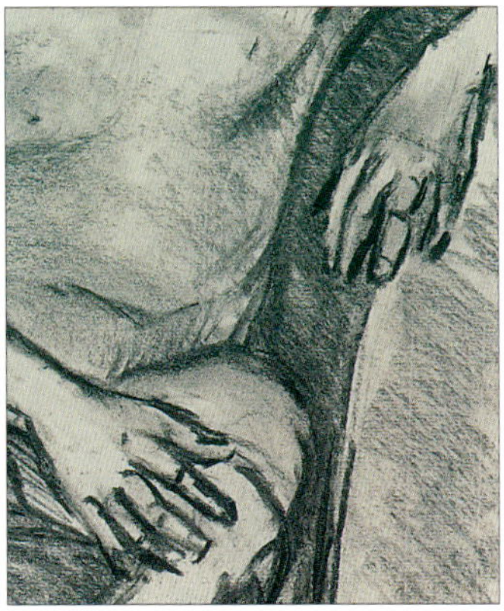

7 Use a kneaded eraser to gently clean up and create more contrast between the lightest and darkest parts. Darken the spaces between the fingers and indicate the segments of the fingers to show how they articulate.

Assessment time
Assess the tonal contrast of the figure as a whole to see where more shading or highlights are needed. For example, the lower part of the torso is slightly shaded by the ribcage as the model slumps back on the sofa, and this area needs to be darkened.

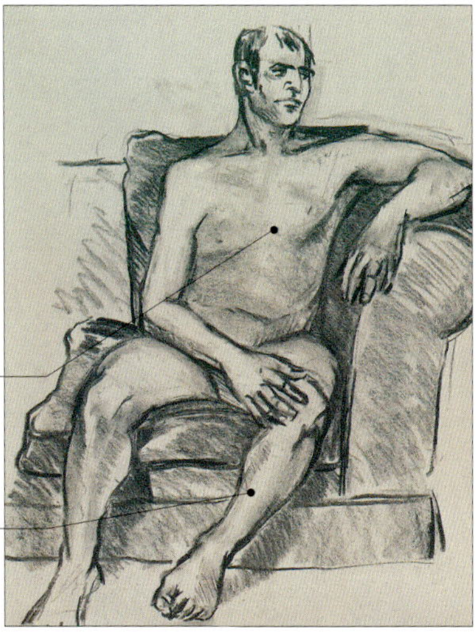

The upper part of the torso is a little too bright.

More shading is needed on the model's left leg. At present it looks rather flat and does not show the muscle tone well.

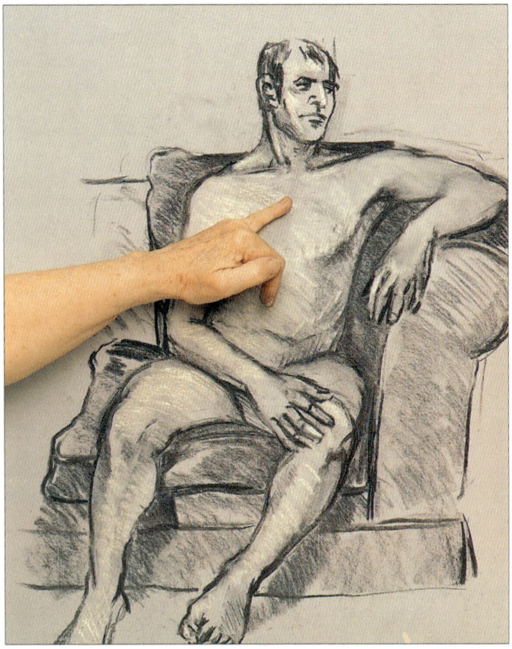

8 Using a very pale cream pastel, put in the highlights on the face, right arm and leg. (Cream is a more sympathetic colour for flesh tones than a stark white.) Even though the limbs are rounded forms, the highlights help to define the different planes. Blend the pastel marks with your fingertip.

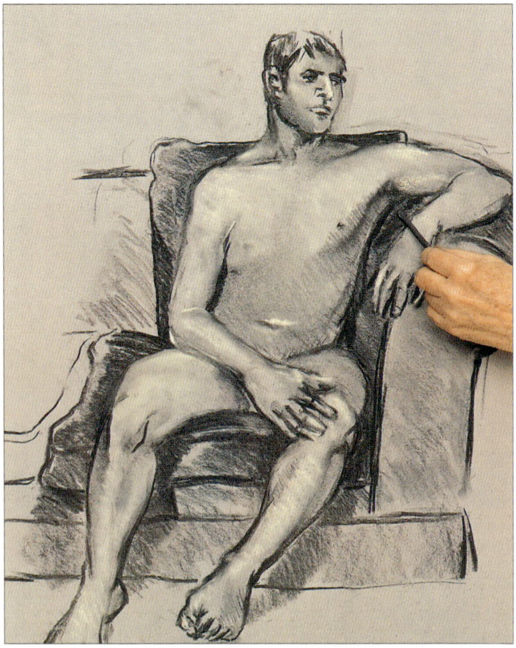

9 Apply more charcoal shading on the lower part of the torso, again blending the marks with your fingertip. (Use your little finger for blending, as it is the driest part of the hand and the risk of smudging the charcoal is reduced.) Darken the sofa under the model's arm, so that he stands out more.

The finished drawing
Although this is not an overly elaborate drawing, it conveys the muscular nature of the model's body. The calves and thighs, in particular, are well developed (this particular model is a professional dancer). Subtle shading reveals the different planes of the body and the combination of dark, intense charcoal marks and soft pastel works well.

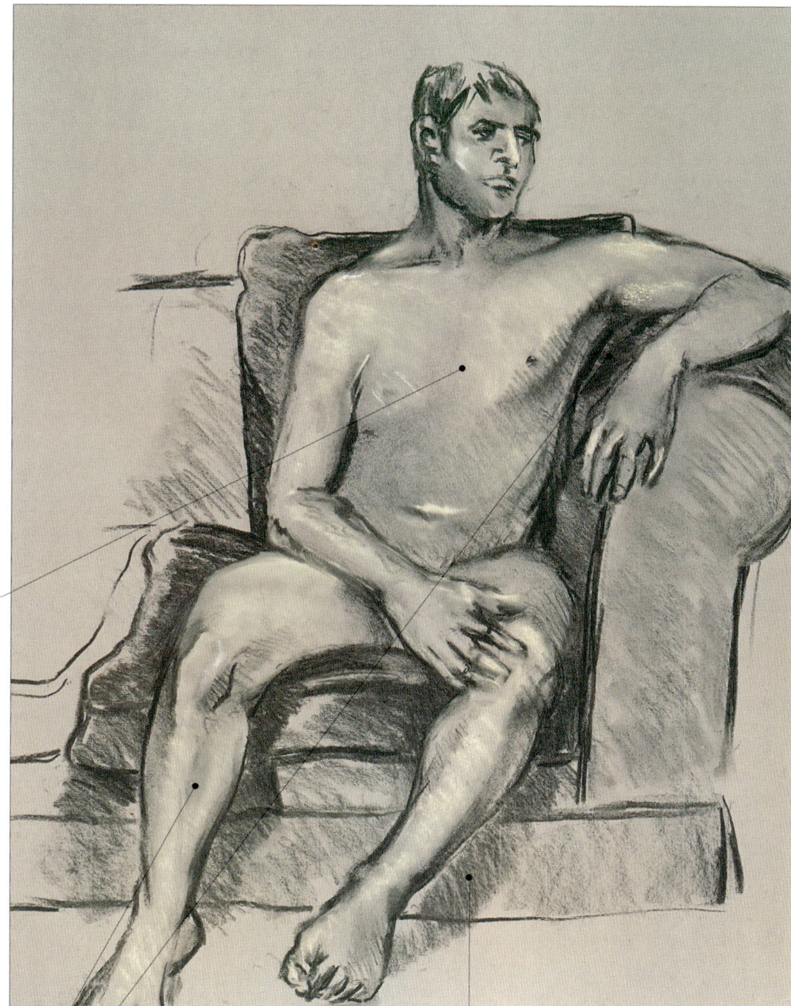

The pastel marks on the torso are blended to convey the smooth skin texture.

Note how effectively shading conveys the muscles in the calf.

The figure stands out well against the dark background of the sofa.

The shadow cast enhances the three-dimensional quality of the drawing.

Curled-up figure in watercolour

This project is about training your eye to see the figure as a whole shape, rather than as a torso with limbs appended. Ask your model to crouch on the floor or curl up, bringing their knees in towards the chest and perhaps wrapping their arms around their legs. Then look at the pose and decide what geometric shape it would fit inside – is it a square, a rectangle, a circle or some other geometric form?

Before you start to draw or paint the pose, lightly sketch the basic geometric shape on your paper or hold the shape in your mind's eye and make sure that the pose is contained within it. (It doesn't matter if some elements, such as a foot or hand, overhang the edge a little; it's the overall shape that's important.) Think of yourself as a sculptor using your pencil or brush to chisel shapes from a lump of marble.

Materials

- *HB pencil*
- *Heavy HP watercolour paper*
- *Watercolour paints: cobalt blue, alizarin crimson, viridian, cadmium yellow pale, Prussian blue, Venetian red, ultramarine blue*
- *Gouache paints: white*
- *Brushes: large flat, medium round, fine round*

The pose

Here, the artist selected a viewpoint slightly above the model, which allowed her to see over the model's shoulder to her bent legs and arms. (If her eye level had been level with the model's back she would have seen only the curve of the spine, which would have made for a less interesting composition.) The main light source was positioned in front of and above the model, so her upper leg and shoulder are brightly lit while her lower back is in shadow. The cool blues and greens of the cushions and throws were chosen to contrast with the warm tones of her skin.

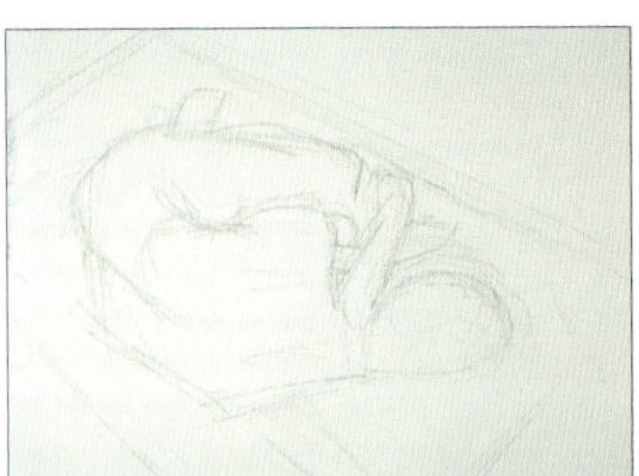

1 Using an HB pencil, roughly sketch the pose. Here, the overall shape of the body is contained within a rectangle. Put in the main curve of the body, the angle of the shoulder, the head and the hands. The straight edges of the bed and cushion are also very useful guidelines.

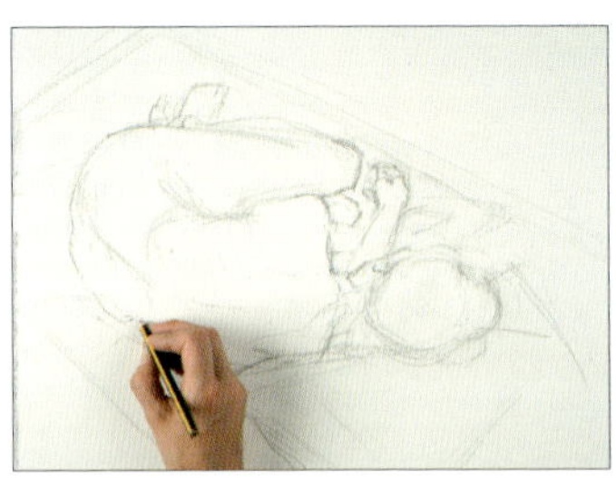

2 Continue until you have all the points of reference that you need. Look for basic shapes. The hands and feet, for example, should be box shapes – don't be tempted to get into drawing the individual digits.

You should also indicate the different planes where the body turns from the light, such as the shoulder blades.

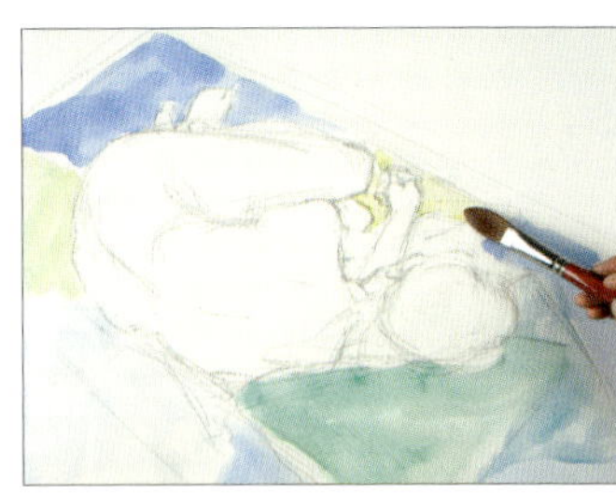

3 Mix a dilute wash of cobalt blue with a tiny bit of alizarin crimson. Using a large flat brush, put in the blue sheet. Use a mix of viridian and cobalt for the underlying colour of the striped blue cushion, and viridian and cadmium yellow pale for the green cushion. Add more yellow to the green mix and paint the bright green of the throw.

4 Wash in the colour of the blue background wall with a dilute mix of Prussian blue. Now wash a very dilute mix of Venetian red and cadmium yellow pale over the body, adding a little more red for the darker areas and remembering to leave the very brightest highlights untouched. Apply a very dilute wash of cadmium yellow pale to the hair.

5 Brush very dilute ultramarine blue, wet into wet, over the lower back, which is in deep shadow. Mix a bright green from viridian and cadmium yellow pale and, using a medium round brush, begin putting in the stripes of the patterned throw. Paint the deep turquoise colour of the throw using a mix of cobalt blue and viridian.

6 Mix a warm reddish brown from Venetian red and cadmium yellow pale and put in the mid tones of the hair. Apply cadmium red to the warmer, darker parts of the skin, such as the shoulder blades. Mix a dark brown from Venetian red and a little Prussian blue and put in the cast shadows under the hand and on the nape of the neck. Mix a dark green from viridian and a little yellow and put in the shadow under the green cushion. Put in the dark stripes and shadow under the striped blue cushion using ultramarine blue.

Tip: Now that you have put in the background, you can erase your original pencil guidelines in these areas.

7 For the cooler shadow on the lower left leg, use a mix of ultramarine blue and alizarin crimson. Use a paler version of this mix for the top edge of the left thigh. Paint the shadows cast by the feet in ultramarine blue. Using the reddish brown mix from the previous step, build up the warmer and darker tones on the skin – for example, the shadow under the shoulder blades, and on the left arm and thigh and the right knee.

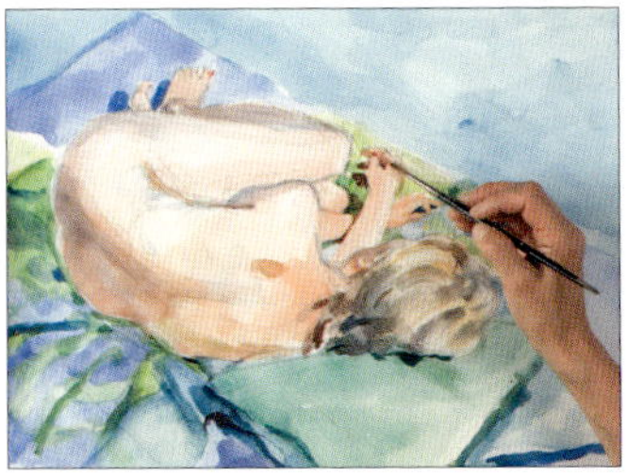

8 Continue building up the skin tones using the same reddish brown mix as before on the lower back. Using a fine round brush, apply the greens and blues of the throw and cushion right up to the edge of the figure to define it more sharply. Apply warm reddish browns where needed on the hands to create some modelling, cutting in with other colours for the negative shapes between the fingers. Carefully dot in the red nail varnish using cadmium red.

Tip: If the initial washes that you applied to the cushion have dried, dampen the area with a little clean water first (taking care not to lift off the underlying colour), so that the new paint spreads wet into wet – otherwise you may end up with rather harsh edges.

Assessment time

As this is intended to be a relatively quick and simple watercolour study, do not be tempted to overwork it, as you may destroy the clarity of the washes and lose the light and airy feel. Just take a few moments to look at the overall balance. Ask if there is sufficient light and shade on the body to make it look three-dimensional and if any more detail is required in the surroundings.

The hair merges into the nape of the neck and the cushion.

The foreground cushions look rather flat and need more tone.

9 Mix cadmium yellow pale with a little white gouache and, using a fine round brush, carefully touch in some of the highlights on the tips of the hair.

10 Using a large round or mop brush and the viridian and cadmium yellow pale mix from Step 3, deepen the colour of the green cushion in the foreground and put in some folds in the fabric. This is the part of the picture that is nearest to us, and having a little more texture in the foreground can help to create a sense of scale.

The finished painting

Although this is a loosely painted, almost impressionistic interpretation of the pose, it has a liveliness and sparkle that are very appealing. The white of the paper also contributes to the feeling of liveliness. The trick with good watercolour painting is to achieve a combination of spontaneity and control – spontaneity in allowing the paint to flow and create lively mixes on the paper, and control in not allowing it to go where you do not want it to. Here, the artist has taken great care not to let any of the background colours spill over on to the body; at the same time, she has worked wet into wet to build up the skin tones and create a very realistic-looking impression of light and shade. Note how some of the pencil underdrawing shows through, the linear marks adding detail and enhancing the soft watercolour washes.

Wet-into-wet washes, built up layer by layer, have been used to build up areas of tone with no hard edges.

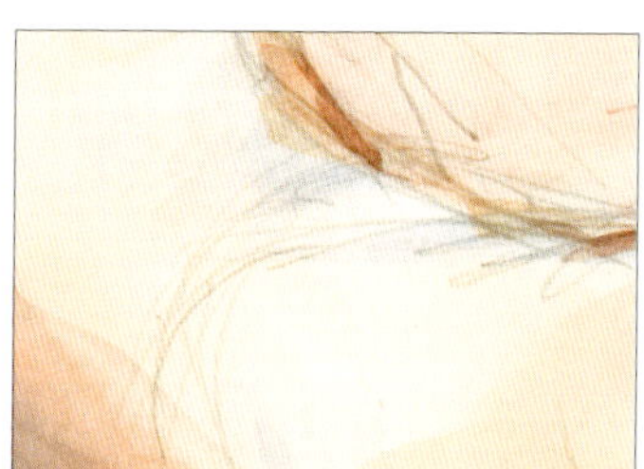

The pencil underdrawing adds a little linear detail and prevents the painting from looking too flat.

The cast shadows are a small but integral part of the composition, adding depth to the image.

Seated female figure in watercolour

You might imagine that posing a seated figure is somehow easier than posing a standing figure: surely all the model has to do is sit still! However, you need to create an interesting composition and make sure that your model can hold the pose in comfort.

A simple seated pose, with the model's back supported by the backrest of a chair or sofa, is certainly easy to hold – but it will not necessarily create a very dynamic picture. From virtually any angle, the model's midriff and thighs will be hidden from view. Viewed from the side, the chair or sofa may dominate your picture. Viewed from the front, the feet will be nearest to the artist and the rest of the body may then appear unattractively foreshortened.

Think about the overall line of the pose: do you want a strong diagonal line, as here, or a softer, more curving shape? Look for interesting angles in the composition: the negative shapes (that is, the spaces between different elements) are critical, as are the angles of the limbs. In the pose selected here, the model's right arm and left leg are bent, forming a zig-zagging line through the composition. Even quite small changes to the pose can make a very big difference to the overall effect, so ask your model to make minor adjustments until you arrive at something that you feel will create a strong composition.

The pose shown here is actually quite hard to hold for any length of time. Much of the model's weight is resting on her left arm, so regular breaks are essential. This is also a difficult pose for the model to resume exactly after a break, so be prepared to make minor adjustments as the painting progresses. Try to put down the basic structure relatively quickly, before the model needs to take a break.

Materials

- *Heavy watercolour paper*
- *Watercolour paints: yellow ochre, ultramarine blue, vermilion, cerulean blue, alizarin crimson*
- *Brushes: medium round*

The pose

The strong diagonal line of the body makes this a very dynamic pose. The bent right arm and left leg neatly counterbalance one another and form a line that zig-zags through the picture, while the triangular negative space between the model's left arm, torso and the cushion adds interest to the whole composition.

1 Mix a dilute wash of a neutral olive green from yellow ochre and ultramarine blue. Using a medium round brush, lightly draw in the main lines of the pose. As always, think of the body as a series of boxes rather than an outline. Use the tilt of the model's shoulders as a guideline to drawing the other elements and remember to look at the negative shapes as well as the positives.

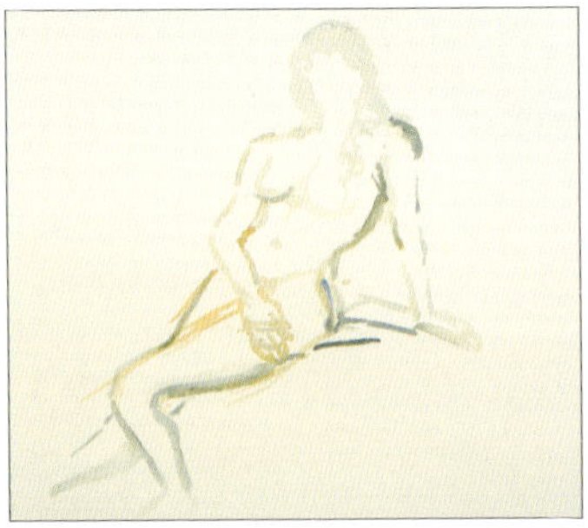

2 Continue until you have mapped out the whole pose. The exact colours are not important, but keep them very pale for this 'underdrawing' and use colours that complement the skin tones you will be using.

3 When you're happy with the basic structure, add a little more ultramarine blue to the mix and refine the shape of the face and shoulders. Use a very dilute mix of the same colour to begin putting in the background. Use a little vermilion to lightly touch in the cushion on which the model is sitting, noting how the weight of her body pushes the edge of the cushion upwards. Apply a stronger wash of ultramarine blue for the fabric.

4 Lightly map in the position of the facial features, using the same blue-green mix as in the previous step for the eyebrows and eyes and a very dilute wash of vermilion for the shaded side of the nose. Mix a very dilute wash of cerulean blue and apply it to the background above the stool.

5 Mix a very dilute, cool purple from alizarin crimson with a tiny amount of ultramarine blue and lightly brush it on to the lower part of the breasts. Brush the same mix over the edge of the left arm, then drop in a little yellow ochre so that the colours blend wet into wet on the paper to create a warm, glowing skin tone.

6 Darken the hair with a mix of alizarin crimson and ultramarine blue. Do not try to put in every single strand, but make your brushstrokes follow the direction of the hair growth. Apply more blue to the background, pulling your brush away from the figure in a series of spiky strokes so that the colour does not bleed into the figure.

7 Carefully brush a little very dilute vermilion over the model's face, remembering to leave the very brightest highlights untouched. Using slightly darker versions of the previous mixes, brush a little colour on to the shaded side of the body – the model's left side.

8 Refine the facial details, using the bluish-purple mix for the eyes and vermilion for the nostrils, mouth and the dimple in the chin. Put more colour into the hair, using the same mix as in Step 6. Remember to leave some slight gaps for the highlights.

Assessment time

The painting is taking shape well, and the character and detail are starting to come through. Some modelling has been created on the left-hand side of the model's body, but the other side of the body has been left largely untouched, even though this area is receiving a lot of light and consequently contains some bright highlights, for which you need to reserve the white of the paper. More tone needs to be added to the figure as a whole, to differentiate the light and shaded areas more clearly and give the figure some form. The stool on which the model is sitting needs to be painted in order to set the figure in context, and applying more colour around the model would help to differentiate her from the background, and frame her better. The skin tones also need warmth.

This area has received virtually no paint at all.

This area is in deep shadow and needs to be much darker in tone.

9 Using the same mixes as before – warm reddish purples and yellow ochre – build up the skin tones across the body as a whole, working wet into wet. Remember to leave the very brightest highlights untouched. Intensify the blue background and red cushion with stronger washes of ultramarine blue and vermilion respectively.

10 Strengthen the tones on the legs if necessary, so that they stand out from the background. Use yellow ochre to put in a suggestion of the wooden floorboards. This is quite a loose, impressionistic painting so do not attempt to put lots of detail into the surroundings: the figure should dominate the composition.

The finished painting

The main purpose of this study is to concentrate on the figure, and so the artist has put in just a suggestion of the background. However, the cool blue cloth acts as a foil to the warm colours of the skin and allows the figure to stand out.

By paying attention to the light and dark areas and allowing the skin tones to blend wet into wet on the paper, the artist has created lively mixes that capture the effect of the light falling across the figure.

The edge of the arm is very brightly lit and has been left unpainted, so the background is essential in order for it to stand out.

Although much of this area has been left unpainted, the cool, dark shadows under the breast convey the form.

Lively, flowing brushstrokes and various colour mixes create an impression of the hair without putting in every single strand.

Seated figure in Conté

This project uses Conté – an extremely versatile medium – in both pencil and stick form. The pencils are hard and sharp enough for you to be able to create crisp, linear detailing and delicate hatching, yet soft enough for the marks to be smudged to create large areas of tone. Although the pigment in Conté sticks is relatively powdery, the sticks are slightly harder and more oily than soft pastels, so you can lay one colour on top of another, allowing the underlying colour to show through. This enables you to create lively mixes of colour on the paper – perfect for skin tones.

Here, the artist also used a dip pen and ink to outline part of the figure – a lovely touch, as the dip pen creates slightly irregular marks that have great liveliness and energy, yet contrast well with the softness of the Conté. You can make lines of different widths by varying the amount of pressure you apply and by twisting the pen as you work.

Materials

- *Good-quality drawing paper*
- *Conté pencils: various shades of yellow ochre, pink, yellow, blue, purple, brown, green, black*
- *Conté sticks: black, brown*
- *Dip pen*
- *Sepia ink*

The pose

In order to give some height to the image, the model was asked to pose sitting on the back of a sofa. Resting his head on his hand not only provides a useful support in a pose that has to be held for a long time, but also frames the face. As the walls of the room are painted white, coloured fabrics were hung behind his head so that the figure would stand out from the background. A dressing gown placed on the sofa darkens the bottom left corner of the image and, together with the background drapes, frames the figure.

1 Using a yellow ochre Conté pencil, map out the pose, looking at the body as a series of geometric blocks at first. Put in the centre line of the head and lines to indicate the position of the facial features.

2 Begin blocking in some of the background cloths, using pink and yellow Conté pencils. This is to use the negative spaces around the figure to help define it more precisely. Put in some of the more deeply shaded areas on the body, such as chest between the arms and the area under the model's right arm, at the same time.

3 Use a blue pencil to put in the line of the hair and beard. Put in the facial features using a purple pencil. Use the same colour to outline the left shoulder, so that it stands out. Lightly hatch brown (for the darker tones) and yellow ochre (for the mid tones) over the body so that you begin to get some sense of light and shade.

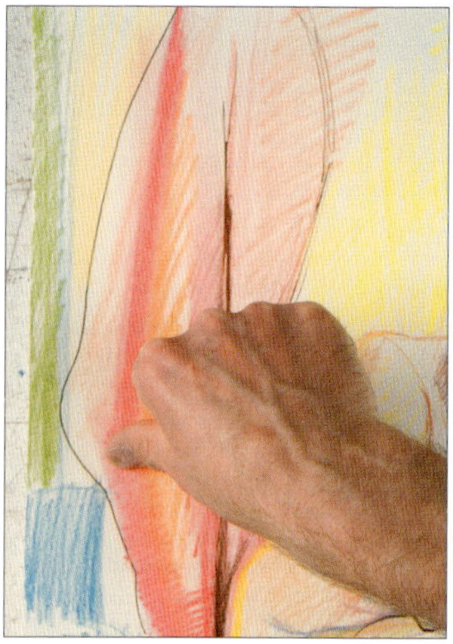

4 Using a dip pen and sepia ink, put in the folds in the background fabrics. Rub the background pink and yellow hatching with a rag or your fingertips to soften and blur the marks, making the fabric look soft and fluid.

5 Scribble in the green of the model's gown, looking at how the fabric drapes and folds. Using a dip pen and sepia ink, delineate the edges of the head and limbs and put some spiky detail in the hair.

6 Stroke the side of a black Conté stick over the darkest areas of tone on the body, then smudge the marks with your fingers.

7 Using a purple Conté pencil, put in the wood panelling in the background, lightly hatching the panels and using strong, linear marks for the lines between them. Smudge the hatching lines with your fingers. Use a cool blue pencil for the skirting board, which is in shadow.

8 Using a brown Conté stick, hatch in the underside of the model's left hand. Lightly hatch pale yellow ochre Conté pencil over the light parts of the patterned fabric. Using a green Conté pencil, put in some of the patterning on both the fabric and the model's gown.

Assessment time

In the final stages of the drawing, concentrate on developing the modelling on the figure and on making sure that it stands out from the background. At present, the different planes and sinews of the legs are not sufficiently clear and the side of the torso also lacks form. The facial features, too, are rather indistinct and the flesh tones are too uniformly yellow in colour. The lower legs, in particular, require more definition. The left leg and foot almost merge into the background fabric, and the outer edge of the right leg needs to be strengthened in order to distinguish it more clearly from the left leg. The patterned fabric of the sofa could be built up a little more, but take care not to overdo fabrics and backgrounds, in case you overpower the main subject.

The modelling on the body needs to be built up more.

The facial features are a little indistinct.

The left leg merges into the background.

9 Using a black Conté pencil, draw in the eyebrows and hair. Put in a blue shadow on the side of the face and the eyes and lines around the eyes in blue. Reinstate any lines that have been lost – for example, the edge of the left hand, which is lost against the face. Using a purple Conté pencil, hatch over the most deeply shaded parts of the torso and legs, smudging the marks with your fingers to create the different planes on the legs. Add a little more modelling to the left shoulder.

10 Add a little more detail on the fabrics and any missing shadows, such as the one under the thigh.

Tip: Aim for a general impression of the fabric patterns, rather than a detailed rendering, otherwise the fabric may begin to overpower the portrait.

The finished drawing

Although it is generally not advisable to place the figure centrally in the frame, here the central placement evokes a feeling of calm that is entirely in keeping with the pensive, reflective expression of the model.

Despite this, the image is far from static. The diagonal tilt of the head and body is counterbalanced by another diagonal line running in the opposite direction down from the tip of the model's right shoulder to his left foot. The striped fabric and the strong vertical lines of the tongue-and-groove panelling in the background also add visual interest to the composition.

Improving the modelling on the figure and adding a little more depth and detail to the fabrics in the final stages have given the drawing much more of a three-dimensional feel. Several techniques have been used to build up the modelling, from simple hatching and cross-hatching to smudging the Conté marks with the fingers to build up areas of soft tone. Using a dip pen to outline part of the figure is a lovely touch, as it adds irregular marks that give the figure energy and vibrancy.

Linear detailing is created using both the tip of the Conté pencils and a dip pen, which has a lovely organic feel.

Cross-hatching one colour over another builds up areas of tone and allows you to create lively optical mixes of colour.

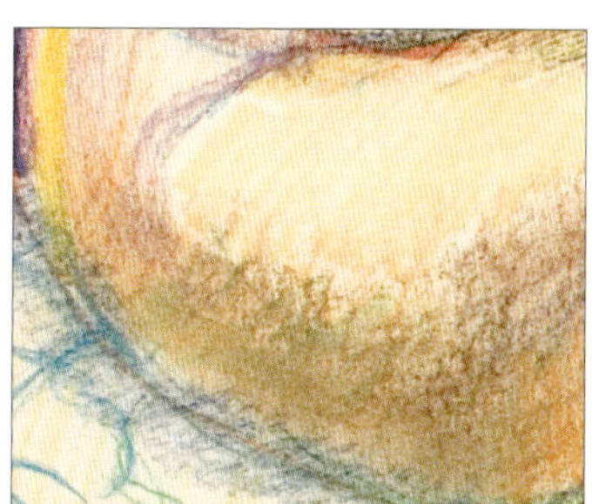

There is just enough detail in the fabric to provide visual interest without overpowering the drawing.

Seated figure in soft pastels

Once you've gained some experience of drawing and painting the figure against a plain backcloth, why not try including more of the setting in your picture? Often, just a hint of the surroundings – a rug on the floor, a vase of flowers or a book on a nearby table – is enough to create a sense of atmosphere. Props, such as the lily that the model is holding in this project, can also help create a 'story' – and, on a purely practical level, they give the model something to do with his or her hands. And strong, sculptural shapes like the lily can be used to cast interesting shadows, which you can use in your composition. Remember, however, that the figure should always remain the main focus of your painting. If you have a very complicated element in the background, such as wallpaper (or the rug in this scene), it's perfectly acceptable to simplify it in your painting and merely hint at the colours and pattern.

This project is worked in soft pastel, which is a wonderfully versatile medium. It allows you to make both strong, linear marks using the tip of the pastel and broad sweeps of colour using the side; you can also blend the marks with your fingers to create soft, smooth textures while still allowing several colours to mix optically on the paper.

Soft pastels come in a huge range of colours and there may be several shades of the same colour in a large set. The colour names may also vary from one manufacturer to another, so it can be hard to compare different brands; in fact, some brands have no colour names, only numbers. When choosing colours, be guided by your eyes.

If you have only a small set of pastels, white may be the only colour you have for the highlights. If this is the case, put down the highlight as white, and then apply another colour on top and blend in with your finger to create a pale tint.

Materials

- *Dark green pastel paper*
- *Soft pastels: various shades such as Naples yellow, pink, raw sienna, burnt umber, black, white, olive green*

The pose

The artist has included just enough of the room to provide a context for the pose without detracting from the figure. This is an easy pose for the model to hold, as her back is well supported. As the light is coming from the side, there are some fairly strong cast shadows on the sofa, which add interest to the composition. A few carefully chosen props – an open book, a lily and a couple of cushions and throws – complete the scene.

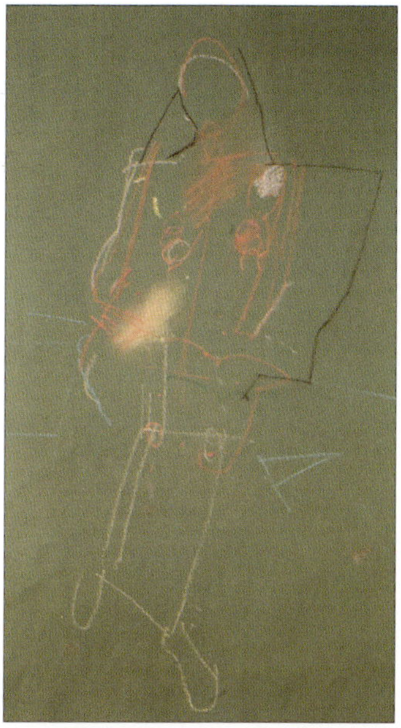

1 Establish the main lines of the pose and make sure that you can fit everything into the picture space. The first stages of a drawing are all about mapping out where features are in relation to each other. Here, for example, the right knee is almost directly below the right nipple. Put in the basic 'egg' shape of the head, which is slightly tilted here. Look for things like the relative size and angles of the feet, and think of the rest of the body as a series of geometric blocks to get the model's proportions right.

Tip: See if there's anything in the surroundings that you can incorporate in your first stage drawing as a guide to where things are placed. Here, for example, the artist has outlined the cushion behind the model's head and the triangle of light that breaks up the shadows cast on the sofa.

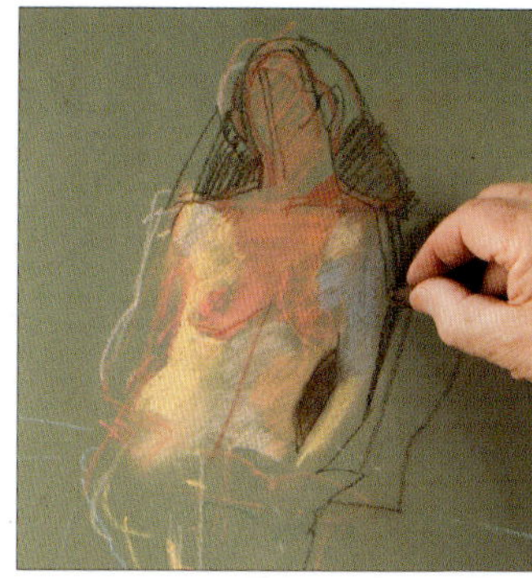

2 Begin to put down blocks of warm and cool colour as you work on your drawing. The right-hand side of the model's upper chest, for example, is very warm, but her left-hand side, which receives less direct light, is cooler in tone. There is quite a lot of reflected light on the breasts. Block in the cushion, as this will help to define the shape of the model's left arm.

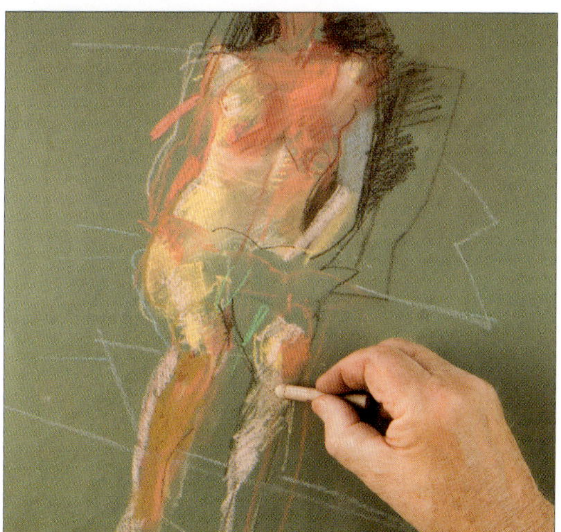

3 Continue working down the torso and legs, putting in the warm and cool tones. Don't try to be too precise at this stage: just establish the general shapes of the different areas.

Tip: Keep checking the proportions to make sure the body does not become too elongated and that you have left plenty of room for the feet.

4 Put in highlights around the face – for example, on the edge of the nose and on the model's right cheek and forehead – and on the shoulders, so that you start to develop the form. Establish the position of the facial features, without attempting to put in much detail at this stage. Gradually build up the flesh colours on the upper chest. Block in the dark cushion; this will help to define the edges of the figure without drawing a crisp, sharp line.

5 Continue developing the modelling on the figure, looking all the time for the strong highlights and shadows that will reveal the form. Use a combination of short, linear marks that imply the muscle masses or bone structures beneath the skin (the rib cage, for example) and soft finger-blending for smooth areas such as the highlights above the right breast. Begin blocking in the shape of the lilies on the model's lap. (Use the dark green of the paper for the leaves in parts.)

6 Refine the facial features, looking for the highlights and shadows as before. Using the tip of the pastel, put in more of the general lines of the model's wavy hair.

Tip: If necessary, break your pastel stick to get a clean, sharp edge so that you can draw fine lines and details.

7 Roughly block in the striped throw and the sofa behind the model. As with the cushion in Step 4, this will help to define the edges of the figure. Note how the stripes on the throw change direction as the fabric folds and drapes.

8 Roughly draw in the open book beside the model. The white of the pages accents the turn of her wrist and emphasizes its shape. Begin putting in any cast shadows that you can see. The lily casts a shadow on the model's leg; put this in using a warm, reddish brown. Elsewhere on the legs, look for the highlights and shadows that delineate the calves.

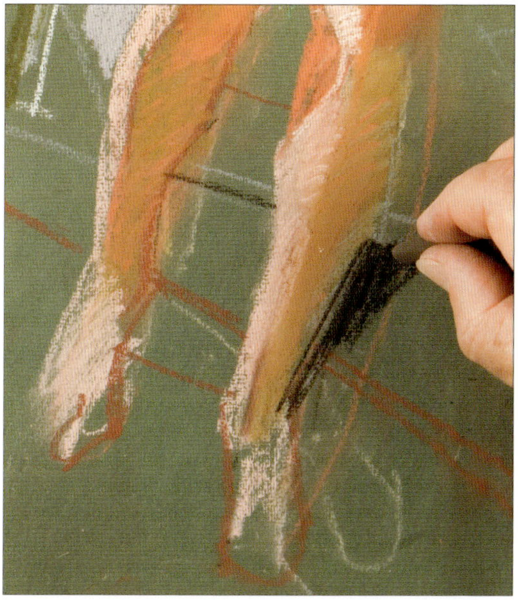

9 Block in the dark shadow under the sofa, as well as the line of the rug on the floor.

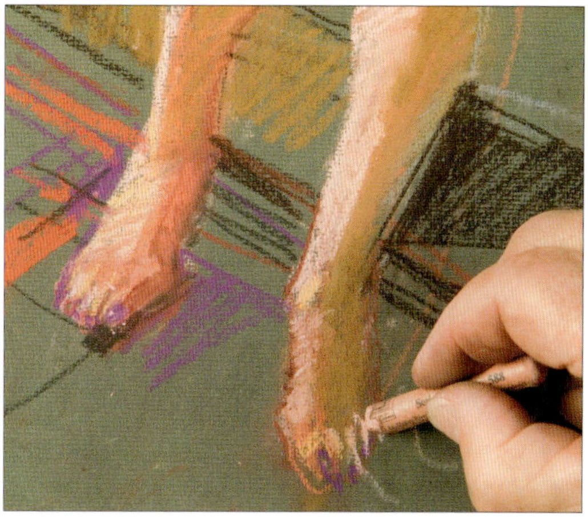

10 Put in as much of the pattern of the rug as you wish, taking care not to allow the rug to overpower the rest of the drawing. The feet themselves should be drawn initially as simple geometric shapes before you attempt to put in any detail such as the individual toes. As always, create a sense of their form by looking for the lights and darks and the warm and cool areas; the instep of the right foot, for example, is very warm in tone, so use a relatively dark purple.

11 The cast shadows are a subtle but important part of the overall composition of this picture. Put in the shadow of the lily on the sofa using a pale, cool grey, and then the shadow that the body casts on the sofa using a dark green. You can smooth out and soften the pastel marks later if necessary – just block in the general shapes for now.

12 Using warm pinks, put in any missing highlights on the upper left arm and torso, where the bony protuberances of the collar and shoulder bones catch the light. This area receives much less light than the other side of the model's body, so you will notice that even the highlights are relatively dark in tone.

Assessment time
With the exception of a few key highlights to really emphasize the bone structure, the drawing of the model is virtually complete. The light falling across the figure from the left creates lovely modelling. Although the artist has included no more than a suggestion of the patterned rug in the foreground, and has simply blocked in the background quite roughly, there is just enough detail around the model to add interest to the composition without detracting from the figure.

When creating your own life drawing projects you may choose to leave out personal jewellery, or indeed ask your model to wear a necklace or similar that you feel adds a certain 'personality' or colour to the pose. The blue jewellery has yet to be added to this drawing, and will add a constrasting cool highlight to the flushed, warm area beneath the model's throat.

13 Using a mid-toned olive green, block in the shaded front edge of the sofa, then blend the marks with your fingers. The parts of the sofa not in shadow were put in with a pale mauve. It's perfectly acceptable to use a little artistic licence for things like this; here, the artist felt that the mauve complemented the skin tones and was a more lively colour than the actual grey of the fabric.

14 Put in any final details and finishing touches such as the model's jewellery. Use white for the silver chains and green overlaid with a bright blue for the turquoise stones. Finally, put in any missing highlights on the neck and clavicle using a light raw sienna.

The finished drawing

Although the artist has included enough of the surroundings to create a sense of place, nothing is allowed to dominate the figure. Peripheral details such as the open book and the rug on the floor are put in only sketchily (although you could draw them in more detail if you wished). The strong side lighting has created interesting shadows that the artist has made an integral part of the composition. By carefully assessing the light and dark tones, the artist has created a convincingly three-dimensional portrayal.

The highlight area on the arm is broken up by the shadow cast by the left breast.

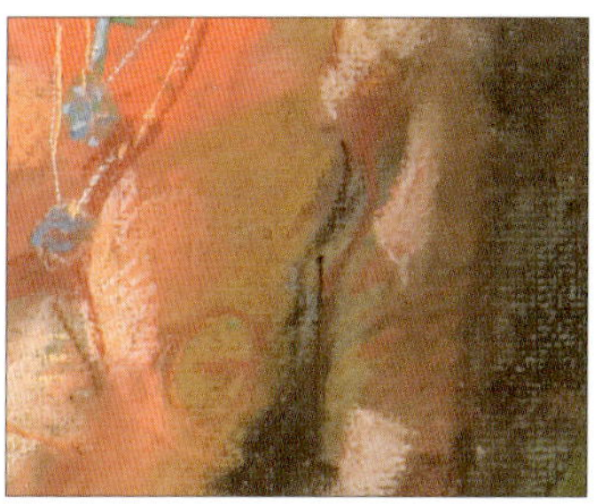

The open book lying beside the model contributes to the overall 'story', and suggests something about the subject.

A combination of linear marks and soft finger blending is used to convey the skin tones and the form of the figure.

The cast shadow of the lily forms a graphic compositional element in its own right and breaks up an otherwise empty space.

Standing figure in mixed media

The best advice to anyone setting up a pose in a domestic interior is to keep things simple. It's very easy to get carried away with adding colourful props and details, to the point where you end up with a painting of the setting rather than of the figure.

Think about using the furnishings as a kind of 'frame' for the main subject, or arranging them in such a way that the viewer's eye is led through the scene to the figure. In the scene here, for example, the draped fabrics almost function as arrows, pointing towards the figure. Look at how the negative spaces around the figure contribute to the composition: often they can be used to define the shape of the subject.

Finally, pay attention to the lighting. Side lighting is perhaps the best way of creating good modelling on your subject, and both side and top lighting can produce interesting shadows that you can use in your composition.

In terms of the model's pose, you need to look at the overall shape. Compositionally, a straightforward standing pose, with the model's weight evenly distributed over both feet and the arms hanging by the side, can be very boring. Instead, ask your model to bend his or her arms or legs, or perhaps stretch one leg out. In addition to making a more interesting shape, this will also tense the muscles, affording you the opportunity to closely examine different muscle groups and how they affect the figure.

Materials

- *Watercolour paper*
- *Conté pencils: various shades of raw sienna, blue, purple, pink*
- *Gouache paints: cobalt blue, white, vermilion, yellow ochre, alizarin crimson, ultramarine blue, carmine red, lemon yellow*
- *Brushes: medium flat, medium round, fine round*

The pose

The model was asked to stretch out his arms to create a more dynamic shape; it would be incredibly tiring to do this without any support, so the window ledge provided a practical solution. The cast shadows on the wall are an integral part of the composition and need to be treated as shapes that have substance in their own right. The draped fabrics add colour and interest.

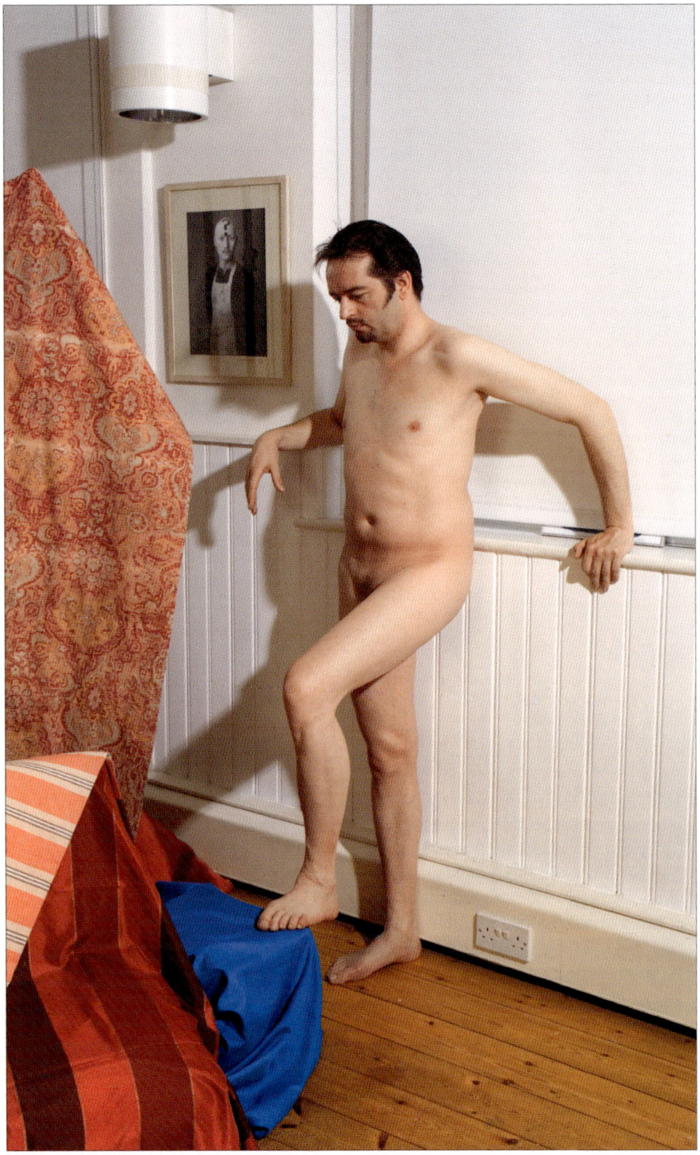

1 Using a raw sienna Conté pencil, put in construction lines as a guide to where things are positioned – for example, the nipples and navel form an inverted triangle. Look for different planes, such as those on the legs, and mark them lightly. Elements beyond the figure can be used as guidelines, too – such as the vertical line of the window.

2 Continue until you have mapped out the entire pose, continually measuring and referring to your points of reference in order to make sure that everything is the right size and in the right place.

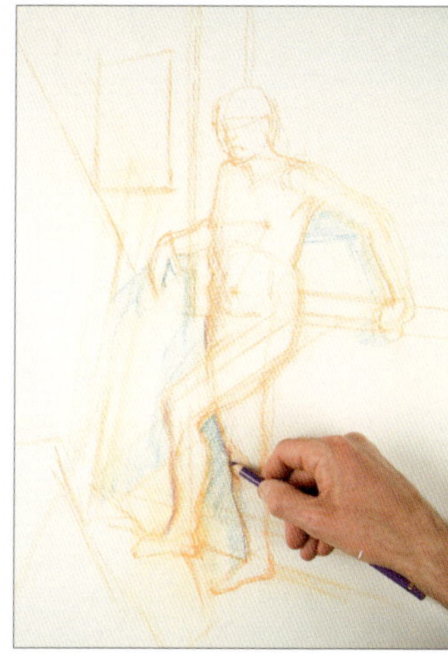

3 The cast shadows form part of the overall composition, and putting them in early on in the drawing gives you another useful guide to use when checking where things are placed. Using the side of a blue or purple Conté pencil, depending on whether you feel a warm or a cool tone is appropriate, lightly shade them in.

4 Use a pink Conté pencil to go over the outline of the warm-coloured backcloth. Add a touch of warm shading (purple) to the right-hand side of the model's face, hand and chest.

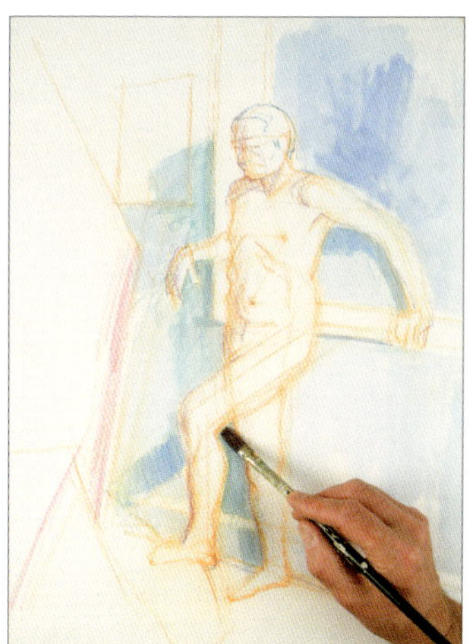

5 Mix a pale, dilute blue from cobalt blue and white gouache. Using a medium flat brush, apply this over the background. Then brush clean water over the Step 3 Conté pencil shadows, so that the marks blend in.

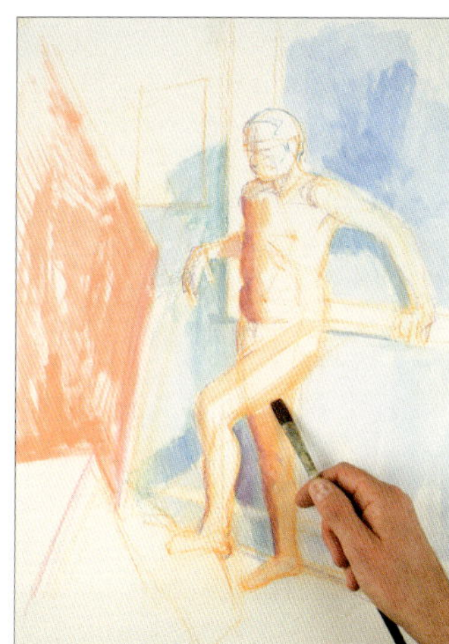

6 Mix a pink tone from vermilion, white and a little yellow ochre and scumble it loosely over the backcloth. Mix a violet shadow colour from alizarin crimson, ultramarine blue and white and paint in all the shadows.

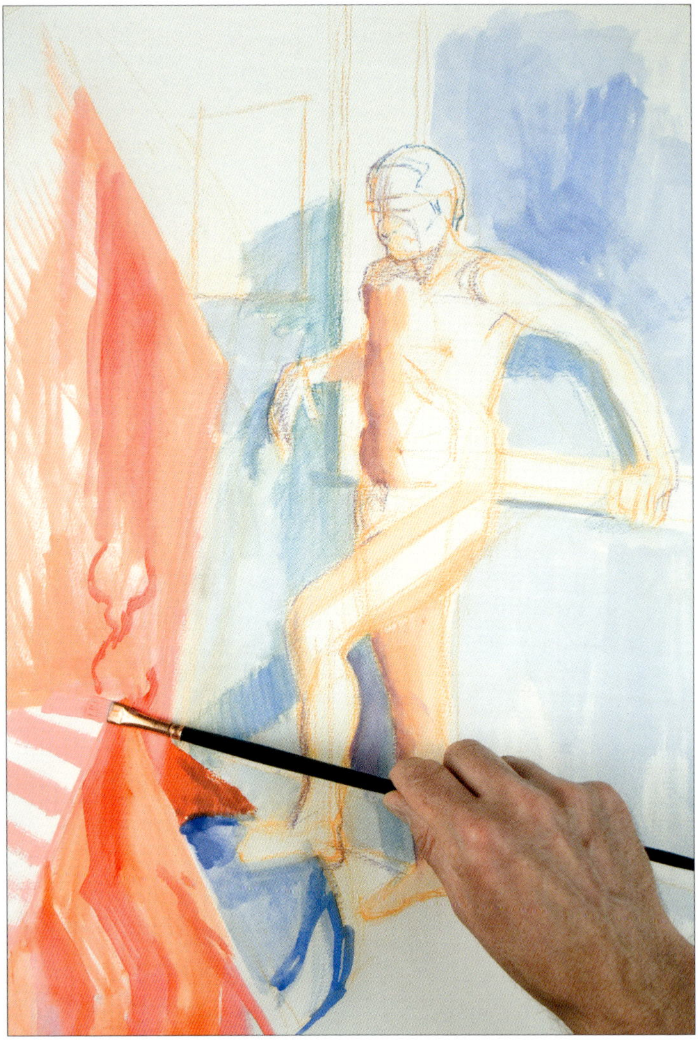

7 Apply a very thin wash of yellow ochre over the mid-toned areas of the legs. Loosely put in the blue fabric of the stool on which the model's left foot is placed, using a mix of white and ultramarine blue. Next, apply the pink tone from Step 6 over the light parts of the plain red throw. Then mix a brighter pink from carmine red and alizarin crimson for the stripes of the other throw. You can use the same colour to begin sketching in the rough shapes of the patterned backcloth.

Tips:

- To maintain the tonal balance of the painting, it's important to keep everything moving along at the same rate, so don't be tempted to finalize one area before you move on to the next. Alternate between working on the subject and the background.
- To avoid changing brushes often, when you have one colour on your brush look for somewhere else you can use it.

8 Using an almost dry brush, apply a little of the bright pink over the mid-tone areas of the left leg, leaving some of the paper showing through for the very brightest highlights. Use the violet mix from Step 6 for the deep shadows on the legs and again for the eyes and beard. Gradually build up the modelling on the chest, using cool green (mixed from yellow ochre and ultramarine blue) or warm purple-pink tones as appropriate.

9 Using a medium round brush, scumble on a relatively thick mix of yellow ochre for the floorboards, and brush the same colour over the shaded underside of the left arm and into the lower stomach area.

10 Using a fine round brush, paint in the picture frame to the left of the model's head in a pale mix of yellow ochre and white, adding a little blue to the mix for the centre of the frame. Using ultramarine blue, brush in the folds of the fabric on the footstool. Paint the reflected shadows on the skirting board in various dilute pinks and blues, as appropriate. Using a combination of the pink mix and yellow ochre, add the dark tones on the legs.

11 Use ultramarine blue to put in the lines of the panelling, applying dilute yellow ochre for the panels themselves. Block in the hair with a thin mix of ultramarine blue and white. Use the violet mix from Step 6 to draw in the shadow cast by the model's left hand. Relocate the cast shadows with a mix of ultramarine and white.

Assessment time

Virtually all the elements of the image have been put in, although the skin tones on the figure, which is the main focus of the picture, are too pale overall and there is insufficient modelling on the body. The facial features also need to be given more emphasis. The background behind the figure is too cool and blue, and the cast shadow on the wall – which is an important part of the composition – still looks too insubstantial. When you make these final adjustments, remember to keep looking at the picture as a whole, continually assessing each element in relation to all the rest, so that you do not concentrate on one area at the expense of others.

This cast shadow needs to be strengthened to create a stronger sense of light and shade.

The facial features need to be more distinct to convey the model's mood and character.

More modelling is needed on the figure, particularly on the torso and upper left arm.

12 Add texture to the hair by applying a mix of alizarin crimson and ultramarine blue, using short, spiky brushstrokes. Use the same colour to darken the beard and eyebrows. Build up the modelling on the figure, using a range of warm tones and exaggerating the tonal differences in places for a more dramatic effect. Warm up the cool blue background with a mix of yellow ochre and white. Apply lemon yellow to the sunlit side and ledge of the window frame, with white on top to provide a warm, golden glow.

13 Put in the lines of the floorboards, using a neutral brown/grey mix. Use the brush to cut in around the feet and refine their shape.

14 Tone down the very brightest highlights on the chest with a pale mix of pink, white and lemon yellow.

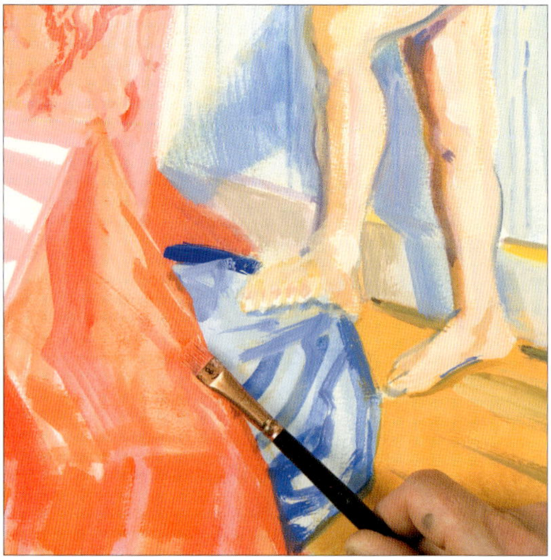

15 Darken the fabric along the sofa edge to create more of a three-dimensional effect.

The finished painting

This is a colourful, lively painting that demonstrates the chalky, opaque nature of gouache paint well. The figure is positioned just off centre, which is almost always more effective than a central placement. The background is relatively sparse, allowing the figure to stand out. The slanting lines of the floorboards and the colourful fabrics all help to direct the viewer's eye to the main subject, yet compositionally they are balanced by the strong vertical lines of the figure and the tongue-and-groove wood panelling. The warm yellow light filtering through the edge of the closed window blind and the cool cast shadows give the painting a lovely sense of light and shade.

The shadows and hint of yellow sunlight create a lovely feeling of light and shade.

A few vivid colours are echoed in the skin tones, making the composition work well as a whole.

The modelling on the figure has been painted with care.

The lines of the floorboards point inwards, directing our attention towards the figure.

Foreshortened male in acrylics

Drawing and painting the figure in perspective can make for a much more interesting pose than a static standing or seated pose, in which the whole body is positioned at more or less the same distance from the artist.

In this pose, the model's head and torso appear considerably larger than his feet, simply because they are much closer to the artist. Plot exactly where each element of the figure goes before you begin painting. You may even decide to exaggerate the pose very slightly, as the artist has done here, in order to emphasize this particular model's muscular arms and upper body for dramatic effect.

Your model will have to hold this pose for a considerable length of time, so make sure that he or she is aware of this before you begin. Here, the model was lying on a thin sheet on a hard wooden floor; placing a cushion under his elbows made the pose much more comfortable and thus easier to hold for longer. Even the best and most experienced of models will have to take occasional breaks, so do whatever you can to ensure that the model can get back into the same position. For example, it's a good idea to put masking tape on the floor around the model's feet (and elbows, in this case) to use as a guide to get back into exactly the same position as before. You could also ask your model to focus on a specific point, such as a painting on the wall, so that they can redirect their gaze to this point when they resume the pose.

This painting is done in acrylics. You can use very thin paint for an under-painting to establish the main lines and the shadows, and build up the skin tones little by little. To create a deeper texture you can use thick, impasto-like applications using a palette knife or (as the artist did here) your fingertips.

Materials

- *Canvas board*
- *Acrylic paints: ultramarine blue, yellow ochre, lemon yellow, vermilion, alizarin crimson, white*
- *Brushes: medium flat, large flat*

The pose

Ask your model to move around until he or she finds a pose that can be held relatively easily for a long period. Aim to get interesting angles and shapes within the composition: here, for example, the model initially stretched both legs out behind him in a straight line, but bending the right knee gave a much more dynamic shape to the pose.

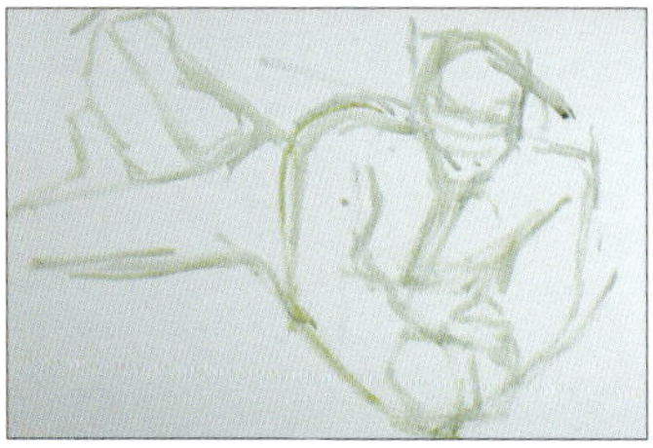

1 Mix a dilute wash of cool green from ultramarine blue, yellow ochre and a touch of lemon yellow. Using a medium flat brush, carefully but roughly map out the pose, remembering to think of the figure as a series of geometric blocks. Think of the head as a foreshortened box, for example. Look for features that line up, such as the right elbow and the right knee, as well as the clasped hands, right shoulder and the bulge of the left calf. Also, pay particular attention to the way the legs in this pose are very foreshortened, and the torso seems rather twisted, so that you can see more of the model's belly than of his back.

2 Continue with the underpainting until you think you've got down any lines that you can use as guides. Put in the position of the facial features, still remembering to maintain the 'box' shape of the head. Then roughly put in the line of the blue background cloth and some of the creases in the fabric.

Tips:

- Keep things very rough and loose at this stage and use very thin paint that can easily be covered over.
- For your underpainting, use cool colour tones to interplay with later warm ones.

3 Roughly scumble in the background cloth on which the model is lying. The exact colour isn't important at this stage, provided that you do not use something that will overpower the later painting; all you are doing now is establishing the basic structure.

4 Mix a dilute wash of yellow ochre for the floorboards. Using a large round brush, apply this colour above the head so that the figure begins to stand out from the background.

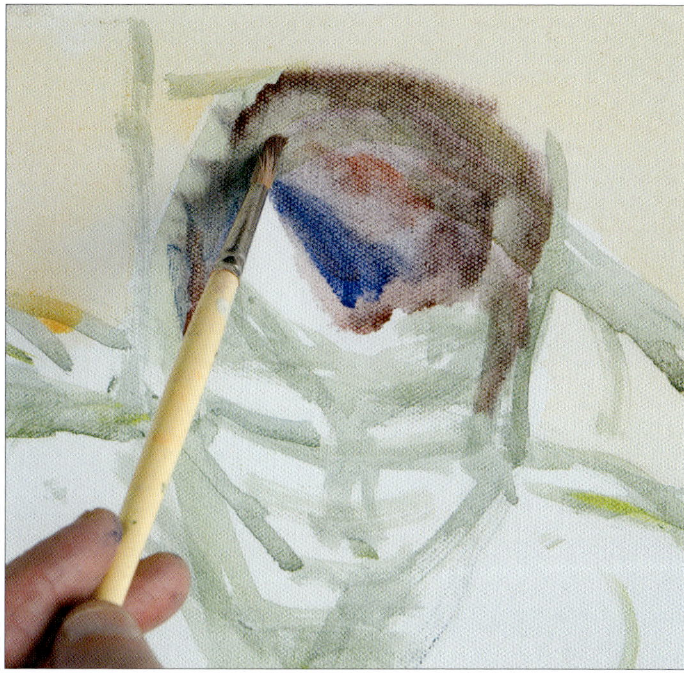

5 Mix a purplish blue from vermilion and ultramarine blue and apply it over the hair. Try not to make the colour too uniform: vary the depth of colour, and also leave some gaps for the highlights. Don't worry about getting all the colours just right at this stage. This is still the underpainting: you will be building up the colour and adjusting the tones gradually as the painting progresses.

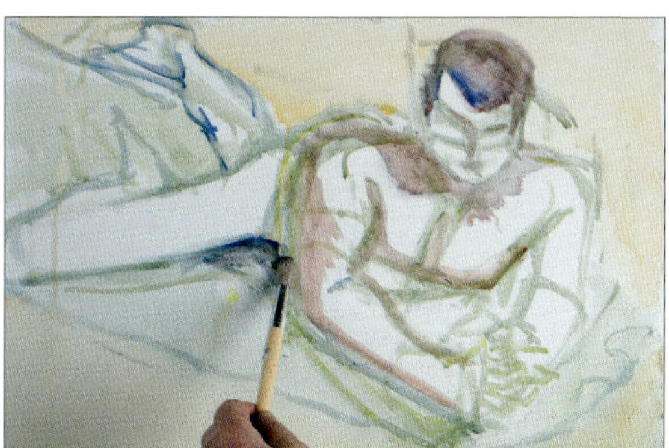

6 Use the same dilute purple mix for the eyebrows and the line of the nose and mouth. Now begin to apply it to the very warmest, reddest parts of the body – the shoulders, the outer edge of the model's right arm, which is largely in shadow, and the chest muscles.

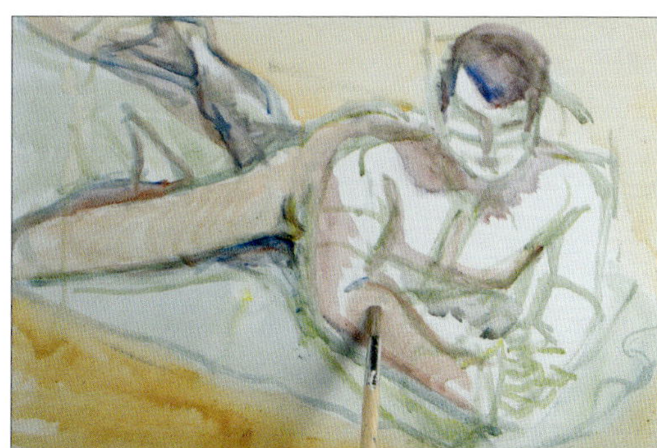

7 Wash a stronger mix of yellow ochre over the foreground floor. Mix a wash of a pinky flesh tone from vermilion, white and a touch of yellow ochre and apply it to the back leg. Dilute the mix and apply it to the foreground leg. Add a little more vermilion to the mix and wash it over the arms, which are more tanned and warmer in tone than the legs, using curving brushstrokes that echo the form of the limbs.

8 Now start to build up the tones on the head, using a bluer mix on the hair than in Step 5 to create some tonal variation in the hair mass. Using the same warm flesh tones as before (mixed from vermilion, white and a touch of yellow ochre), apply more paint across the model's suntanned shoulders and right arm. Note the strong shadow on the neck.

Tip: Keep the brush quite dry. You can scrub the paint on quite vigorously at this stage, as you're simply establishing the underlying skin tones: more precise modelling will be done later on.

9 Add more water to the flesh tone mix so that it is very dilute, and apply it to the face, dropping in more yellow ochre on the right side, which is warmer in tone. Go over the shadow under the breastbone with a thicker, orangey mix to create some modelling on the torso. Use the same colour to separate the right arm from the torso.

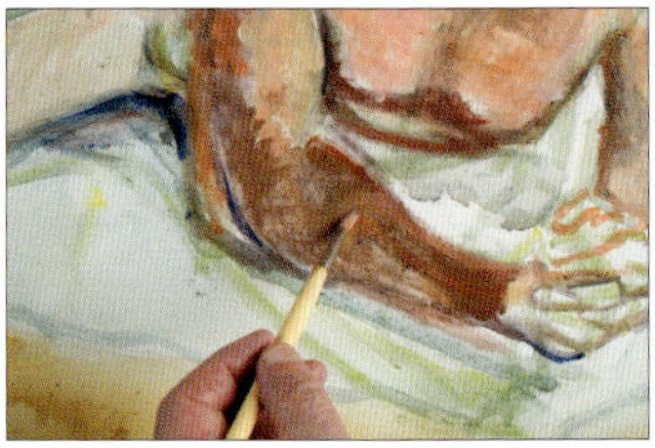

10 Roughly block in the chest with a dilute mix of vermilion, white and a little yellow ochre. Ensure you use varied tones, otherwise the colour will look flat. Scrub a darker mix of yellow ochre and vermilion over the right arm, with curved strokes that follow its form.

11 Darken the skin tones on the legs, using the same mixes as before. Note, however, that the colour is much cooler and bluer here than in the chest area. Add a little more ultramarine blue to the mix to paint the deep shadow under the body.

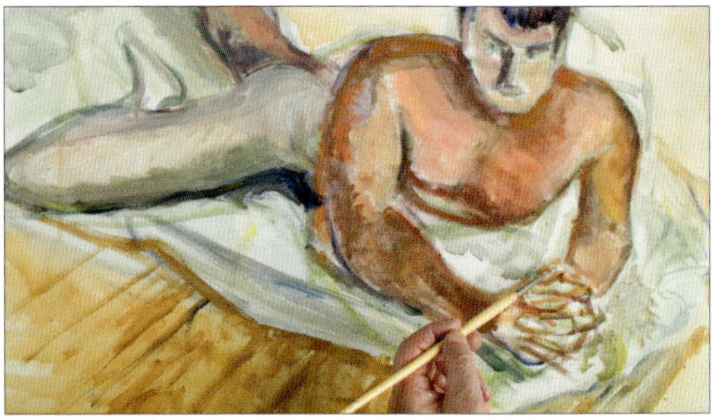

12 Paint the lines of the floorboards using a thick mix of yellow ochre, making sure you get the angle right. Scrub a more dilute, slightly paler mix of yellow ochre over the boards. Add a little more tone to the background fabric. Begin to delineate the different planes of the fingers.

Assessment time

All the underlying skin tones have been established, but the painting still looks a little flat. The final stages of the painting will be about making gradual adjustments, refining details such as the facial features and improving on the modelling in order to make the figure look convincingly three-dimensional.

The highlights and shadows are evident, but the limbs do not look rounded.

The right arm is too dark, and jumps forward in the image.

The facial features have been mapped out but more detailing is needed.

13 Using a small flat brush, deepen the hair colour, using the same mixes as before. Apply more colour to the face, looking carefully at the cheekbones to see which areas require a darker mix. Build up contouring on the arms, again switching between warm and cool, light and dark mixes.

14 On the legs, apply a warm mix of vermilion and white to the upper part of the front leg, which is in the light, and a cooler, yellowy green (ultramarine blue plus yellow ochre) to the underside of the leg, which is in shadow. Use curved brushstrokes to convey the rounded shape of the leg.

15 Touch in warm, dark purple mixes of alizarin crimson and ultramarine blue on to the more shaded areas of the fingers. Tone down any overly dark or red areas of the right forearm with a pinkish mix of vermilion and white.

16 Use various thick mixes of white, lemon yellow and ultramarine blue to suggest the folds in the cloth on which the model is lying. You may find it easier to use your fingers to smooth and blend the paint.

17 Continue refining the details and contouring on the face, using the same colour mixes as before. Remember to look for where the shadows fall and at the contrasts between warm and cool tones.

18 Using the same tones as before, refine the fingers. Take care not to lose sight of the fact that the fingers are rounded forms: use a darker, purplish mix for the shaded planes and a lighter, pinker mix for those that are in the light.

19 You're nearing the final stages. Use a clean brush to blend the wet paint on the canvas and soften the transition from one colour to another. This is important on the background, as harsh lines there might distract attention.

20 Make final adjustments to the skin tones on the body. Here, the artist used mixes of vermilion, white and a little yellow ochre to create a little more modelling on the torso, blending the colours wet into wet with his fingers.

The finished painting

This painting concentrates attention firmly on the model's strongly developed upper body and arms; it's perfectly legitimate to over-emphasize features a little for the sake of making a more dynamic composition, as painting is more about how you perceive your subject than about creating a photo-realistic interpretation that is 'correct' in every detail. The flesh tones are built up gradually through wet-into-wet washes. The wonderful textural quality of acrylic paints is also exploited here, with thick, impasto-like applications of paint on the cloth the model is lying on.

The foreground floorboards are painted in more detail than those in the background, creating an impression of distance.

Thick paint, smoothed out on the canvas with the fingers, creates texture in the cloth on which the model is lying.

Modelling is created through subtle blends of colour and the juxtaposition of warm and cool tones.

Strongly lit figure in oils

In this project, the way that light plays on the figure is as important a part of the composition as the figure itself. The model kneels in a pool of light coming through a window – but the window is covered in a Venetian blind, which casts stripes of light and shade on the body. The body itself casts a shadow on the wall in the background, forming an important – if secondary – part of the composition and filling up what would otherwise be an empty space.

The shadows cast by the blinds also help to define the surface: note how the lines change direction as they hit the different contours of the body. Look, too, for where a shadow stripe changes from warm to cool. Where a shadow is cast on a brightly illuminated part of the body, it is warm; where it is cast on a shaded part of the body, it is cool.

If you have to make your painting over several sessions, remember that the direction of light shifts during the day – so if light streams through your window and illuminates your model in the morning, it will not in the afternoon. The quality of the light may change, too: even if you paint at the same time each day, there may be days when the sky is overcast and the light is flat and dull, which means that shadows will not be so evident. Taking photographs may help you overcome this issue.

Over the sessions, it's inevitable that the model's position will change slightly. So long as the overall balance of warm and cool areas looks right, slight shifts of position really make very little difference to the pose as a whole.

Materials

- *Acrylic-primed linen canvas*
- *Oil paints: cadmium red, cadmium orange, ultramarine blue, burnt umber, yellow ochre, raw umber, alizarin crimson, titanium white, Venetian red, lemon yellow, cadmium yellow deep*
- *Brushes: a selection of filberts in various sizes*

The pose

The slats of the Venetian blinds are partially open so that light slants across the figure. The light also casts the shadow of both the model and the blind on the wall behind. The brightly coloured backcloth picks up the warm skin tones and also provides pattern and texture.

1 Mix a dull orange from cadmium red and cadmium orange. Using a medium filbert brush, map out the figure. Mix a dark grey from burnt umber and ultramarine blue and block in the cast shadow of the body. Add yellow ochre to the mix and scumble on the dark shadow in the top right, above the light coming from the window.

2 Using a more dilute version of the cast shadow mix, tentatively block in the darkest areas of the model's body – the shadows between and under the breasts, under the left arm and on the right knee.

3 Scumble a raw umber and alizarin crimson mix on the backcloth, with more alizarin around the head. Where the cloth is lit, block in with a thickened orange mix from Step 1, then add the shadows cast by the blinds with alizarin crimson.

4 Now begin to put in some of the flesh tones. Mix a pinkish mid-tone from titanium white, yellow ochre and cadmium orange and apply this across everything except the very brightest highlights. For the darker areas, mix Venetian red, yellow ochre and a little burnt umber and apply on top of the earlier mix, blending the paints on the canvas. Put in some guidelines for the facial features – the central line through the head and the line of the eyes.

5 Add cadmium red to the alizarin and burnt umber mix on the background. Roughly block in the initial hair colour in yellow ochre, adding titanium white for the lighter hair colour. Begin to put in the first slats of light on the figure, using a slightly warmer version of the pink tone from Step 4. Brush a mix of ultramarine blue and white into the cast shadow to blend with what's already there, and use the same colour in the shadows on the flesh.

6 Mix a cool yellow from lemon yellow and white and scumble it on to the light area of the background. Next, mix a dark blue-grey from ultramarine blue, burnt umber and a little white and put in the striped shadows on top of the yellow 'light' area.

7 Using thin paint, block in the fabric at the base of the image in cadmium red and the wooden floor in yellow ochre. Using the blue-grey mix from the previous step, reinforce the shadows on the body and indicate the position of the eye socket and navel.

8 Now begin to put in the strips of light on the body, using the lemon yellow and white mix from Step 6.

9 Paint the warm stripes on the right arm using the flesh tone from Step 4. Mix a rich orange from cadmium yellow deep and cadmium red. Using this, and alizarin crimson where appropriate, put in some patterns on the background fabric.

10 Build up the texture and colours in the hair, alternating between the warm lemon yellow and white mix and a cool mix of white and ultramarine blue. Begin to create some modelling on the head, using the blue-grey mix for the dark parts of the face, such as the line under the cheekbone and the eyes, and white tinted with a hint of pink for the very brightest areas.

11 Continue building up the striped shadows on the figure, using a combination of warm and cool mixes depending on where the shadows fall. Look carefully at the stripes to see how they change direction as they hit different contours of the body.

Assessment time

Once you've completed the cast shadows on the body, only minor adjustments will be needed. This is the time to make a final assessment of the shapes and proportions of the limbs. As you're painting in oils, which remain soft and workable for a long time, it is relatively easy to paint over any parts of the body that are too dominant, such as the left knee. Check the edges of the body in particular: here, the model's right foot almost disappears into the background fabric and needs to be redefined. Look, too, at the position and intensity of the cast shadows: are they all in place? Are they the right tone in relation to the rest of the painting? Finally, check the background: if it's dominating or fighting with the figure in any way, then you need to redress the balance. Here, for example, the lemon yellow on the wall is much too harsh and acidic a colour.

The cast shadows are missing from the left arm, and those on the left leg need to be strengthened.

The lemon yellow in the background is too harsh and needs to be toned down a little to balance with the colours in the rest of the painting.

The shape of the right foot is indistinct.

The stomach area is a little too light in tone and needs more modelling.

12 Apply a pale, cool blue-grey to the base of the right foot, which is just catching the edge of the light. Redefine the shape of the hands and make the right foot separated from the body with a shadow mix of alizarin crimson and ultramarine blue. Using the same mixes as before, finish painting the striped shadows cast on the body by the blinds and adjust the warm and cool tones on the body where necessary. It is the transition from warm to cool tones, as the body turns away from the light, that will make the figure look rounded and three-dimensional.

Tips:

• The stripes are quite thin, so use a fine filbert brush.

• Try to paint both the stripes and the spaces in between them with bold, confident strokes following the direction of the shadows – although, as the oil paint remains soft and workable for some time, it's easy to make corrections if you suddenly find your lines become a little wobbly or are running in slightly the wrong direction.

• The mixes of paint used for the shadows help to define the shape of the hands, legs and feet, as well as giving some modelling.

13 Use the ultramarine and alizarin mix to define the shape of the navel and the spaces between the fingers, and to strengthen the shadow area between the right arm and torso.

14 Darken the shadow cast on the wall by the model's body by scumbling on the ultramarine blue and burnt umber mix from Step 1. Knock back the very bright yellow of the shadow cast by the blinds with a mix of white tinted with a tiny amount of the pink/ochre flesh tone.

The finished painting
Through his skilful assessment of warm and cool tones, the artist has created a convincingly three-dimensional image and captured the intriguing play of light and shade on the figure. Oils are a wonderful medium for subtle transitions of tone and colour temperature, as the paint remains malleable for a long time and you can blend colours wet into wet on the canvas. The dramatic shadows are an integral part of the composition, and this colourful backcloth sets the figure off beautifully.

There is just enough detail in the backcloth to provide interest without detracting from the figure.

Note how the cast shadow colours change from warm to cool as the body turns away from the light.

The relatively warm yellow tints the cooler white applied on top of it, so the overall effect is still one of warmth.

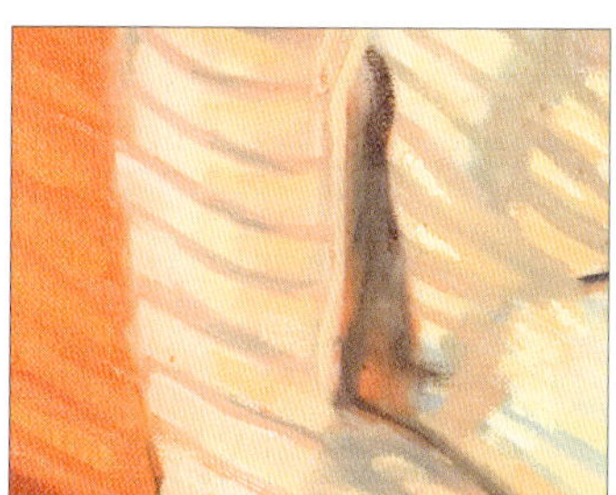

Foreshortened figure in soft pastel

We all have a preconceived idea of what the proportions of the human body are, but when you draw a foreshortened figure it becomes more important than ever to abandon these notions and make careful measurements. You must learn to trust your actual measurements and observations rather than rely on what you think you know.

To make precise measurements, it is absolutely vital that you remain in exactly the same place. If you move around, your viewpoint in relation to the model will change – and this will affect any measurements that you take. Do not start by trying to draw the whole outline; instead, put down light 'markers' to establish the extremities of the body – the top and bottom of the head, the outer points of the shoulders, the tip of the hand, the tilt of the knee and so on. It may not be obvious to others what these marks relate to, but if they mean something to you, that's fine.

Keep the setting and any props relatively simple. You have enough to contend with without having to worry about drawing complex surroundings. And remember that you can define your subject by what's around it, as well as by outline. If you are finding it too difficult to discern the exact shape of a particular part of the figure, shift your attention to the surroundings instead and draw the point at which they butt up against the figure.

Preliminary sketch

As a foreshortened pose is quite complex to draw, start by making a few quick sketches – no more than a couple of minutes each – to work out a composition that appeals to you.

Materials

- *Buff-coloured pastel paper*
- *Soft pastels: various shades of Naples yellow, burnt sienna, raw umber, white, pink, pale blue, pale green, grey*

The pose

In this pose, the model's feet are nearer the artist than her head, which means that her body is foreshortened; for example, compare the apparent length of the right arm with that of the right hip. The bed forms a diagonal line through the picture space, which makes a more interesting composition than simply looking straight down the full length of the bed. The throws and blankets have been kept deliberately simple in colour, so as not to distract from the model, but they add an interesting contrast in texture.

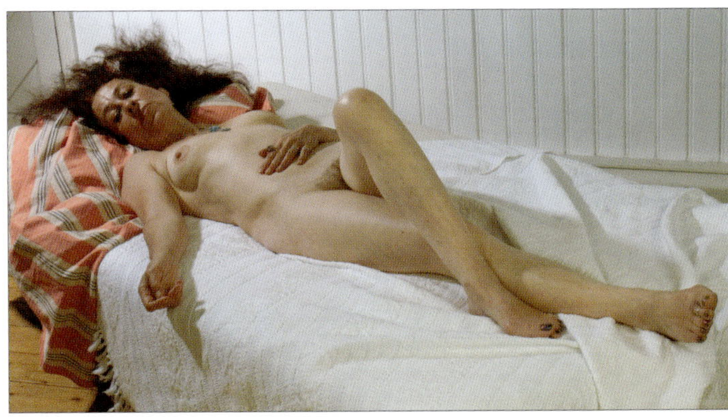

1 Begin by mapping out the composition, taking measurements and making sure that you can fit the whole figure on the paper. Look for strong lines within the pose that you can use as 'landmarks' – the line across the shoulders, for example, and the diagonal line of the crossed knee. Select colours that approximate to those in the finished drawing (pink where the head and arm come into contact with the striped throw, yellow for the other limbs and the outline of the body on the white throw), so that you can use them to keep track of where you are in the drawing.

2 Put in stronger marks to define bones beneath the skin such as the pelvic bones and the rib cage. Use warm and cool colours to differentiate the planes of the body. Here a cold grey has been used to block in the shape of the rib cage, with warmer yellows on the stomach and chest areas. The rib cage projects out to a greater depth than the head. Even if you can't see the outline clearly, remember its shape: rather like an upside-down basket, with the ribs curving down on either side of the central spine.

3 The upper right arm is very foreshortened: from this viewpoint, it appears roughly the same length as the line that runs down from the model's armpit to the body. Define the outer edge of the arm by using the colours of the striped throw around it. Within the arm, put in the main light and dark tones. Use a medium tone of burnt sienna for the dark areas on the outer and inner edges and Naples yellow for the lighter, more brightly lit areas, then smooth out the pastel marks using the tips of your fingers.

4 Move on to the central torso and look for the ridge of the pelvic bone, which is very pronounced. Note how the lines are angled here to indicate the different planes of the body. Roughly scribble in the hair in black pastel, using the overall shape to define the facial area. Establish the position of the facial features, and use a mix of warm and cool tones so that you begin to create a hint of modelling on the face.

Tip: Note the tilt of the head. When you draw this, it's important that you do not tilt your own head – otherwise the angle and tilt will be incorrect. Observe everything with your head in exactly the same position.

5 Look for any cast shadows that you can use to help build up the modelling on the figure. Here, for example, the right breast casts a strong shadow on the thorax. Put in some of the stripes in the throw behind the model's head, noting carefully where the stripes change direction.

6 Begin to refine the shape of the model's right hand. Think of it as a geometric block rather than a series of individual fingers, and look for the warm and cool tones. The palm, for example, is cooler (yet darker) in tone than the fingers; it is drawn in a slightly bluer, more purple tone than the fingers. Put in the very bright highlight area of the lower arm in white pastel, making your hatching lines run across the forearm to imply its rounded form.

7 Roughly block in the white throw to establish the flat planes of the bed. Again, look for any cast shadows that may be helpful in the composition: here, the right arm casts a distinct shadow on the bed, so block it in with a pale, cool blue and blend the marks with your fingers to create a smooth area of tone.

8 Parts of the torso are very strongly lit. Use cool yellows and white to put in these highlit areas. There is a bright highlight line running along the model's right thigh. Put this in lightly in white and use it as a guide to the different planes of the leg. Much of the left leg, in contrast, is very dark, yet warm in tone: start by putting in the line of the shin in raw umber, then hatching over it.

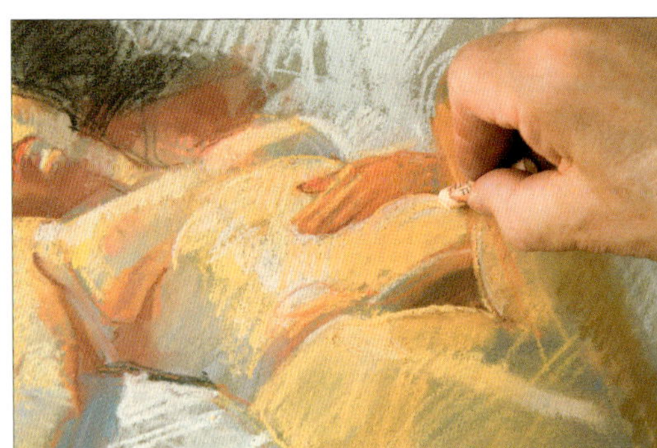

9 Note how the left hand rests on and presses into the stomach: you can use the shape of the hand to imply the curve of the stomach. Think of the left hand as an overall shape, rather than drawing each finger individually. The fingers catch the light, while the back of the hand is in shadow. Pick out the individual highlights that catch the edge of each finger in a warm Naples yellow, and the remaining parts of the hand in warm shades of burnt sienna. The colours you use around the hand will also help to define it.

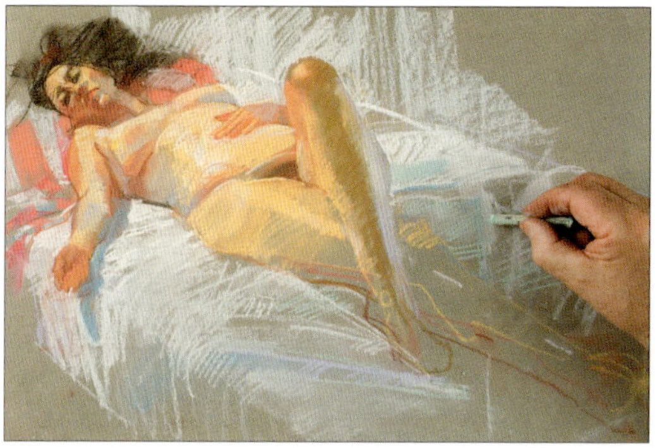

10 One side of the left leg catches the light and is warm in tone, while the other side is in shadow and is cool. Use a warm Naples yellow and a cool very pale blue to convey this. Note that a little of the left thigh is also visible from this angle; draw this in too. Now move back to the background: put in any stripes on the pink throw that are not obscured by the hair, and block in more of the white throw using the side of the pastel. Put in any folds and shadows on the white throw using a cool, pale blue or green.

11 Note that the right leg is not foreshortened, as it goes across the artist's line of vision. The left leg casts a dark shadow on the side of the right knee; block this in using the side of a raw umber pastel. Use the highlight line along the centre of the model's right shinbone to help you define the form of the leg. Below it, use warm pinks, with burnt sienna on the foot. Above it, use cooler yellows. Define the feet, using Naples yellow, raw umber and burnt sienna, and put in the toe nails, noting how much of each nail is actually visible.

Assessment time

Here, the artist has toned down the very warm tones on the right leg by applying cool blue-greys on top of the initial warm tones. The colours mix optically on the paper, creating a lively sense of shimmering light. More minor adjustments are still required. Although the white throw should not dominate the drawing, here it is a little insubstantial: quite a lot of the original paper colour shows through. Some of the skin tones need to be adjusted in order for the different planes of the body to stand out more clearly. The only major problem here is the right arm, which is too foreshortened. It's a good idea to fix the drawing at this stage, so that you can incorporate stronger lines if necessary – but do remember to wait until the fixative has dried before going ahead and making any final changes.

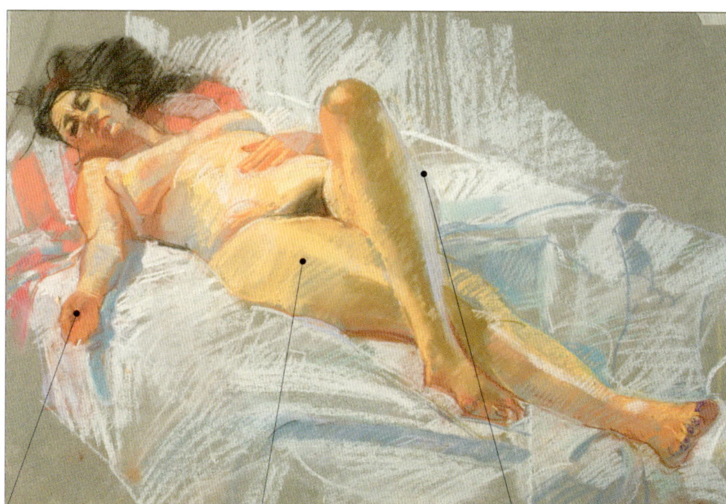

The right arm looks a little too foreshortened. The tips of the fingers should actually be more or less level with the left heel.

This area is too warm and uniform in tone. The colour looks rather matt. The torso, in contrast, is too cool in tone, and the colour between the hip and belly needs blending.

There is not a clear enough distinction between the lower leg and upper thigh.

12 With soft pastels, it is relatively easy to make changes, even in the later stages of a drawing. Here, the artist has redrawn the right arm, making it a little longer. This is the point at which you can also make a final check on the skin tones: because of the direction and angle of light, the right arm is relatively dark, so use warm siennas to strengthen the shaded underside of the arm and tone down the very bright highlights by applying yellow over the existing white.

13 The left hand has been drawn in greater detail than the rest: all you want to do is create the feeling of it resting on the surface of the model's stomach. By toning down the very bright yellow highlights on the fingers and evening out the tones, you can draw attention away from the fingers. The reflected light on the back of the hand is cooler than that on the group of fingers, so use a slightly bluer tone here to differentiate the planes of the hand.

14 The right hip receives a lot of direct light, so tone down the yellow by applying more white on top and blending the marks with your fingertips. This also has the effect of differentiating the different planes of the torso more clearly. To use a landscape analogy, if you think of the side of the torso and the flank as being a near vertical 'cliff', then the stomach is a more or less a horizontal 'plateau' above them.

15 Using the side of the pastel, roughly block in the white wood panelling in the background. It's up to you how much detail you include in the surroundings, but make sure they do not dominate the portrait.

16 Adjust the skin tones, adding final highlights to the feet and calves and re-defining the shape of the ankles. Do this by bringing the pale surroundings right up to the ankle, not by darkening the line of the ankles.

Tip: It's important to keep moving around the picture, between the figure and the background, in order to keep everything moving along at the same rate. This allows you to continually reassess one part of the drawing against another and adjust as necessary.

The finished drawing

Soft pastel allows you to make both strong, linear marks using the tip of the pastel and broad sweeps of colour using the side; you can also blend the marks with your fingers to create wonderfully soft, smooth textures, while still allowing several colours to mix optically on the paper. Here, the artist has exploited the potential of the medium to the full to create a lively drawing that shimmers with light. The foreshortening of the body and the contrasts between areas of light and shade have been meticulously observed.There is just enough background to enhance, not detract from, the figure.

The warm colour of the striped throw under the model's head frames and draws attention to her face. It also reflects some colour into the skin tones.

There is enough linear detail in the white throw to hint at the pattern and the cool blue shadows reveal that the fabric is slightly ruffled.

Note how the strong highlights and shadows along the shinbones help to define the different planes of the legs.

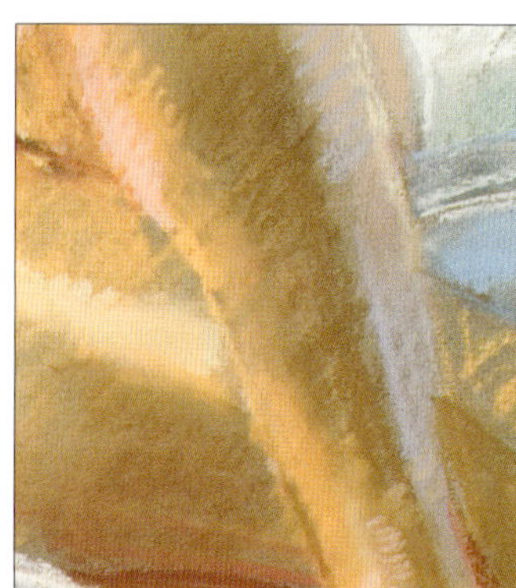

Portraits

Although portraiture is sometimes perceived as being one of the most difficult subjects for artists, the truth is that, provided you train yourself to look and measure carefully, it's no more difficult than anything else; it's all based on keen observation.

This chapter begins with a gallery of portraits by professional artists, which gives you the opportunity to see how artists working in a number of different media have tackled a range of portrait topics and challenges. This is followed by a series of quick sketches – a great way of grabbing a few minutes' drawing practice when you are short of time.

A good portrait is about much more than simply capturing a likeness. You have to try to get to the heart of your subject and convey something of their character. The chapter ends with 13 detailed step-by-step portraits of people of all ages, from a tiny baby just a few days old to elderly subjects with a lifetime's experience. There are indoor and outdoor portraits; there are smiling faces and more contemplative expressions; there are formally posed portraits and those painted from hastily taken snapshots, in which the 'sitter' is unaware of the artist's presence – in short, something for everyone. Study these projects to find out how to tackle various challenges, or simply to see how another artist (whose style may be very different to your own) works.

Gallery

From self portraits and studies of individuals to groups of two or more people in more complicated settings, this section features portraits in varying styles and media. Study them carefully for ideas and approaches that you can apply in your own work – and don't be tempted to dismiss something simply because it doesn't suit your own personal taste. You can learn as much from things you dislike as from things you enjoy.

Painting in monochrome ▶
In this unusual oil painting, *Self Portrait at 32 Years*, Gerald Cains has ruled out colour altogether, while using highly expressive brushwork. The effect is extraordinarily powerful. It can be a useful discipline to work in monochrome, as it helps you to concentrate on composition and tonal balance without the distraction of colour.

Plain background ▼
Ian Sidaway's initial work on *Lydia and Alice* was made using wet-into-wet washes and the features were then sharpened using wet on dry. Gum arabic was used in many of the mixes. This has the effect not only of intensifying the colour but also of making the washes more transparent. Gum arabic also makes dry paint soluble if it is re-wet, so you can wash off dry paint and make any necessary corrections – a very useful facility when painting portraits. The background is deliberately omitted to focus attention on the sitters.

Limited palette ▲

Working over a careful pencil drawing using wet-on-dry washes in *Sisters*, Ian Sidaway achieved harmony by using a limited range of colours. Interestingly, the two girls were painted at different times. The poses were carefully chosen so that the figures could be combined on the support. If you are doing a portrait from a photograph,the background elements can be altered or added to as you work. Alternatively, if you are painting someone in their environment, work on the background and setting at the same time as the figure to avoid the portrait looking as if it has simply been pasted in.

Form through colour ►

As a general rule, the colours in shadows are cooler – that is, bluer or greener – than those in the highlight areas, and Gerry Baptist has skilfully exploited this warm/cool contrast to give solidity to the head in his acrylic *Self Portrait*. Note, too, how the different planes within the head are painted using simple blocks of colour rather than subtle transitions from one tone to the next – an approach that requires bold, confident brushwork. Although all the colours are quite heightened, they are nevertheless based on the actual colours of flesh, and the picture is successful in its own terms.

►

Startling realism ►
This self portrait by Paul Bartlett demonstrates the versatility of the pencil to perfection. Here the effect is almost photographic in its minute attention to detail and texture and its subtle gradations of tone.

Outdoor setting ◄
Light is an important element in Timothy Easton's *The Summer Read* and he has described the sitter more by posture, clothing and general shape than by detailed depiction of the features. With careful observation you will find that it is perfectly possible to paint a recognizable likeness without showing the face at all, just as you often recognize a familar person from a distance by their posture. The square format might seem a slightly unusual choice for a portrait, but here the setting is as important as the sitter, who occupies only a relatively small proportion of the picture space. The table and chair virtually fill the entire width of the picture space, with the flower border providing both background colour and detail and a visual 'full stop'. The viewer's eye is led around the image in a circular movement from the sitter's head, around the table and back again.

Expressive use of watercolour ▶

At first sight, Ken Paine's expressive portrait *Amelia* might well be mistaken for an oil painting, but in fact it is watercolour with the addition of Chinese white. The artist made no initial pencil drawing, but started immediately with a brush and thin paint, gradually increasing the amount of white. The background is reduced to a minimum, very loosely painted, thus concentrating attention on the face.

Figure groups ▼

In landscape painting, a distant figure or group of figures is often introduced as a colour accent or an additional focus for the eye, but where figures form the whole subject, as in Sally Strand's charming *Crab Catch*, it is necessary to find ways of relating them to one another. Like many such compositions, this has an element of storytelling, with the boys sharing a common interest, but the artist has also used clever pictorial devices, notably the shapes and colours of the towel and bucket, to create a strong link between the two figures. The boys' absorbed expressions, and the fact that they are facing one another, also help to direct our attention to the centre of the scene – the contents of the bucket.

▶

Portrait of a group ▲

Figure groups are not the easiest of subjects to tackle in watercolour, as it is not possible to make extensive corrections, but Trevor Chamberlain's *Still-life Session at the Seed Warehouse* shows that in skilled hands there is nothing the medium cannot do. Each brushstroke has been placed with care and, although the artist has worked largely wet into wet, he has controlled the paint so that it has not spread randomly over the surface. The result it a fresh, lively painting with a wonderfully spontaneous feel. If you're attempting a subject like this, spend as much time as you can observing the scene before you commit brush to paper. Even though it may seem at first glance as though your subjects are continually moving, you'll find that when people are engrossed in an activity like this, they tend to revert to the same positions and postures; once you've recognized the essentials of each individual's 'pose', you'll find it much easier to set them down on paper.

Quick, expressive portrait in ink ►

Pen and ink can achieve intricate and elaborate effects, but it is also a lovely medium for rapid line drawings. In this figure study *Girl in an Armchair*, Ted Gould has caught the essentials of the pose in a few pen strokes, sometimes superimposing lines where the first drawing was incorrect or where it needed clarifying.

Composing a figure study ►
In a figure painting you must decide where to place the figure, whether or not to crop part of it, and whether you need to introduce other elements as a balance. Peter Clossick's *Helen Seated* gives the impression of spontaneity because it is so boldly and thickly painted, but it is carefully composed, with the diagonal thrust of the figure balanced by verticals and opposing diagonals in the background.

Painting children ▲
Painting an adult engaged in some typical pursuit can enhance your interpretation, but in the case of children it is a question of necessity; they seldom remain still for long, added to which they look stiff and self-conscious when artificially posed. In her delightful, light-suffused study of *Samantha and Alexis* (oil) Karen Raney has worked rapidly to capture a moment of communication between her two young subjects.

Form and brushwork ►
As the human face and head are complex and difficult to paint, even before you have considered how to achieve a likeness of the sitter, there is a tendency to draw lines with a small brush. This is seldom satisfactory, however, as hard lines can destroy the form. In Ted Gould's *Sue* (oil), the features, although perfectly convincing, are described with the minimum of detail and no use of line, and the face, hair and clothing are built up with broad directional brushwork.

►

Using the paper colour ▶
In portraiture and figure work it is particularly important to choose the right colour of paper, especially if you intend to leave areas of it uncovered, as in Ken Paine's superb *Young Girl*. The painting is almost monochromatic, with the lights and darks built up from the mid-tone of the brown paper.

Freestyle in pen ▲
A fine fibre-tipped pen has been used for this self-portrait by Hazel Harrison, and the forms have been constructed in a spontaneous way, with the pen moving freely over the paper.

Symmetry ◀
One of the so-called 'rules' of composition is to avoid symmetry, but rules are made to be broken and Elizabeth Moore has deliberately flouted them in this unnamed portrait, to produce an oil painting that almost has the quality of an icon. The central placing of the head on the canvas and the outward gaze impart a sense of strength and dignity to the image.

Building tonal structure ▶
Ken Paine exploits the directness and expressive qualities of pastel in his *Head of a Young Woman*. He works with great rapidity, usually beginning by building up the tonal structure with a monochrome "underpainting" made with broad strokes of short lengths of pastel. Linear definition and bright colour accents are left until the final stages. The coloured paper is still visible in areas.

Quick sketches

The only way to get better at drawing and painting is to practise, so try to get into the habit of sketching every day. All you need is a small notebook and a pen or pencil. Carry them around with you wherever you go and do a bit of 'people watching' when you've got a few minutes to spare – on the train or bus to work, in a café during your lunch break, even when you're waiting to collect the kids from school.

Before you embark on really detailed portraits, start by practising getting the features in the right places. Draw heads from different angles so that you get used to how the relative positions of the features change when the head is tilted.

Sketch profiles as well as faces viewed from directly in front and look at where the nose breaks the line of the cheek and at how much of the eye on the far side of the face is visible. Look for different planes within the head and face. Ask friends or family members to pose for you so that you get used to drawing lots of different people. You'll be amazed at how quickly your powers of observation improve.

In the sketches shown on these two pages, the construction lines have been exaggerated so that they show up more clearly. In your own sketches, use very light lines and marks. You can cover or erase these as your artwork develops.

Soft pastel, 15 minutes ►
The central axis of the face runs down through the nose, but because the sitter's head is turned slightly to one side, we can see more on one side of this line than on the other. The features are contained within an inverted triangle that runs from the outer corners of the eyes to the centre of the lips (the philtrum), while the centre of the eye is in line with the outer corner of the mouth.

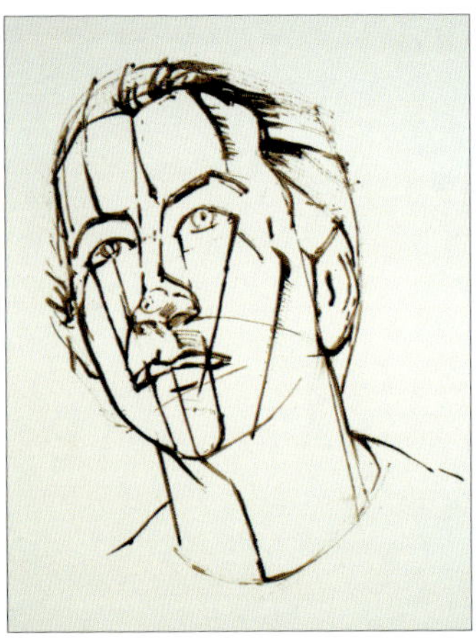

Dip pen and ink,15 minutes ▲
As ink is indelible and virtually impossible to cover up if you make a mistake, the artist began by putting in tiny dots to mark the outer corners of the eyes and mouth and the nostrils. Note how large the area between the nose and chin appears in relation to the head as a whole when the head is tilted upwards like this.

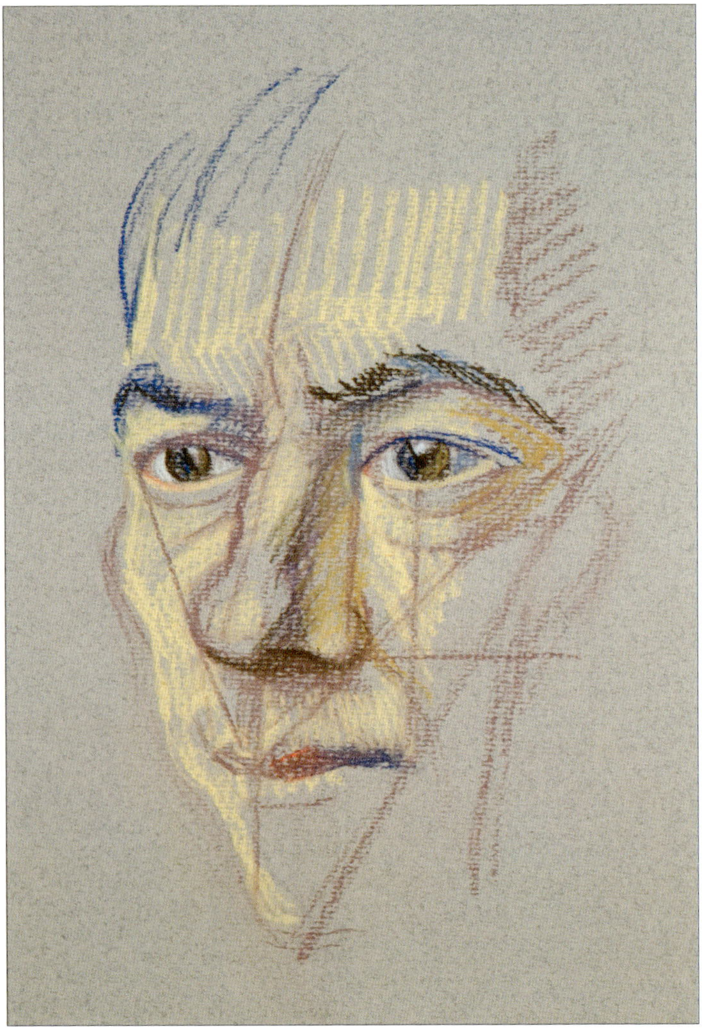

Charcoal, 10 minutes ▲
In this sketch the artist began by wiping the side of a stick of charcoal over the paper to create a broad area of tone, which he then softened by gently wiping with a paper tissue. On top of the basic 'egg' shape of the head, he has indicated the major planes of the face and cranium, as well as the hairline. Although this is intended as nothing more than an exercise in observation, making sketches like this is a good way of training yourself to look for the different planes of the head. Gradually, you'll find that you can use tone, rather than line, to express the transition from one plane to the next.

Acrylic, 15 minutes ▲
Here the artist roughly blocked in the shape of the face in yellow ochre paint to approximate to the skin tones, before adding the construction lines in a darker tone. Note how he established the underlying shape of the cranium before roughly scumbling on colour for the hair. He has also roughly marked in the major planes of the forehead and the side of the face, and applied a slightly darker tóne to the shaded side of the sitter's face to create some sense of modelling.

▶

Make quick sketches – say 15 to 30 minutes – to train your eye to see subtle differences in tone in people's faces as the different planes turn towards or away from the light source. Look to see where the deepest shadows and the brightest highlights fall, and then try to assess the mid tones in between. Remember that there are many minor planes within the face and head, as well as major planes such as the sides of the nose. These minor planes – high or recessed cheekbones, furrows in the brow – are often what help you to capture the individuality of your sitter.

The way that you convey tone depends, of course, on the medium in which you're working. In pencil or pen and ink, you can use hatching or cross-hatching, making your hatching lines close together for dark tones and spacing them further apart for lighter tones. In charcoal and soft pastel you can create a broad area of tone by using the side of the stick, pressing hard for a very dark tone and applying less pressure for lighter areas – and of course in both these media you can wipe off pigment with a soft tissue or torchon to create lighter tones.

In watercolour, you can build up tones gradually, applying several layers of paint until you get the effect you want. In oils and acrylics, depending on the texture you want to create, you can either scumble the paint on quite roughly or apply it as a thin wash.

Remember that the colour of the support can play an important role, too. When working in soft pastels, artists often choose a coloured paper, while in oil and acrylic portraits it is accepted practice to tone the ground before you begin to paint. Select a colour that approximates to the mid tones in your subject, so that you can allow the colour of the ground to show through in the portrait. In watercolour sketches and drawings, you can allow the white of the paper to stand for the very brightest highlights. Letting the paper work for you in this way both speeds up the process and gives a feeling of spontaneity and light to your work.

Conté stick, 20 minutes ◄
Here, the sitter was lit very strongly from one side. On this side of the face, a few faint mid-tone lines convey the creases in the skin around the mouth and nose. On the shaded side of the face the artist created mid and dark tones in two ways: he hatched in small, precise areas such as the nose using the tip and the sharp edge of the square Conté stick and blocked in broad areas on the side of the face and neck with the side of the stick.

Acrylics, 15 minutes ◄
Using just two or three colours, the artist has created a wide range of tones. The white paper stands for the brightest highlights, while the lighter mid tones of the skin are a wash of yellow ochre. The mid and dark tones are varying dilutions of burnt umber, applied as a thin wash in some places and scumbled on more thickly and vigorously in the deep shadows on the side of the face and neck. Applying the paint with a flat brush has created a wide range of marks, from fine lines made by holding the brush almost vertically and using the tip, to broad areas of wash, as on the forehead.

Pastel pencil, 10–15minutes ▲
In this sketch the buff-coloured pastel paper stands for the mid tones, with white pencil hatching being used for the highlights on the side of the face and neck and purple hatching for the shadows. Note how the density of the hatching varies depending on the depth of tone required, with lines drawn close together in the darkest areas (on the far side of the face and under the nose, for example) and spaced more widely in the hair.

The eyes, step by step

Before you embark on full-scale portraits, why not try making some small, quick sketches of individual features such as the eyes or mouth? Homing in on details like this is a great way of sharpening your powers of observation as it forces you to look really hard at shapes and tones. There are lots of undulations across the surface of the face that reveal the shape of the skull beneath and, whatever medium you work in, it's vital that you vary your flesh tones in order to convey these changes in surface form.

Structures such as the eyes and ears are particularly intricate and contain lots of tiny highlight and shadow areas that you need to render with great care. In addition to light and dark tones, remember to use both warm and cool mixes. Warm colours appear to advance, while cool ones recede – and you can exploit this fact to make prominent features such as the nose come forward in the painting.

This demonstration was made in watercolour, which, because of its natural translucency, is a lovely medium for painting the reflective, liquid surface of the eye. Take care not to lose the white of the paper, as this is the lightest tone. The painting took about 45 minutes to complete.

Materials

- *Rough watercolour paper*
- *Watercolour paints: yellow ochre, alizarin crimson, ultramarine blue, burnt umber, cadmium red, cerulean blue*
- *Brushes: Fine round, large flat*
- *Kitchen paper*

The pose

A three-quarter profile was chosen for this sketch, as both eyes are visible and it gives you the chance to explore the way the eyes relate to the nose. Note how, from this angle, the bridge of the nose partially obscures the far eye.

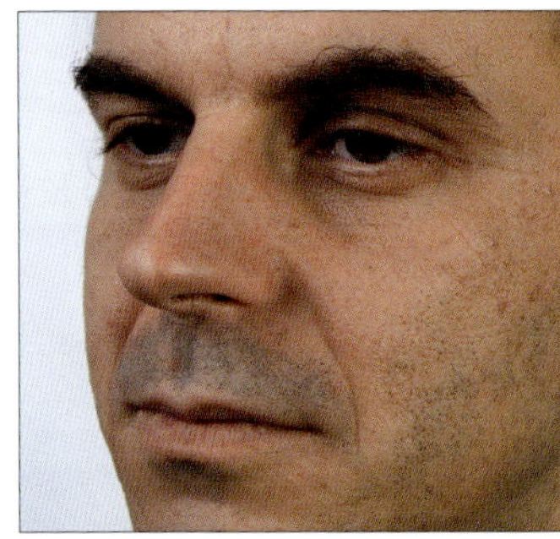

1 Lightly brush the area of paper that you are going to use with clean water so that you can work wet into wet, without creating any hard-edged marks in the early stages. Establish the axis of the eyes and, using a fine brush, dot in the outer corners of the eyes to mark their position. Using a pale mix of yellow ochre and alizarin crimson, outline the almond shape of the eyes, the eyebrows and the line of the nose.

2 Using a grey mix of yellow ochre and ultramarine and short, spiky brush marks, paint in the eyebrows. Using a stronger version of the yellow ochre and alizarin mix, strengthen the line of the upper lids. Add a little ultramarine to the mix and, working wet into wet, put in the deep, recessed shadow around the inner corner of the near eye. Paint the irises using both burnt umber and ultramarine blue as appropriate, remembering to leave the white of the paper for the highlights.

3 Using a very dilute mix of cadmium red, paint the lower lids, leaving the edges white where they catch the light. Paint the dark shadows under and around the inner edge of the near eye in the yellow ochre and alizarin crimson mix. Mix a warm orangey red from yellow ochre and cadmium red and apply it over the upper edge of the upper lids. Use the same colour for the line of the nose.

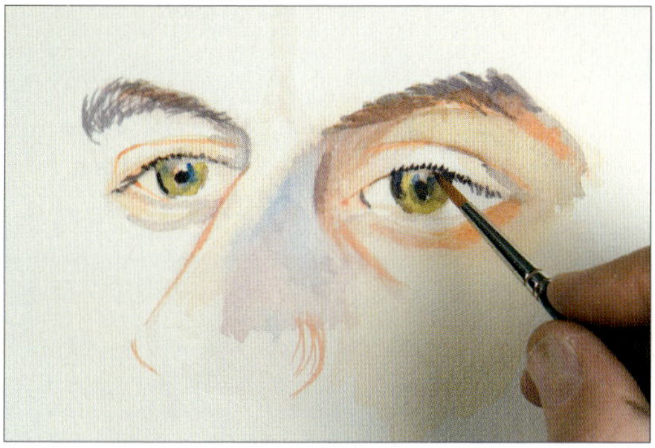

4 Brush the pale cadmium red and yellow ochre mix over the rounded socket of the near eye. Brush clean water over the cheek under the near eye, then drop the pale cadmium red and yellow ochre mix into it, wet into wet. Darken the yellow ochre and alizarin mix by adding ultramarine blue, then paint the line of the eyelashes, using short, spiky brush marks and dots. Use the same colour in the eyebrows.

5 For the shadow in the white of the eye, use a very pale cerulean blue. Dab it off almost immediately with kitchen paper so that there's only a tiny hint of colour. Apply a warm mix of yellow ochre and a little cadmium red to the far cheek, using a slightly darker version of the mix just under the eye. Using the yellow ochre, alizarin crimson and ultramarine mix from Step 2, model the shaded side of the nose, leaving the bridge of the nose (which is in the light) untouched.

6 Put in the nostrils with a deep cadmium red. Using a large flat brush, wash the yellow ochre and cadmium red mix over the near cheek and the warm areas on the side of the nose, modulating the blue mix applied in Step 5 and remembering to leave the highlights white.

The finished sketch

This sketch clearly shows the eyeballs as spherical forms in deep, recessed sockets. Note how much larger the sitter's left eye is than his right; although we tend to assume that both eyes are the same size and shape, they are often asymmetrical. Allowing the white of the paper to stand for the brightest highlights gives this little study real life and sparkle.

The ear, step by step

Just like any other human feature, ears can vary considerably from one person to another. Some people have long earlobes, while others have short ones. Some people have ears that stick out while others have ears that lie flat, close to the skull. The basic structure is the same in everyone, however – an outer and an inner fold, known respectively as the helix and antihelix, which lead around in a curve to the central cavity, or concha. Once you're aware of this structure, you're aware of what to look for. As always, it's the contrast between light and dark tones, and warm and cool colours, that gives a sense of form to drawings and paintings of the ear. Look to see where light catches the bony cartilage of the helix and antihelix and at where darker tones indicate the recessed concha, or central cavity.

This demonstration was done in acrylic paint, which looks slightly darker when it is dry than when it is wet – so always wait until the paint is dry before deciding if you need to adjust the tones. Because acrylic paint is opaque, you can put down dark tones first and then paint highlights on top if you wish, in the same way that you can apply oil paints or oil pastels. If you were to attempt the same sketch in watercolour, you would have to work from light to dark instead. This sketch took about 45 minutes to complete.

Materials

- *Paper*
- *Acrylic paints: yellow ochre, white, brown oxide, alizarin crimson, cadmium red, vermilion, lemon yellow*
- *Brushes: medium filbert, fine filbert*
- *Stay-wet acrylic palette*

The pose

In this profile view you can clearly see the structure of the ear – the outer fold, or helix, which runs around the outer edge and into the central cavity known as the concha, the antihelix (the inner fold) and the fossa (the 'ditch' or groove between the helix and antihelix).

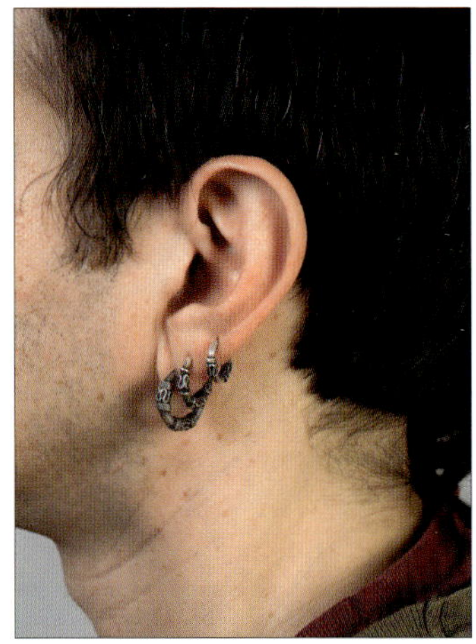

1 Mix yellow ochre and white to form a basic flesh tone and, using a medium filbert brush, scumble it on to the support. Using a fine filbert brush and brown oxide acrylic paint, map in the dark tones on the inside of the ear, looking at the shapes of the shadows in the recesses of the ear.

2 Using a cool purple mix of white, brown oxide and alizarin crimson, put in the curves of the helix and antihelix. Use brown oxide to establish the curve of the outer ear.

3 Add a little ultramarine to the brown oxide and, using vigorous vertical brushstrokes, begin putting in the hair around the ear. Using the same mix, fill in the cool shadows inside the ear; already you are beginning to develop a good sense of the three-dimensional structure.

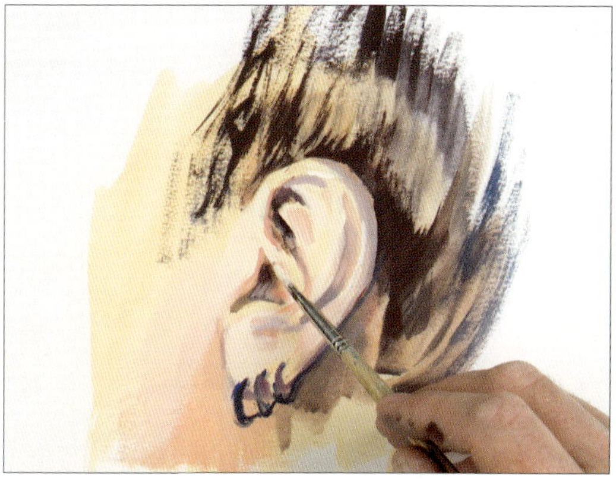

4 Build up texture in the hair, using brown oxide for the darkest parts and the ultramarine and brown oxide mix for the cooler shadows. 'Draw' the earrings in ultramarine blue. Using varying mixes of brown oxide, alizarin crimson and yellow ochre, put in the flesh tones and adjust the tones inside the ear, adding more alizarin for the area under the ear.

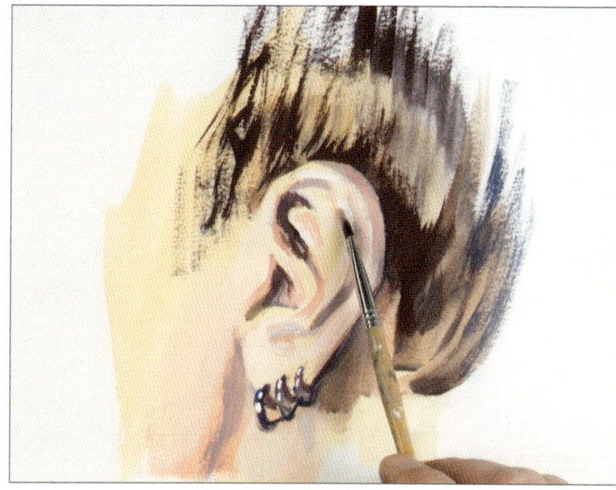

5 Using the same cool purple mix that you used inside the ear, put in the shadow around the jawline. Use pure white to paint the tiny highlights on the earrings and on the inside of the ear.

6 Soften any shadow areas that are too deep, and scumble more colour into the hair, making sure that your brushstrokes follow the direction of the hair growth.

The finished sketch
The contrast between light and dark tones and warm and cool colours has created a strong, three-dimensional sketch. Note, too, how the ear casts shadows on the hair and the nape of the neck, indicating that it does not lie flat against the skull.

The hands, step by step

Hands can be such an expressive part of a portrait that it is well worth devoting lots of time to practising drawing them. The sketch on these two pages took just under an hour to complete and the artist spent as much time measuring and checking as he did drawing.

Hands are quite complicated forms and beginners are often very nervous of even attempting them, but the trick is to start by searching out the overall shape instead of laboriously drawing each finger in turn. When two hands are linked together, as in this sketch, it is often better to think of them as a single form rather than two separate shapes.

When you start putting in details such as creases and wrinkles in the skin, decide which ones are most important structurally and aim for a general impression rather than slavishly copying every single line. If you put in too much of this superficial detail, it can easily detract from the overall shape and structure and dominate the sketch, thus destroying the three-dimensional illusion that you've built up.

Finally – although it sounds obvious – make sure you put in the right number of fingers and that each finger has the correct number of joints!

Materials

- *Good-quality drawing paper*
- *Red Conté stick*

The pose

Here we see each hand from a different angle. The sitter's left hand is angled away from us and is therefore slightly foreshortened: the back of this hand looks a lot shorter than the fingers. Note how the shapes of the fingernails appear to change depending on whether they are angled towards or away from our view.

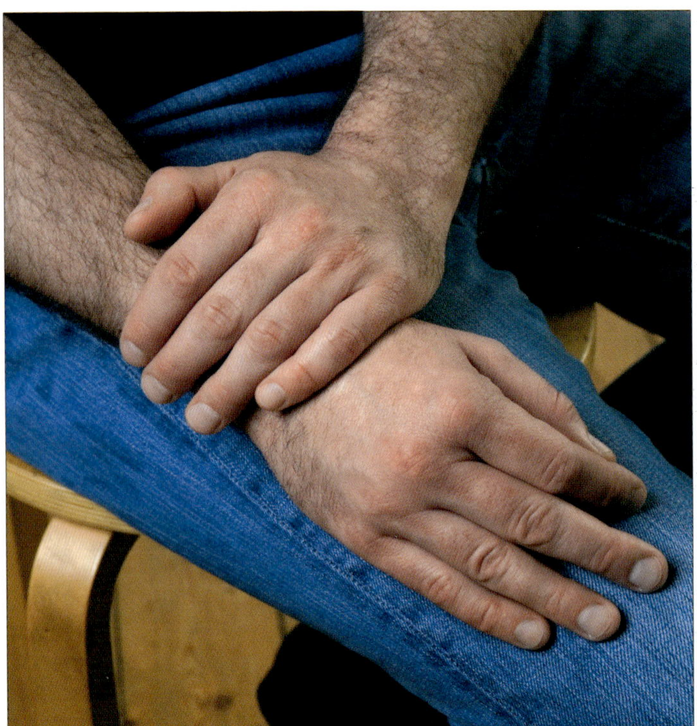

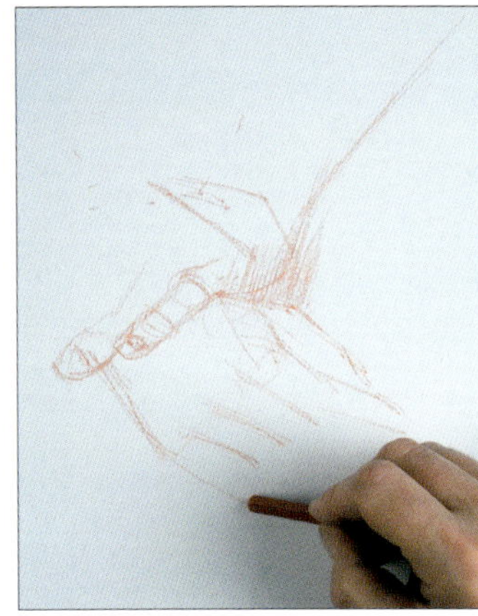

1 Using a red Conté stick, put in faint guidelines to establish the outer limits of the composition. Try to think of the hands as a single unit and start by establishing where the different planes lie. Carefully measure the individual fingers and look at where each one sits in relation to its neighbour.

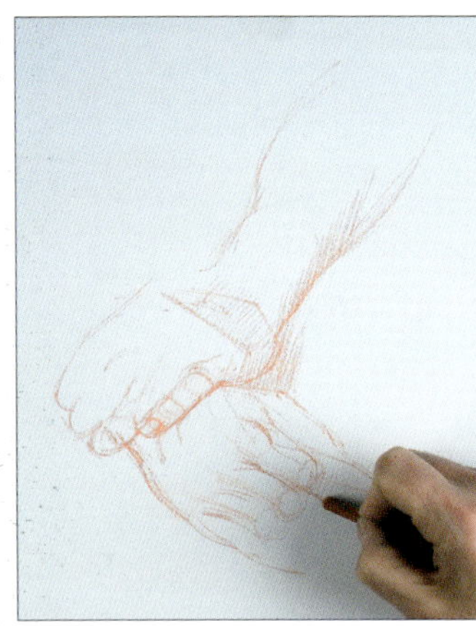

2 Using light hatching, put in some of the shadow on the underside of the sitter's left arm and wrist. (At this stage, the shading is intended mainly to indicate the planes of the arms, so don't do too much detail.) Begin to delineate the individual fingers, using a light, circular motion around the joints to imply their rounded form.

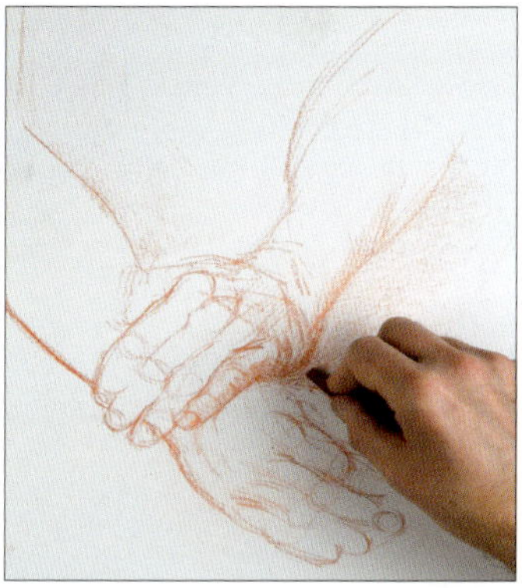

3 Continue delineating the fingers, observing carefully the shapes of the individual fingernails and where the joints occur. You can also begin putting in some of the more important creases and wrinkles in the fingers. Then put in the shadows on the little finger of the left hand. Using the side of the Conté stick, lightly block in the background.

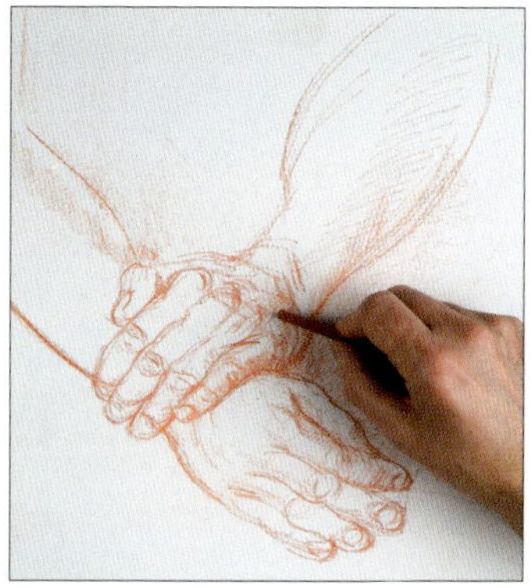

4 Continue working on the linear detail and the shading on the back of the hand and fingers, using the tip of the Conté stick. (Note how much difference in tone there is.) Try to keep the whole drawing moving along at the same pace, rather than concentrating on one area at the expense of the rest.

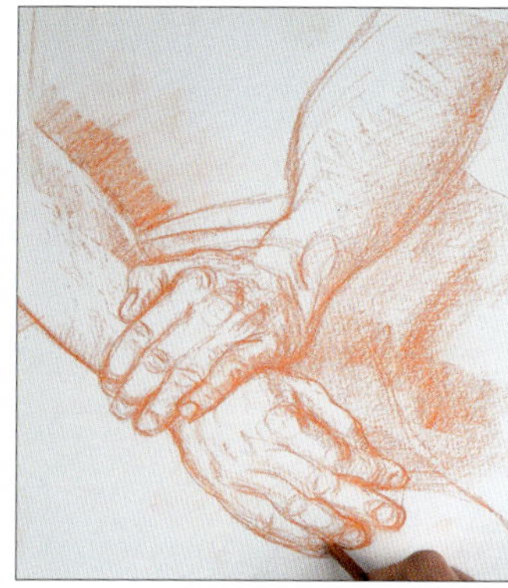

5 Adjust the tones as necessary over the drawing as a whole, using the side of the stick to block in large, dark areas such as the jeans and the tip for crisp, sharp detailing.

Tip: Use the negative shape of the background – in this case, the sitter's denim jeans – to help establish the shape of the arms and hands. You may well find it easier to put in the negative shape of the background first than to outline the positive shape itself – particularly in very small areas, such as the gaps between the fingers.

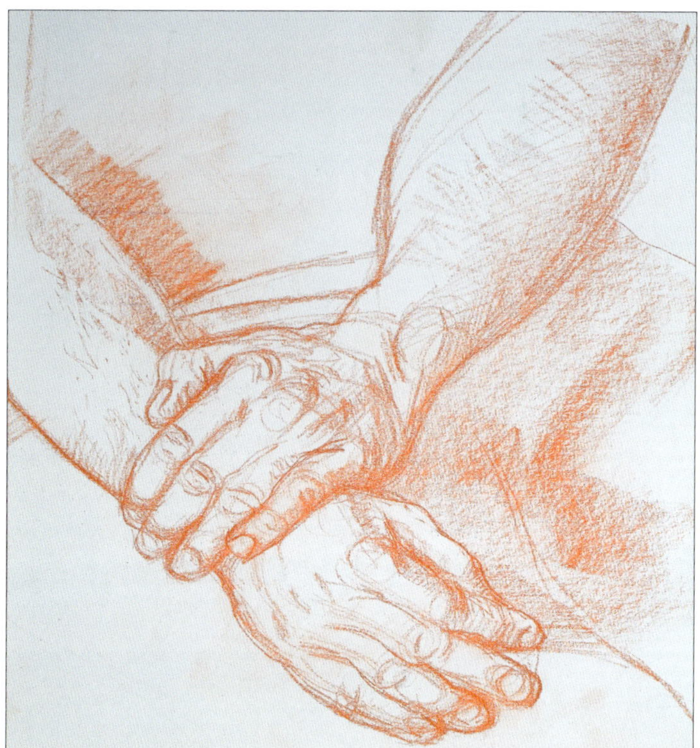

The finished sketch
In this sketch the artist has used a combination of sharp, linear detailing (in the fingers and hatched shadows) and broad, sweeping areas of mid and dark tone, allowing the white of the paper to stand for the brightest highlights. He has included just enough of the background to provide a context for the sketch and make it clear that the sitter's hands are resting, with relaxed muscles, on a solid surface.

Head-and-shoulders portrait

Painting a portrait from life for the first time can be a daunting prospect. Not only do you have the technical aspects to deal with, but you are working with a live model, who will almost certainly fidget and demand to see what you are doing. Before you embark on your first portrait session, practise drawing and painting from photographs to build up your skills and confidence.

This project is done in watercolour, which is the medium of choice for a great number of leisure painters. It is a wonderful medium for painting skin tones, as you can gradually build up layers of soft washes, allowing the paint to merge wet into wet to create soft-edged transitions from one tone to another. Put a lot of care into your underdrawing. If you can get the facial features in the right place and know where the main areas of light and shade are going to be, then you are well on the way to success.

Finally, don't try to do too much. Details like clothing are relatively unimportant in a head-and-shoulders portrait. Instead, try to capture your subject's mood and personality by concentrating on the eyes and expression.

The pose

If you are new to portraiture or to painting with a model rather than from a photograph, a simple pose, with the model looking directly at you, is probably the best way to begin. The eyes are the key to a good portrait, and this pose shows a strong, direct gaze that attracts the attention.

Place a strong light to one side of the model, as it will cast an obvious shadow on the back wall and make it easier for you to assess areas of light and shade on the face, which will assist you with your modelling work. Most importantly, make sure your model is seated comfortably, with good support for her back and arms, as she will have to hold the same pose for some time. You may find it helpful to take photographs for reference so that you can work from these once the model has left.

Select a plain background that does not draw attention away from your subject. You can rig up plain drapes behind the model to achieve this, and choose colours that suit the mood of the portrait or complement the model's skin or hair colour.

Materials

- *HB pencil*
- *300gsm (140lb) HP watercolour paper, pre-stretched*
- *Watercolour paints: light red, yellow ochre, alizarin crimson, sap green, sepia tone, neutral tint, ultramarine blue, ultramarine violet, cobalt blue, burnt umber, cadmium orange, cadmium red*
- *Brushes: large round, medium round, fine round*

Tips:

- From time to time, look at your drawing in a mirror. This often makes it easier to assess if you have got the proportions and position of the features right. Also hold your drawing board at arm's length, with the drawing vertical, to check the perspective. When you work with the drawing board flat, the perspective sometimes becomes distorted.
- Over the course of a portrait session, you will probably find that your model will drift off into a daydream, and the eyelids and facial muscles droop, creating a bored, sullen-looking expression. If this happens, ask your sitter to redirect his or her gaze towards you (ideally without moving the head!); this immediately resolves the problem.

1 Using an HB pencil, lightly sketch your subject, putting in faint construction lines as a guide to help you check that the features are accurately positioned.

Resist the temptation to start the face by drawing an outline. If you do this, the chances are that you will find you haven't allowed yourself enough space for the features. Start by working out the relative sizes and positions of the features and then worry about the outline overall.

It is always a good idea to put in faint pencil guidelines – a line down through the central axis of the face and lines across to mark the positions of the eyes, nose and mouth. As a general rule, the eyes are level with the ear tips and approximately halfway down the face. The nose is roughly halfway between the eyes and the base of the chin. The mouth is usually less than halfway between the nose and chin. The sitter in this portrait appears at first glance to have a very symmetrical face, but be aware that most faces are not exactly symmetrical and look carefully at the differences between the left and right side.

2 Begin to put in some indication of the pattern in the model's blouse. You do not need to make it detailed.

3 Mix light red and yellow ochre to make the first warm but pale flesh tone. Using a medium round brush, wash this mixture over the face, neck and forearms, avoiding the eyes and leaving a few gaps for highlights. This is just the base colour for the flesh. It will look a little strange at this stage, but you will add more tones and colours later on.

4 You have to work quickly at this stage to avoid the wash drying and forming hard edges. While the first wash is still damp, add more pigment and a little alizarin crimson to the first skin tone and paint the shadowed side of the face to give some modelling. Add more alizarin crimson to the mixture and paint the lips. Leave to dry.

5 Touch a little very dilute alizarin crimson on to the cheeks and some very pale sap green into the dark, shaded side of the face. Mix a warm, rich brown from sepia tone and neutral tint and start to paint the hair, leaving some highlight areas and the parting line on the top of the head completely free of paint.

6 Mix a very pale blue from ultramarine blue and a hint of ultramarine violet. See where the fabric in the blouse creases, causing shadows. Using a fine round brush, paint these creases in the pale blue mixture.

7 Go back to the hair colour mixture used in Step 5 and put a second layer of colour on the darker areas of hair. Paint the eyebrows and carefully outline the eyes in the same dark brown mixture.

8 Mix a very light green from yellow ochre with a little sap green and, using a fine round brush, paint in the irises, leaving a white space for the highlight where light is reflected in the eye. Strengthen the shadows on the side of the face and neck with a pale mixture of light red and a little sap green.

9 Use the same shadow colour to paint along the edge of the nose. This helps to separate the nose from the cheeks and make it look three-dimensional. Mix ultramarine violet with sepia tone and paint the pupils of the eyes, taking care not to go over on to the whites.

Assessment time
The portrait is nearing completion and it is time to stand back and decide what adjustments to make and what final details to add. Beware of overworking a portrait like this. The key to its success is its directness.

The model does not stand out clearly from the stark white background.

Successive washes of colour give the hair depth and sheen.

The creases and shadows in the blouse imply the contours of the body underneath the fabric.

10 Mix a dark green from sap green, cobalt blue and burnt umber. Using a large round brush, carefully wash this mixture over the background, taking care not to allow any of the paint to spill over on to the figure. (You may find it easier to switch to a smaller brush to cut in around the figure.)

11 While the background wash is still damp, add a little more pigment to the green mixture and brush in the shadow of the girl's head. Mix an orangey-red from cadmium orange and cadmium red and, using a fine round brush, start putting in some of the detail on the girl's blouse.

12 Continue building up some indication of the pattern on the girl's blouse, using the orangey-red mixture from Step 11, along with ultramarine blue and sap green.

Tip: Don't try to replicate the pattern exactly: it will take far too long and will change the emphasis of the painting from the girl's face to her clothing. A general indication of the pattern and colours is sufficient.The face should always be the most noticeable part of any portrait.

The finished painting

This is a sensitive, yet loosely painted portrait that captures the model's features and mood perfectly. It succeeds largely because its main focus, and the most detailed brushwork, is on the girl's eyes and pensive expression. Careful attention to the shadow areas has helped to give shape to the face and separate the model from the plain-coloured background.

Althought the hair is loosely painted, the tonal variations within it create a sense of volume.

The detailed painting of the eyes and mouth helps to reveal the model's mood and character.

In reality, the pattern on the blouse is much more detailed than this, but a more accurate rendition would have drawn attention away from the girl's face.

The shadow on the wall helps to separate the model from the background and gives the image more depth.

Head-and-shoulders portrait in acrylics

The surroundings and the clothing in this head-and-shoulders portrait have been kept deliberately simple in order to give you an opportunity to practise painting skin tones.

You might think it would make life very simple for artists if there was a ready-mixed skin colour that could be used in all circumstances. However, although you may come across a so-called 'flesh tone' in some paint manufacturers' catalogues, it cannot cope with the sheer variety of skin tones that you are actually likely to encounter.

Even in models with the most flawless of complexions, the skin will not be a uniform colour in all areas. The actual colour (particularly in fair-skinned individuals) can vary dramatically from one part of the subject to another: the cheeks, for example, often look redder than the forehead or chin simply because the blood vessels are closer to the surface. And, just as with any other subject, you need to use different tones to make your subject look three-dimensional. To understand this, look at black-and-white magazine photographs of models with good bone structure: note how the cheekbones cast a shadow on the lower face. Even though (thanks to make-up) the skin colour may be virtually the same all over the face, in strong light there may be differences in tone.

You also need to think about colour temperature: using cool colours for the shadows and warmer ones for the lit areas is a good way of showing how the light falls on your model. Although cool blues and purples might seem strange colours to use for painting skin, it is surprising how using them with warmer colours can bring a portrait to life.

The same principles of colour temperature also apply to the light that illuminates your subject. Although we are generally unaware of the differences, the colour of sunlight is not as warm as, say, artificial tungsten lighting. It's hard to be precise about the colours you should use for painting skin tones, as the permutations are almost infinite, so the best advice is simply to paint what you can actually observe rather than what you think is the right colour.

Materials

- *Board primed with acrylic gesso*
- *B pencil*
- *Acrylic paints: Turner's yellow, cadmium red, titanium white, burnt umber, cadmium yellow, lamp black, phthalocyanine blue, alizarin crimson, yellow ochre*
- *Brushes: large flat, medium flat, small flat*

The pose

A three-quarters pose with the light coming from one side, as here, is generally more interesting to paint than a head-on pose, as it allows you to have one side of the face in shadow, thus creating modelling on the facial features. It also means that the sitter can look directly at you, which generally makes for a more dramatic portrait. The lighting also creates highlights in the model's dark eyes, which always helps to bring a portrait to life. Although this model was sitting in front of a very busy background, the artist chose to simplify it to a uniform background colour in the finished portrait to avoid drawing attention away from the face. He also placed more space on the side of the picture space towards which the model is facing: it is generally accepted that this balance of composition creates a more comfortable, and less confrontational, portrait.

1 Using a B pencil, lightly sketch your subject, indicating the fall of the hair, the facial features and the areas of shadow. Put in as much detail as you wish; it is particularly important to get the size and position of the facial features right.

2 Mix a light flesh tone from Turner's yellow, cadmium red and titanium white. Using a medium flat brush, block in the face and neck, adding a little burnt umber for the shadowed side of the face.

3 Add a little more cadmium red to the flesh-tone mixture and use it to darken the tones on the shadowed side of the face, under the chin and on the neck. Mix a red-biased orangey mix from cadmium red and cadmium yellow and paint the cheek and the shadowed side of the neck as well as the shaded area that lies immediately under the mouth. Immediately the portrait is taking on a feeling of light and shade.

4 Mix a pale bluish black from lamp black and phthalocyanine blue and begin putting in the lightest tones of the hair, making sure your brushstrokes follow the direction in which the hair grows. When the first tone is dry, add burnt umber to the mixture and paint the darker areas within the hair mass to give the hair volume. Add more phthalocyanine blue to the mixture and paint the model's shirt.

5 Mix a pale brown from cadmium red, burnt umber, Turner's yellow and titanium white and loosely block in the background, painting carefully around the face. You may find it easier to switch to a larger brush for this stage, as it will allow you to cover a wide area more quickly.

6 Mix a rich, dark brown from lamp black, burnt umber, cadmium red and a little of the blue shirt mixture from Step 4. Using a small flat brush, paint the dark of the eyes and the lashes, taking care to get the shape of the white of the eye right. Use the same colour for the nostril.

7 Use the same colour to define the line between the upper and lower lips. Mix a reddish brown from burnt umber and phthalocyanine blue and paint the shadows under the eyes and inside the eye sockets.

8 Paint the mouth in varying mixes of alizarin crimson, cadmium red and yellow ochre, leaving the highlights untouched. The highlights will be worked in later, using lighter colours.

9 Darken the flesh tones on the shaded side of the face where necessary, using a mixture of alizarin crimson, phthalocyanine blue and a little titanium white, adding more blue to the mixture for the shadow under the chin, which is cooler in tone.

10 Mix a dark but warm black from burnt umber and lamp black and paint the darkest sections of the hair, leaving the lightest colour (applied in Step 4) showing through in places. This gives tonal variety and shows how the light falls on the hair.

11 Add more water to the mixture to make it more dilute and go over the dark areas of the hair again, this time leaving only a few highlights showing through as relatively fine lines.

12 Mix a dark blue from phthalocyanine blue and lamp black and paint over the shirt again, leaving some of the lighter blue areas applied in Step 4 showing through. Your brushstrokes should follow the direction and fall of the fabric.

▶

13 The beauty of acrylics is that you can paint a light colour over a dark one, without the first colour being visible. If you think the background is too dark and there is not sufficient differentiation between the model and the background, mix a warm off-white from titanium white, yellow ochre and burnt umber and, using a large flat brush, loosely paint the background again.

14 Using a small flat brush, cut around individual hairs with the background colour, carefully looking at the 'negative shapes'.

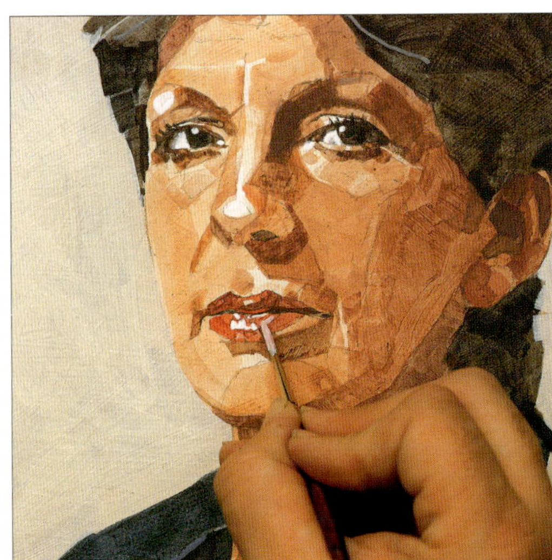

15 Using a fine round brush and titanium white straight from the tube, dot the highlights on to the eyes, nose and lower lip.

The finished painting

This is a relatively simple portrait, with nothing to distract from the sitter's direct gaze. Although the colour palette is limited, the artist has achieved an impressive and realistic range of skin and hair tones. Interest comes from the use of semi-transparent paint layers and allowing the directions of the brush marks to show through.

Carefully positioned highlights in the eyes make them sparkle and bring the portrait to life. The direct, critical gaze is an essential element of the portrait.

Variations in the skin tone, particularly on the shaded side of the face, help to reveal the shape of the face and its underlying bone structure.

The highlights in the hair are created by putting down the lightest tones first and then allowing them to show through subsequent applications of paint.

Portrait in oils on a toned ground

This portrait was painted from a photograph – you cannot expect a model to hold an expression as animated as this for any length of time.

Here, the artist opted for a head-and-shoulders portrait. Your most important decision when setting up a portrait is how much to include. If you leave out the shoulders, you will end up with what looks like a disembodied head; if you include much more of the torso than shown here, emphasis will be drawn away from the face and the balance of the portrait will be wrong.

In order to be able to start from a mid tone, the artist began by toning the canvas using a rich, warm mix of Venetian red and yellow ochre. Working on a white ground can be too strong a contrast. The artist was able to leave some of the ground showing through in the final painting for the brickwork and the mid tones of the model's skin.

The next stage was to make a thin underpainting in order to map out the basic pose. The advantage of using very thin paint for the underpainting is that if you make a mistake you can easily wipe it off with an old rag that has been dipped in turpentine.

In all portraits, it's important to continually refer back to your original points of reference – the width of the eyes, or the distance between the tip of the nose and the chin, for example – to check that your measurements and the proportions of the face are still correct. Be prepared to make adjustments as your work progresses.

Materials

- *Stretched oil-primed linen canvas*
- *Oil paints: Venetian red, yellow ochre, terre verte, burnt umber, titanium white, ultramarine blue, alizarin crimson, lemon yellow, lamp black, cadmium red*
- *Turpentine*
- *Old rag*
- *Brushes: selection of filberts in various sizes*

The pose

The model was posed in front of a brick wall, which provides texture and interest without detracting from her expression and features. The photograph was taken in late afternoon, so the sunlight that streams in from the left is both warm in colour and low in the sky, providing good modelling on the face.

1 Tone the canvas with a dilute mix of Venetian red and yellow ochre and leave to dry. Dilute terre verte oil paint with turpentine to create a thin mix. Using a fine filbert brush, map out the overall structure of the portrait. Start by putting in the shoulder line (which in this case forms a strong diagonal through the composition), neck, facial area and the approximate area occupied by the hair. Then put in the facial features in burnt umber.

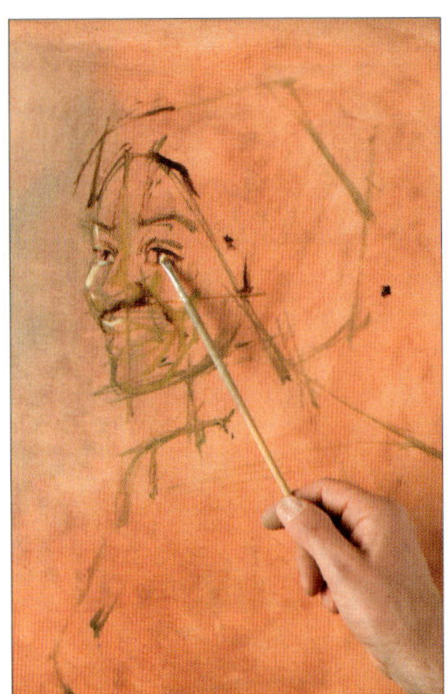

2 Put in more lines that you can use as a point of reference, such as the central line through the head. Begin putting in some of the mid tones, such as the bridge of the nose, with a yellowy mix of yellow ochre and terre verte. Mix titanium white with a little yellow ochre and put in 'markers' that you can refer back to later in the painting for the highlights – on the edge of the right cheekbone and top lip, for example. Carefully touch in the whites of the eyes.

Tip: The exact colour of your reference marks is not critical – but varying the colours a little makes it easier for you to differentiate these new marks from the previous ones and keep track of where you are in the portrait.

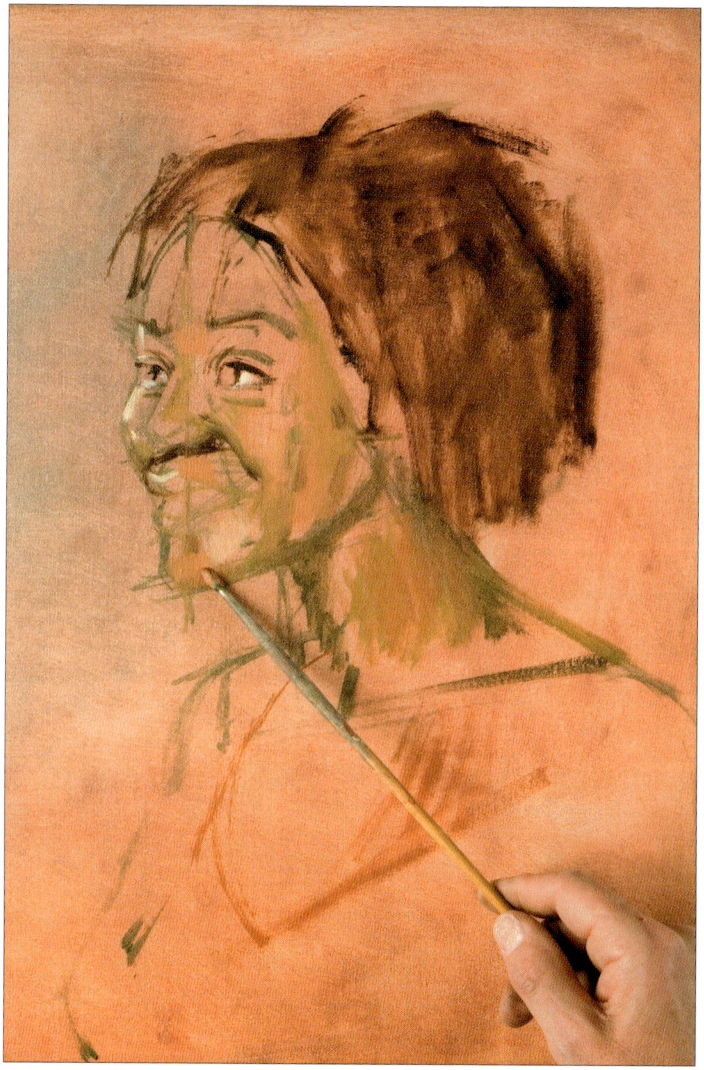

3 Scumble burnt umber over the hair, allowing some of the toned ground to show through in places. Roughly scumble the yellowy green mix used in Step 2 on to mid-toned shadow areas such as the neck and the side of the face. Mix a reddish brown from Venetian red, yellow ochre and a little titanium white and apply this on top of the earlier mix, allowing the colours to mix optically on the surface of the canvas. This generally creates a much more lively mix than physically mixing the same colours in the palette.

Tip: Look for changes in tone across the face and neck that express the muscles underneath the surface of the skin.

4 For the mid- to dark tones on the face – for example, down the centre of the brow and the bridge of the nose – use a mix of Venetian red, yellow ochre and burnt umber. Add white to this and put in some of the light highlights – on the left cheek and around the mouth, for example. Add ultramarine blue to the original mix for the shadow under the chin, and scumble a little of the same blue mix into the hair to create tonal variation.

5 Paint the dark tones on the chin with a mix of Venetian red and yellow ochre. Using the brush tip, put in some light marks for the teeth and paint the gums in alizarin crimson. On the model's right shoulder and chest, scumble on a light mix of white and yellow ochre for the highlight areas.

6 Refine the shape and position of the teeth. Mix a yellowy green from lemon yellow, a little terre verte and white and scumble it on to the background, leaving spaces for the mortar lines of the bricks. Looking at the negative spaces around your subject makes it easier to see the positive shapes.

7 Continue to build up the modelling on the face, alternating between warm and cool mixes and light and dark tones. Remember that warm colours tend to advance, while pale ones recede – so if you want an area such as a cheekbone to come forward, use a warm tone.

8 Put in the darkest tones in the hair, using a relatively thin mix of lamp black and ultramarine blue. Allow some of the canvas texture to show through.

9 Put in the white of the left eye with a mix of white with a hint of lemon yellow, and the white of the right eye with a cooler mix of white and ultramarine, so that it appears to recede slightly. Reassess the facial highlights and adjust if necessary. Begin blocking in the camisole in cadmium red.

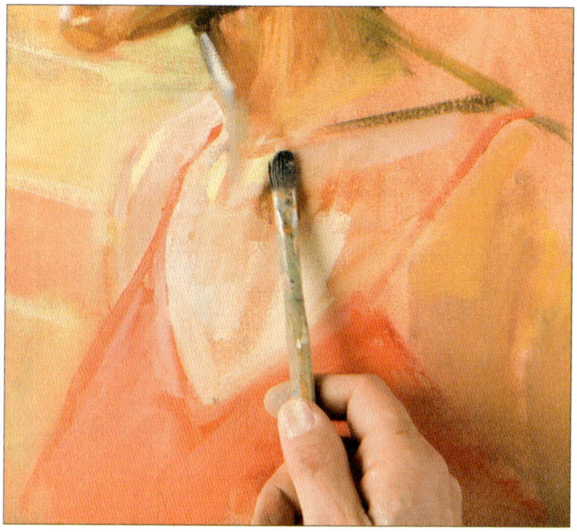

10 Now look at the highlights on the chest and shoulder. The collar bones are very prominent and catch the light, so use a warm mix of white and lemon yellow.

11 Scumble a mix of lemon yellow and white over the brick background, toning it down with a little terre verte in places and leaving the yellowy-green mix from Step 6 showing through for the mortar between the bricks.

12 Add more terre verte to the mix and scumble it over the bricks on the right-hand side. Block in the shape of the model's red top more precisely with cadmium red, adding white to the mix in parts so that the colour is not flat. As you improve the modelling on the chest, look for the highlights.

13 Build up the modelling on the arm, using the same mixes as before. Put in the dark crease under the arm in a mix of burnt umber and terre verte.

Assessment time

When you feel you're getting near the end of any painting, it's important to take time to look critically at what you've done and see what changes, if any, are required. Here, although the modelling on the face is virtually complete, there are a few gaps remaining – particularly around the hair line – where the toned ground shows through. The arms and shoulders almost merge into the background and need to be brought forward. Some of the skin tones are a little too dark in places and need to be toned down; the shadow under the chin and around the jawline, in particular, is both too dark and too heavy, but this is easy to rectify. In oils, you can apply a lighter colour on top of a dark one. You can even wipe off colour using a rag dipped in turpentine if necessary.

14 There are places on the head that have received no paint, allowing the toned ground to show. Block these in using the same skin tones as before. Strengthen the shadow on the back of the neck; because of the way the light falls, this area is quite dark. Lighten the shadow under the chin using a mix of Venetian red, yellow ochre and terre verte, and soften the edges.

15 Cover any gaps and build up more texture in the hair with a deep blue-black mix of burnt umber and ultramarine blue.

Tip: Don't try to put in every strand of hair, but make sure your strokes follow the direction of growth.

16 Using cadmium red paint, darken the red top. Note, however, that the colour is not totally uniform: creases and folds in the fabric create slight shadows that reveal the form beneath.

The finished painting
This is a lively portrait that perfectly captures the model's expression and personality. The artist began by toning the canvas with a mix of Venetian red and yellow ochre, which was similar in colour to both the mid-tones of the model's skin and the brick wall in the background. This enabled him to allow some of the ground to show through in his finished painting, unifying the surface. Although the colour palette is relatively restricted, the bright highlights and the white of the eyes and teeth really sing out and help to bring the portrait to life. Note, too, the effectiveness of the contrasts in texture – the smoothness of the skin, achieved by blending the paint wet into wet, versus the roughly scumbled paint on the background and the short, spiky brushstrokes used for the hair.

Paint has been lightly scumbled on to the brick wall, exploiting the texture of the canvas.

Because the light is so bright, the highlighted skin areas are paler than you might expect.

Energetic, spiky brushstrokes capture the texture of the hair.

Baby in watercolour

The birth of a baby is a really special time for all the family. What better way to commemorate it than by making a watercolour sketch of the newborn?

Many artists begin their portraits by making a pencil underdrawing to check they've got the proportions right and have positioned all the features correctly before they start applying the paint. On this particular subject, however, the colours and washes are so pale that any underdrawing might show through in the finished painting. The trick is to work with very pale mixes in the initial stages and only apply stronger colour when you're absolutely sure that everything is correctly placed. Remember, too, that watercolour always looks a little lighter when dry. Start light and build up gradually.

Generally speaking, if a brightly lit area (such as the baby's left cheek in this case) is warm in tone, then the shaded areas will be cool. Although babies' faces are rounded and the cheekbones are not as discernible as they are in adults, there is still a point at which you will need to veer away from a warm tone and towards a cool one, otherwise your painting will look very flat and the whole face will appear to be on the same plane.

There is a lot of white in this subject. In pure watercolour, the white of the paper is used to convey the brightest whites – but every white contains some shadow areas. Here, there are wrinkled and crumpled areas in the sleepsuit where a darker tone is clearly visible. To capture these, use a very pale, cool blue – and work wet into wet so that you do not create any sharp lines or hard edges. If the paper gets too wet, dab off the excess with kitchen paper.

Materials

- *Heavy rough watercolour paper*
- *Watercolour paints: ultramarine blue, yellow ochre, lemon yellow, raw sienna, cerulean blue, alizarin crimson, Venetian red, cadmium red*
- *Brushes: large mop, medium round, fine round*
- *Kitchen paper*

The pose

This is the kind of portrait that any parent would be thrilled to have. The yellow blanket in which the newborn baby is wrapped forms a frame for his head and adds a subtle but important contrast in colour to the white of his clothing and the sheet.

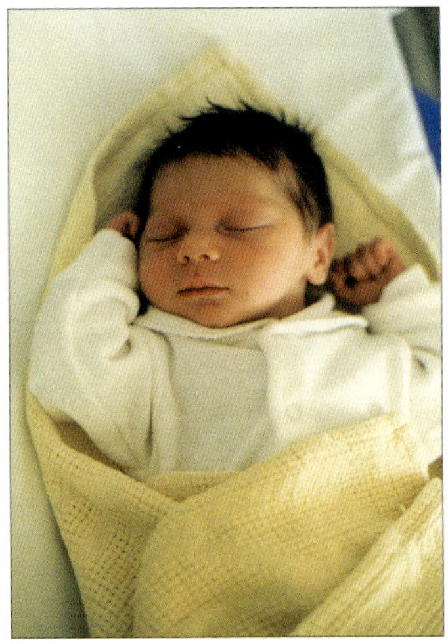

1 Work out roughly where the blanket and baby will be positioned on the paper. Dip a large mop brush in clean water and 'draw' some of the main folds and shadows of the white sheet. Then dip the brush into a dilute wash of ultramarine blue and drop the colour wet into wet onto the dampened area. The colour will spread and blur to give soft marks with no hard edges.

2 Mix a very dilute wash of yellow ochre with a touch of lemon yellow and brush in the shape of the blanket around the baby.

3 Mix a reddish brown colour from raw sienna and yellow ochre. Using a medium round brush, establish the position and shape of the head and left hand. At this stage you should be thinking only about the composition, not the detail.

4 Use tiny dots of colour to establish the inner and outer points of the eyes and the nostrils. Note that the baby's head is tilted slightly to one side, so the eyes are on a slight diagonal line, rather than horizontal. Using a very dilute version of the same mix, put in the curve of the brow and the eye sockets, and the lips and left ear. Work wet on dry for the features, as you do not want the paint to spread.

5 Mix a very dilute wash of cerulean blue and carefully put in the very faint shadows on the sleepsuit. Use the same mix to mark the collar and button band of the sleepsuit. Using ultramarine blue and a medium round brush, begin putting in the baby's hair, making spiky brushstrokes that follow the direction of the hair growth. Try to use quick yet delicate movements to avoid wobbly brush strokes.

6 Mix a very dilute wash of alizarin crimson. Dampen the baby's cheeks with clean water and then drop the alizarin mix into these areas, wet into wet. Quickly blot off the paint with kitchen paper so that the colour is not too dark or hard-edged.

7 Mix a dilute wash of a warm, purplish blue from ultramarine blue and alizarin crimson and dash it into the spiky tufts of hair. Use the same colour for the deep shadow areas – below the ear, for example – and dot it along his eyelashes. Mix together alizarin crimson and yellow ochre and put in the warm tones on the forehead, leaving the white paper for the brightest highlights.

Assessment time

The skin tones are building up nicely, but the features are still very indistinct. The contrast between the hot tones of the baby's face and the fabrics, which have received virtually no paint, is too stark. Now that the overall structure is established, you should concentrate on the tonal balance and on building up the features into a more life-like portrait.

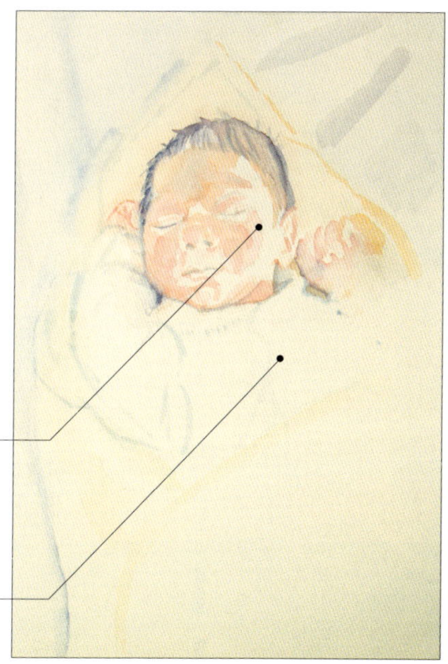

There are the beginnings of some modelling on the baby's cheeks, but the highlights are too bright and the features still too indistinct.

There is virtually no detail in the blanket or slepsuit.

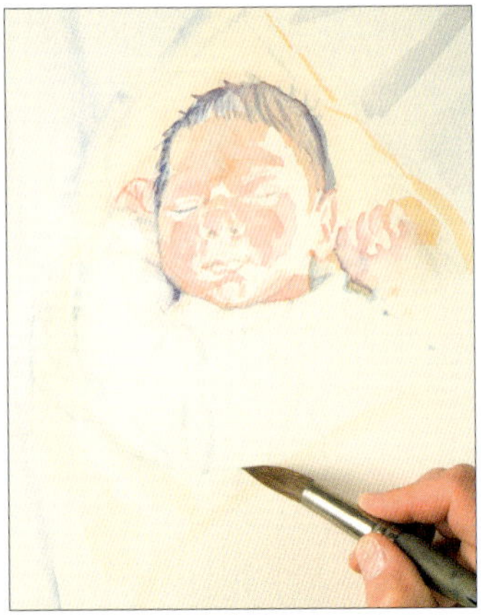

8 Gradually build up the skin tones. Aim for a continual interplay of warm and cool tones – the warm yellow ochre and alizarin mix versus the cooler ultramarine and alizarin. The warm tones appear to advance, while cooler ones recede. Mix a dilute wash of ultramarine blue and alizarin crimson and put in the creases in the sheet and sleepsuit, leaving the white paper to stand for the highlights.

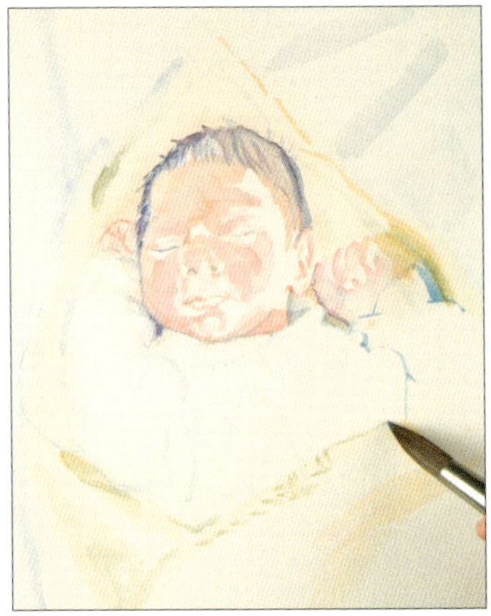

9 Mix a dilute yellowy green from cerulean blue and yellow ochre. Using a dry brush and broad brushstrokes, put in the dark shadow areas on the yellow blanket. Then, using the tip of the brush, begin making dotted and dashed marks across the blanket to create the openweave pattern of the fabric.

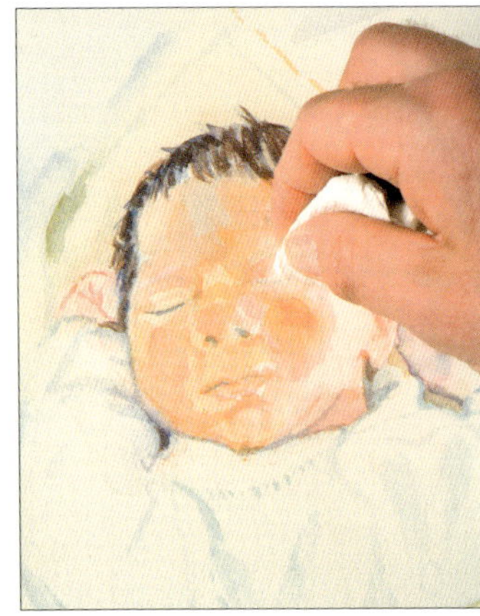

10 Mix a dark, earthy brown from Venetian red and a little ultramarine blue and, using spiky brushstrokes as before, drybrush it on to the hair to create some texture. Apply more warm colours – cadmium red and yellow ochre – to the face, allowing the colours to merge wet into wet on the paper. Wash very dilute cadmium red over the face and blot it off immediately with kitchen paper.

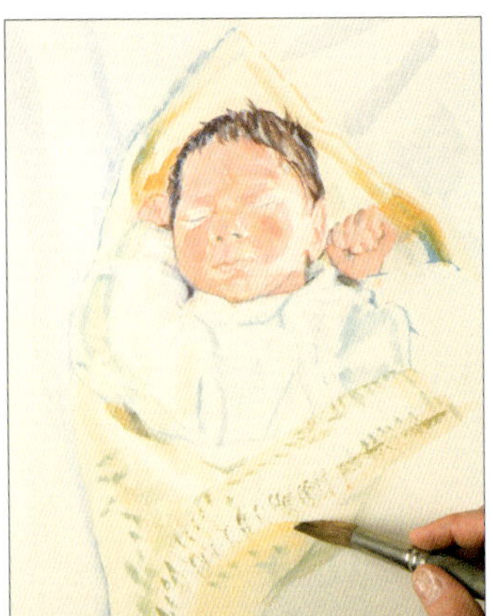

11 Drybrush a mix of cerulean blue and yellow ochre over the blanket as before, using the tip of the brush to create textural marks and break up the monotony of the pale wash. Brush a stronger, more yellow version of the same mix over the edges of the blanket around the baby's head.

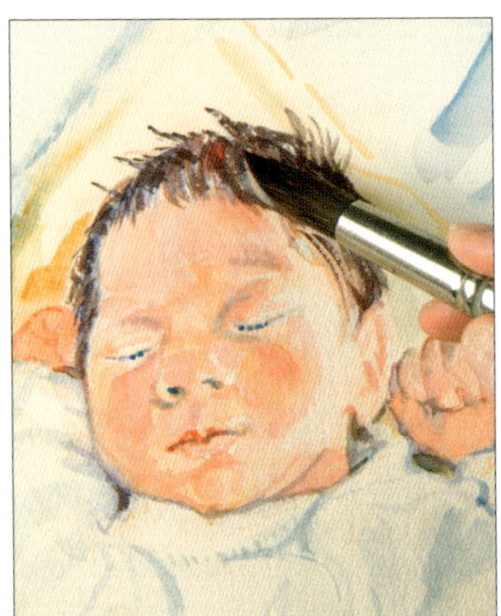

12 Redefine the facial features if you feel they're not strong enough. Here, the shape and colour of the lips was redefined with a little more cadmium red. Dash more of the earthy brown mix from Step 10 into the hair, taking care not to lose the existing spiky texture.

13 Using a drybrush technique and alternating between the yellowy green mix from Step 10 and dilute cerulean blue, build up the texture and patterning on the blanket. Leave to dry. Finally, apply a wash of yellow ochre over the blanket to provide a stronger-coloured 'frame' for the baby.

The finished painting
This is a charming portrait of a newborn baby that exploits the potential of watercolour to the full. The viewpoint, looking down on the sleeping child, emphasizes his fragility and vulnerability, as do the soft, pastel colours.

Using only a limited palette of colours, the artist has applied successive wet-into-wet layers of very dilute, transparent washes to build up the skin tones, allowing the colours to merge on the paper so that there are no hard-edged transitions of tone. The white of the paper shines through, giving the picture lift and sparkle, while drybrush marks on the blanket and the spiky hair add an interesting texture to the painting.

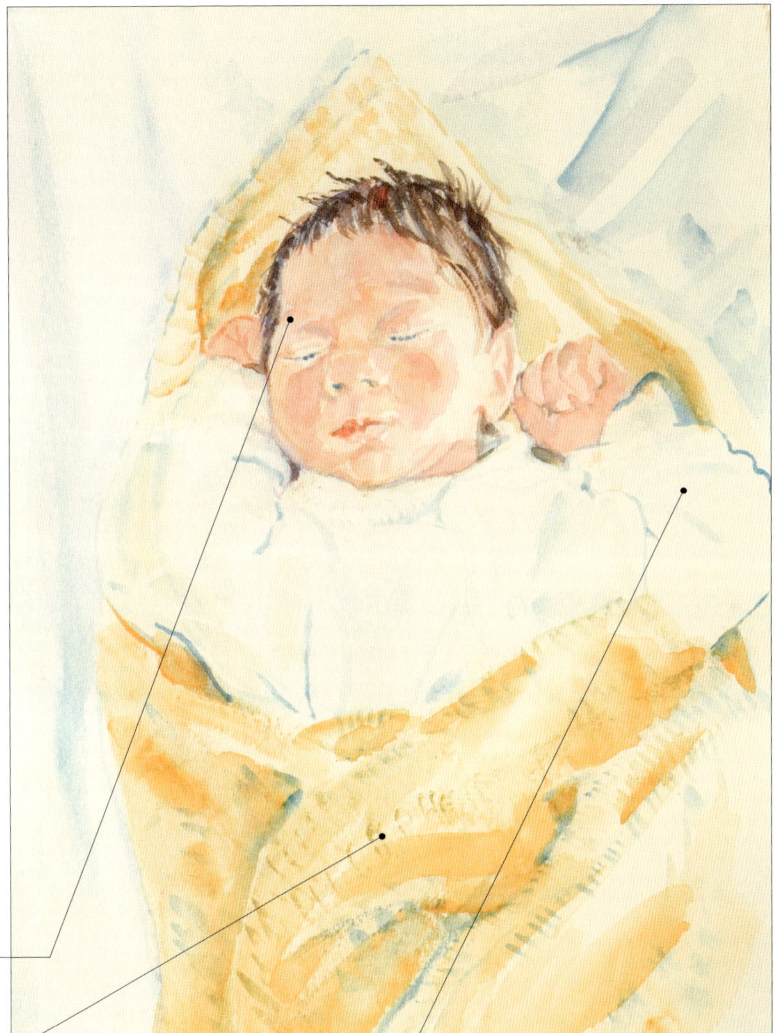

Wet-into-wet washes create subtle transitions of tone on the face, and suggest the delicate quality of the baby's skin.

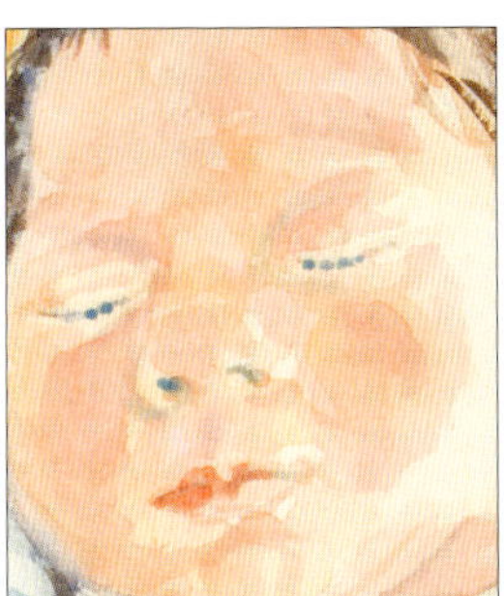

Textural drybrush marks contrast well with the wet-into-wet washes on the skin.

The white of the paper stands for the brightest areas of the white sleepsuit and sheet.

Young child in acrylics

There are several things to remember when drawing or painting a child. The first is that children are very active and have a short attention span: you cannot expect them to sit still for hours while you work on your portrait, and for this reason you will probably find it easiest to work from a photograph.

Second, in children the head is much larger in relation to the overall body size than it is in adults. Although the human race is infinitely varied, as a general guideline the head is about one-seventh of the total height of the body in adults – but in babies it may occupy almost as much as one-third of the total. The little girl in this portrait is about two years old: her head represents approximately one-quarter of her total height.

This project starts with toning the support – a classic technique that was much used by some of the great portraitists such as Peter Paul Rubens (1577–1640). This provides the advantage of starting to paint from a mid-tone background, rather than a stark white ground, which makes it easier to judge the subtle flesh tones and the effects of light and shade cast by the sun. It also establishes the overall colour temperature of the portrait from the outset. In this instance, burnt sienna gives the portrait a lovely warm glow, which is appropriate to the dappled sunlight that illuminates the scene.

Materials

- *Board primed with acrylic gesso*
- *Acrylic paints: burnt sienna, ultramarine blue, titanium white, cadmium red, lemon yellow, alizarin crimson, phthalocyanine green*
- *Brushes: small round, medium flat, small flat*
- *Rag*
- *Matt acrylic medium*

The pose

Relaxed and informal, this child's attention is occupied by something that we cannot see. Note that she is positioned slightly off centre. If a figure in a portrait is looking off to one side, it is generally better to have more space on that side, as this creates a calmer, more restful mood. Placing a figure close to the edge of the frame creates a feeling of tension.

Preliminary sketch

Flesh tones can be tricky, and you may find it useful to make a quick colour sketch experimenting with different mixes, such as the one shown on the left, before you start painting.

1 Tone the primed board with burnt sienna acrylic paint and leave to dry. Mix a dilute, warm brown from burnt sienna and a little ultramarine blue. Using a small round brush, make a loose underdrawing, concentrating on getting the overall proportions and the angles of the head and limbs correct.

2 Mix a darker, less dilute brown, this time using more ultramarine blue. Using the small round brush, put in the darkest tones of the hair, the shadows on the face and under the collar of the girl's dress, and the main creases in the fabric of the dress. These creases help to convey form.

3 Mix a very pale pink from titanium white, cadmium red and a little lemon yellow and paint the palest flesh tones on the face, arms and legs, as well as some highlights in the hair. Add more water and put in the lightest tones of the girl's dress. Note how the colour of the support shows through.

4 Mix a warm purple from ultramarine blue and alizarin crimson. Using a medium flat brush, block in the dark foliage area to the left of the girl. Add more water and ultramarine blue to the mixture and paint the darkest foliage areas to the right of the girl and the shadows under the stool.

5 Mix a bright green from phthalocyanine green, lemon yellow, titanium white and a little cadmium red. Block in the lawn and background foliage. Use less lemon yellow for the shaded grass and more white for the brightest parts.

6 Mix a very pale green from titanium white and phthalocyanine green and brush it loosely over the child's sun-bleached cotton dress.

7 Mix a dark brown from burnt sienna and ultramarine blue and start to put some detailing in the hair and on the shadowed side of the face. Mix a warm shadow tone from alizarin crimson and burnt sienna and build up the shadow tones on the left-hand (sunlit) side of the face, alternating between this mixture and the pale pink used in Step 3.

8 Add titanium white to the purple mixture from Step 4 and paint the stool to the right of the child. Paint the stool on which she is sitting in a mixture of brown and titanium white, with brushstrokes that follow the wood grain. Mix a rich brown from burnt sienna and alizarin crimson and, using a small round brush, paint the shadows at the bottom of her dress.

9 Dab some of the purple mixture (the stool colour) over the foliage in the background. Using the same colour in this area establishes a visual link between foreground and background; the light colour also creates the impression of dappled light in the foliage. Mix a dark, bluish green from ultramarine blue and phthalocyanine green and paint the shadow under the dress collar and any deep creases and shadows in the fabric of the dress.

10 Using the pale pink mixture from Step 3 and a round brush, go over the arms and legs again, carefully blending the tones wet into wet on the support in order to convey the roundness of the flesh.

Assessment time

The blocks of colour are now taking on some meaning and form: for the rest of the painting, concentrate on building up the form and detailing.

The tonal contrasts on the face are too extreme and need to be blended to make the skin look more life-like.

The hands and feet, in particular, need to be given more definition.

The child is not sufficiently well separated from the background.

Tip: To make flesh look soft and rounded, you need to blend the tones on the support so that they merge almost imperceptibly; it is rare to see a sharp transition from one colour to another. Working wet into wet is the best way to achieve this, gradually darkening the tone as the limb turns away from the light. With acrylic paints, you may find that adding a few drops of flow improver helps matters: flow improver increases the flow of the paint and its absorption into the support surface.

11 Mix burnt sienna with a tiny amount of titanium white. Using a small round brush, paint the dark spaces between the fingers and the shadows between the feet and on the toes. Try to see complicated areas such as these as abstract shapes and blocks of colour: if you start thinking of them as individual toes, the chances are that you will make them bigger than they should be.

12 Refine the facial details, using the same mixes as before. Put in the curve of the ear, which is just visible through the hair, using the pale pink skin tone. Mix a reddish brown from alizarin crimson, ultramarine blue and burnt sienna. Build up the volume of the hair, looking at the general direction of the hair growth and painting clumps rather than individual hairs.

13 Using the purple shadow mixture from Step 4 and a small flat brush, cut in around the head to define the edge and provide better separation between the girl and the background. Mix a dark green from phthalocyanine green and ultramarine blue and loosely dab it over the dark foliage area to provide more texture. Using cool colours here makes this area recede, focusing attention on the little girl.

14 Add a little matt acrylic medium to the pale pink flesh tone and go over the light areas of the face, working the paint in with the brush to ensure that it blends well and covers any areas too dark in tone. The matt medium makes the paint more translucent, so that it is more like a glaze. Do the same thing on the arms, adding a little burnt sienna for any areas that are slightly warmer in tone.

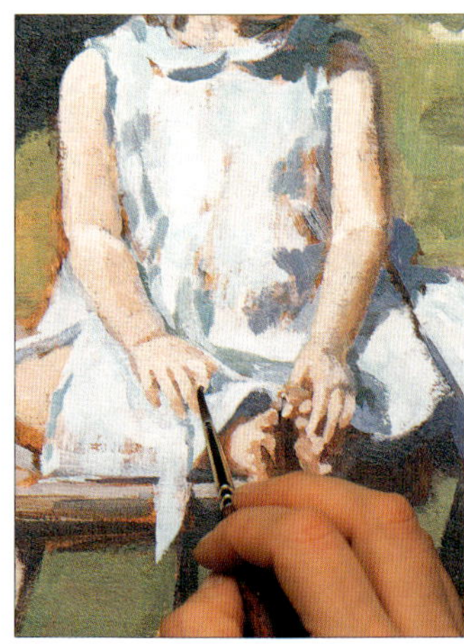

15 Make any final adjustments that you deem necessary. Here, the artist felt that the girl's hands were too small, making her look slightly doll-like; using the pale flesh colour from previous steps, she carefully painted over them to make them a little broader and bring them up to the right scale.

The finished painting

This is a charming portrait of a toddler with her slightly chubby face and arms, rounded mouth, big eyes and unselfconscious pose. There is just enough detail in the background to establish the outdoor setting, but by paying very careful attention to the tones of the highlights and shadows, the artist has captured the dappled sunlight that pervades the scene.

Although no detail is visible in the eyes, we are nonetheless invited to follow the child's gaze.

The subtle blending of colour on the child's arms and face makes the flesh look soft and rounded.

There is just enough background to give the scene a context without distracting from the portrait.

Brushstrokes on the stool follow the direction of the woodgrain – an effective way of conveying both pattern and texture.

Grandmother and child in soft pastels

Family portraits, particularly of very young children, are always popular – and a project like this would make a wonderful present for a grandparent. Soft pastels capture the skin tones beautifully, and you can smooth out the marks with your fingers or a torchon to create almost imperceptible transitions from one tone to another. Build up the layers gradually. You can spray with fixative in the later stages to avoid smudging the colours, but be aware that this could dull or darken the colours that you've already put down. Soft pastel is also a lovely medium for drawing hair, as you can put down many different colours within the hair mass to create depth and an attractive sheen. When drawing hair, look at the overall direction of the hair growth.

Young children have very short attention spans and they certainly can't hold the same pose for the time it takes to draw a detailed portrait. You'll be lucky if they sit still for long enough for you to do anything more than a very quick sketch – so working from a photograph is probably your best option. Even then, it's very hard to get a young child to do exactly as you want if you tell them what to do. Often you either get a shot with the child staring grumpily at the camera, or he or she will wriggle, making a good shot impossible.

One simple solution is to make the photo session into a game by pulling faces, clapping your hands, holding up a favourite toy and generally interacting with the child so that he or she forgets all about the camera. Above all, take lots of shots so you have plenty of reference material to choose from. Then you can combine material from several shots – invaluable if you can't get a shot in which both sitters are smiling at the same time.

Materials

- *Pale grey pastel paper*
- *Soft pastels: pinkish beige, white, dark brown, mid-brown, orangey beige, pale yellow, pinkish brown, reddish brown, dark blue, red, pale blue, grey, pale pink, black*

The pose

This is a happy pose, with both child and grandmother smiling broadly. To help them relax for the shot, the photographer got them to make a little game out of clapping their hands which, in addition to helping them forget that they're having their photo taken, imparts a sense of movement to the pose.

1 Using a pinkish beige soft pastel map out the basic shapes – the heads of the two sitters and the position of the arms. Draw the sleeves and neckline of the grandmother's sweater in white pastel, putting in the most obvious creases in the fabric, and put in the slant of the little boy's shoulders in white, too.

2 Using the pinkish beige pastel again, indicate the position of the facial features by marking a central guideline with the eyes approximately halfway down. The grandmother's head is tilted back, so her eyes are a little above the halfway point. Roughly block in the child's hair and the shadows in the woman's hair in dark brown.

3 Still using the dark brown pastel, put in more of the hair, smudging the pastel marks with your fingers. Indicate the darkest parts of the facial features – the recesses of the eye sockets and nostrils. Apply some flesh tone to the child's face, using mid-brown for the darker parts and a more orange version of the beige used in Step 1 for the lighter parts. Using the side of a pale yellow pastel, roughly block in the base colour of the little boy's shirt.

4 Using the side of a white pastel, block in the grandmother's sweater. Apply a pinkish beige to her face and neck, blending the marks with your fingers.

5 The grandmother's neck is slightly warmer in tone than her face. Use a reddish brown for the slightly darker tones in this area, again blending the marks with your fingers. Use the same colour for the child's lips. Using your fingertips, smooth out the mid-brown on the child's face, leaving the orangey beige for the lighter parts. Use a very dark brown for the child's eyebrows and eyes.

6 Using a dark blue pastel, put in the creases in the fabric of the grandmother's sweater. Block in the arms, using a pinkish brown for the grandmother and a reddish brown for the little boy. Overlay various flesh tones – pinkish beige, orangey beige, red – as appropriate, blending the marks with your fingers. Flesh is not a uniform colour; look closely and you will see warm and cool tones within it.

7 With a dark brown pastel, put in the shadow under the child's chin and around the collar of his shirt. Put in some jagged strokes on the hair so that you begin to develop something of the spiky texture. Darken the child's eyes.

> **Tip**: Think of the eyes as spherical forms rather than as flat circles on the surface of the face.

8 Using the same flesh colours as before, continue building up the modelling on the little boy's face. Add some red to the cheeks, blending the marks with your fingers. Like most toddlers, he has a fairly chubby face, so there are no deep recesses under the cheekbones, but with the mix of light and darker-coloured tones the flesh is starting to look more natural. Using the tip of a white pastel and dabbing on small marks, lightly draw his teeth and apply some tiny, glossy highlights to the lips.

9 Repeat the process of building up modelling on the grandmother's face. Apply pale yellow to her hair.

10 Continue working on the hair, putting in browns and greys to get some tonal variation within the hair. Note, too, how the hair casts a slight shadow on her face. Use a brown pastel to draw in the creases in the little boy's shirt. Draw in the crease lines around the grandmother's nose and mouth with a reddish brown pastel.

Assessment time
The expressions and pose have been nicely captured, but in places the skin tones appear as blocks of colour and need to be smoothed out more. A little more modelling is also needed on the faces and hands. The eyes need to sparkle in order for the portrait to come alive.

The pupils and irises have been carefully observed, but there is no catchlight to bring the eyes to life.

The child's hands, in particular, appear somewhat formless.

11 Continue the modelling on the grandmother's face and neck, gradually building up the layers and fleshing out the cheeks. Use the same colours and blending techniques as before. The adjustments are relatively minor at this stage.

12 Apply more yellow to the boy's shirt, scribbling it in around the dark crease marks. Smudge more brown over the yellow for the stripes in the fabric. A hint of the pattern is sufficient; too much detail would detract from the face.

13 Using the side of the pastel, block in the grandmother's sweater with a very pale blue. Reinforce the dark blue applied in Step 6 to define the folds in the fabric. Apply tiny pale-blue dots around the neckline of the sweater.

14 Draw the little boy's fingernails with a pale pink pastel and apply light strokes of reddish brown between the fingers to separate them. Like his face, the fingers are fairly chubby so you don't need to put too much detail on them. Blend the marks with your fingertips if necessary to create soft transitions in the flesh tones.

15 If necessary, adjust the flesh tones on the boy's arms and fingers. Here, the artist judged that the face was too dark, so she applied some lighter flesh tones – a very pale orangey beige – to the highlights to redress the balance. Apply a range of browns to his hair to build up the texture and depth of colour.

16 Add a thin white line for the grandmother's necklace. Darken her lips and inner mouth; adjust the flesh tones. Redefine the creases around the nose and mouth, if necessary.

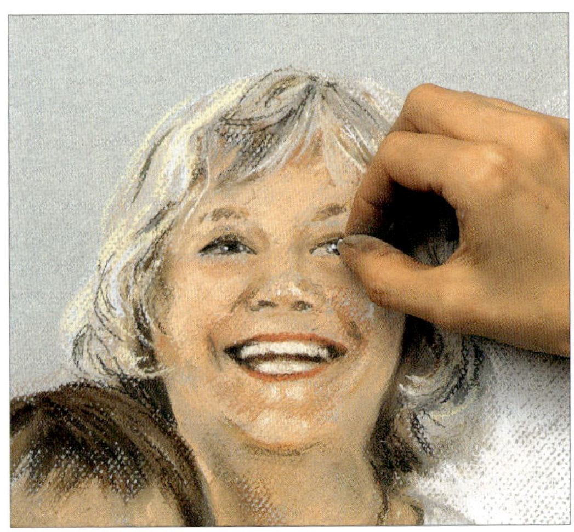

17 The final stage is to put in some detail in the eyes – the black pupils and some tiny dots of white for the catchlights.

The finished drawing

This is a relaxed and informal portrait that captures the sitters' moods and personalities. Using soft pastel has allowed the artist to build up the flesh tones gradually, achieving a convincingly life-like effect. Leaving the grandmother's hands slightly unfinished helps to create a sense of movement as she claps her hands together – in much the same way as a blurred photograph tells us that a subject is moving.

In wide smiles, the lips are stretched taut across the arc of the teeth. We see more of the upper teeth than the lower teeth; sometimes only the tops of the lower teeth are visible and almost never the gums.

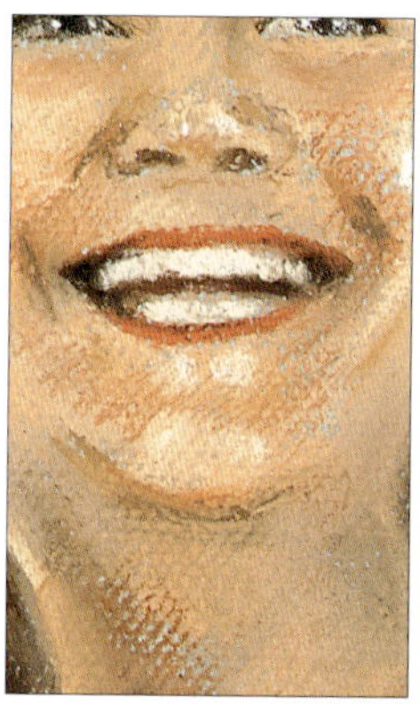

Leaving the hands unfinished creates a sense of movement.

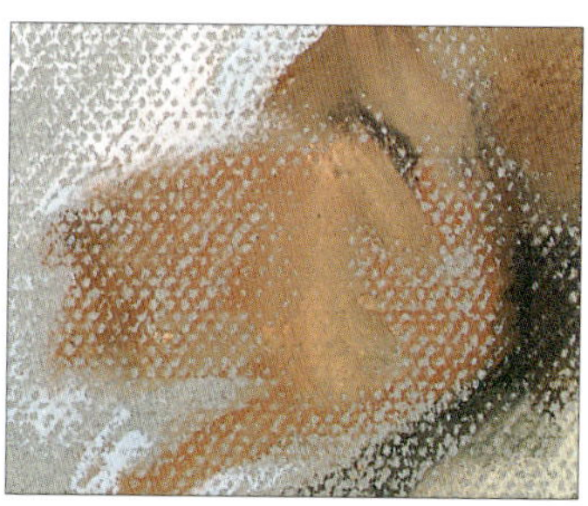

The eyes sparkle: a tiny dot of white is sufficient to bring them alive.

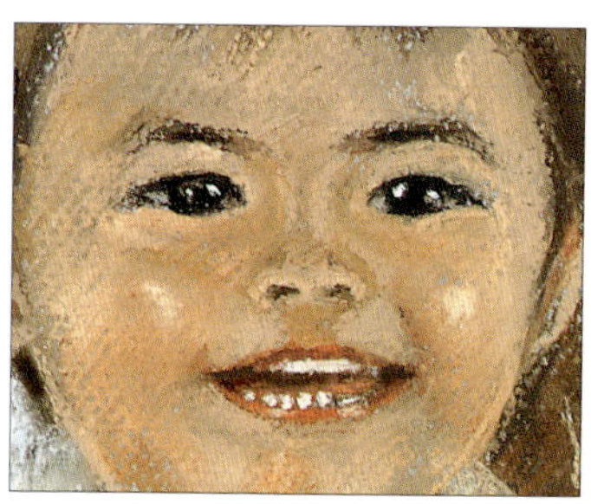

Note how many different tones there are within the hair.

Character portrait in charcoal

Markets are a great place to do quick sketches or take snapshots of people going about their daily business, which you can then work up into more detailed portraits at a later date. People are so engrossed in what they're doing that they're unlikely to take much notice of you – so your photos and sketches may be much more natural.

Here, the artist decided to omit both the background and the woman on the left and to concentrate on making a character portrait of the man – but you could, of course, include the setting, too, provided you kept the main emphasis of the drawing on his face.

This particular portrait gains much of its strength from the fact that there is direct eye contact between the subject and the artist, which immediately brings the portrait to life and makes the viewer feel involved in the scene. His gaze is quizzical, perhaps even slightly challenging, and even without the inclusion of the market setting, his slightly hunched pose and wrinkled face indicate that he leads a hard life.

Charcoal is a lovely medium for character portraits and, like black-and-white reportage or documentary-style photographs, a monochrome drawing has a strength and immediacy that works particularly well with this kind of subject. The same drawing in colour would have a very different feel – and probably far less impact. Why not try the same project in coloured pencil, too, to see the difference?

Materials

- *Fine pastel paper*
- *Thin charcoal stick*
- *Compressed charcoal stick*
- *Kneaded eraser*

The pose

In this scene two market traders in Turkey were spotted by chance rather than asked to pose formally. So these are character portraits. The artist concentrated on the man on the right, as the three-quarters pose, with direct eye contact, is more interesting than the head-on view of the lady. He has a strong profile, while the woman's face is more rounded and her features less clearly defined. The plastic sheeting could be confusing so it was omitted.

1 Using a thin stick of charcoal, map out the lines of the pose. Look at the angle of the shoulders and back and at where imaginary vertical lines intersect, so that you can place elements correctly in relation to one another. Here, for example, the peak of the man's cap is almost directly in line with his wrist.

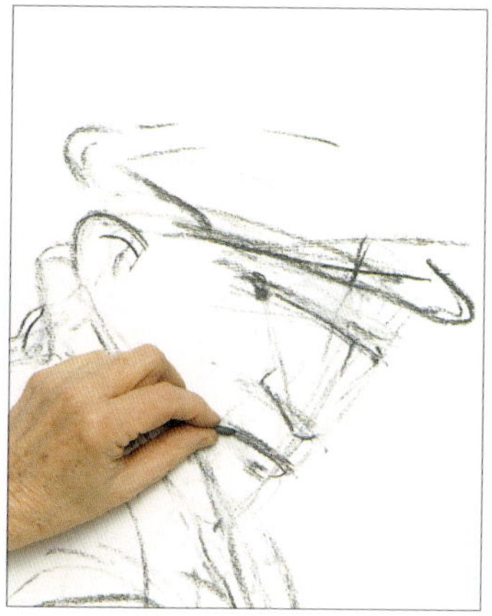

2 Still using the thin charcoal stick, lightly put in guidelines to help you place the facial features. Draw a line through the forehead and down to the bottom of the chin, lines across the face to mark the level of the eyes, the base of the nose and the mouth, and an inverted triangle from the eyes down to the nose.

3 Refine the facial features and roughly block in the fur collar on the man's jacket. (It provides a dark frame for the face.)

4 Lightly draw the curve of the top of the skull. Although you can't actually see the skull beneath the cap, you can use the tilt of the head and the features you've already put in to work out where it should be. Remember that the base of the eye socket is generally about halfway down the face, so the top of the skull is likely to be higher than you might think.

5 Now you can draw the cap. Without the faint guideline of the skull that you drew in the previous step, you'd probably make the cap too flat and place it too low on the head. Draw the eyes and eyebrows and the sockets of the eyes. Already you can see how the form is beginning to develop.

▶

6 Sharpen the line of the far cheek and apply loose hatching on the far side of the face (which is in shadow) and on the forehead, where the cap casts a shadow.

Assessment time

The facial features are in place and most of the linear work has been completed, although the details need to be refined and the eyes darkened. Now you can begin to introduce some shading, which will make the figure look three-dimensional and bring the portrait to life.

The jacket looks flat. There is nothing to tell us how heavy it is or what kind of fabric it is made from.

Shading has introduced some modelling on the far side of the face, but more is needed.

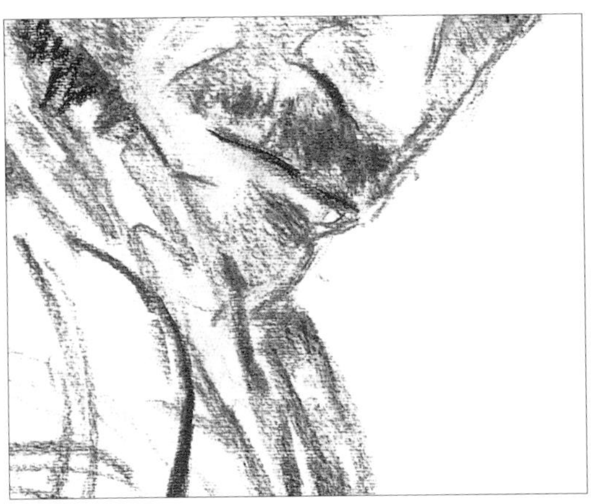

7 Using a compressed charcoal stick, which is very dense and black, put in the line of the mouth.

8 Again, using the compressed charcoal stick, put in the pupils of the eyes, remembering to leave tiny catchlights.

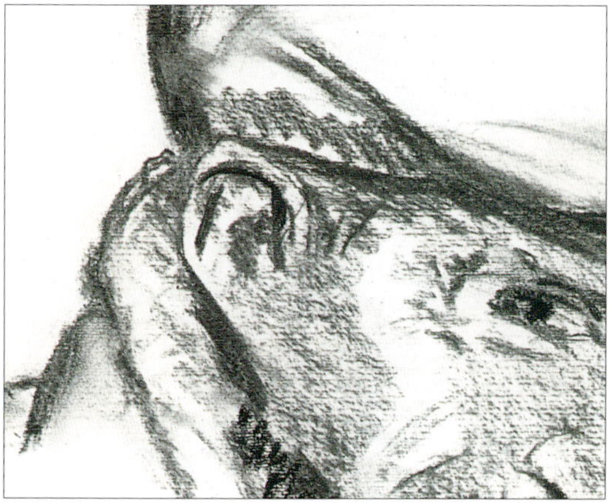

9 Using the side of a thin stick of charcoal, very lightly shade the right-hand side of the man's face. The shadow is not as deep here as on the far side of the face, but this slightly darker tone serves two purposes as it helps to show how tanned and weatherbeaten his face is and also creates some modelling on the cheeks.

10 Using the tip of your little finger, which is the driest part of your hand, carefully blend the charcoal on the right cheek to a smooth, mid-toned grey.

11 Using a kneaded eraser, pick out the highlighted wrinkles on the face, and the whites of the eyes. Each time you use it, wipe the eraser on scrap paper to clean off the charcoal and so prevent smudges.

Tip: To get a fine point on the eraser for intricate areas, mould the eraser with your fingers.

12 Block in the dark, shaded side of the cap, using the side of the charcoal stick. Note that the cap is not a uniform shade of black all over: leave areas on the top untouched to show where the highlights fall.

13 Using compressed charcoal, block in the fur collar on the jacket and smooth out the marks with your fingers. By making slightly jagged marks, you can suggest the texture of the fur. Note how the face immediately stands out more strongly when framed by the dark fur.

14 Put in the dark crease lines of the folds in the jacket. The deep creases help to show the weight of the fabric.

15 Using the side of the charcoal, apply tone over the jacket, leaving highlights on the sleeve untouched.

16 Using the side of your hand in a circular motion, blend the charcoal to a smooth, flat tone.

The finished drawing

This portrait is full of character. Note the classic composition, which draws our attention to the face – the overall shape of the portrait is triangular, with the strong line of the back leading up to the face and forming the first side of the triangle, and a straight line down from the peak of the cap to the arm forming the second side.

In addition, the face is positioned roughly 'on the third' – a strong placement for the most important element in the drawing. The three-quarter viewpoint with the sitter's face turned partway towards the viewer, means that there is direct eye contact, immediately involving the viewer in the painting. The sitter's strong profile is also evident from this viewpoint.

Wrinkles in the skin are picked out using the sharp edge of a kneaded eraser.

The crease lines and variations in tone show the weight and bulkiness of the fabric.

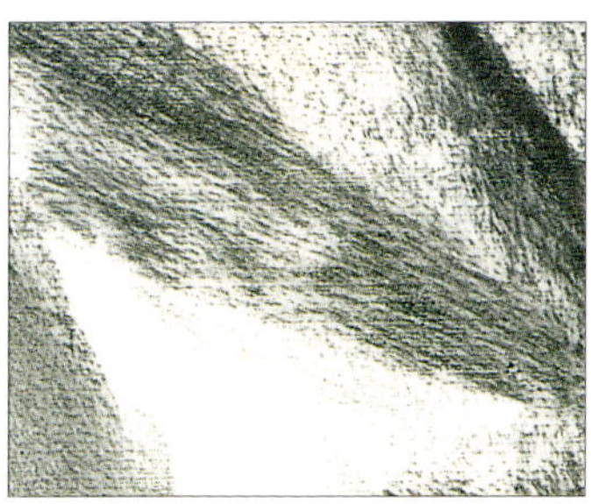

The direct eye contact between sitter and viewer makes this a very strong portrait.

Character study in watercolour

A good portrait is about more than capturing a good likeness of the sitter: it should also reveal something of their personality and interests. You can do this by including things that they would use in everyday life as props. You might, for example, ask a keen musician to sit at the piano. Alternatively, you could depict someone at his or her place of work. The sitter for this portrait loves literature and is an avid reader – hence the book that she is holding and the piles of books in the background. Take care, however, not to allow the background and props to dominate. Here the books are little more than simple, graphic shapes. If elements threaten to overpower, reduce their importance in the composition – or even omit them altogether.

As we grow older, we inevitably acquire a few wrinkles and 'laughter lines', all of which give a face character and expression. Here, the artist decided to make a pencil underdrawing and to allow many of the pencil marks to show through in the final watercolour painting. The result is a fresh, lively portrayal that combines the very best characteristics of two very different media – the linear quality of pencil and soft, wet-into-wet washes of watercolour paint in the skin tones. He primed his watercolour paper with an acrylic gesso, which renders any pencil marks softer and blacker than they would otherwise be and creates an interesting, slightly broken texture.

Don't worry about creating an exact likeness of your sitter in the early stages, or you may get caught up in the fine detail and lose sight of the overall composition and proportions. If you get the basics right, the rest will follow.

Materials

- *Heavy watercolour paper primed with acrylic gesso*
- *B pencil*
- *Watercolour paints: raw sienna, cadmium orange, indigo, ultramarine blue, raw umber, black, vermilion, cerulean blue*
- *Brushes: small and medium round*

The pose

This elderly lady's face is full of character and, by including the book that she is reading and the piles of books in the background, the artist has also managed to tell us a little about her interests. However, the television in the background adds nothing to the scene; in fact, it distracts attention from her face. For this reason, the artist decided to omit it.

1 Using a B pencil, begin your underdrawing by putting in faint marks and dots for the relative positions of features such as the crown and chin and the outer and inner points of the eyes. Then work upwards from the chin, putting in the central line through the head, which tilts here at an angle of about 20°. Put in a little shading on the left side of the face and smudge it with your finger– simply to help define areas rather than to add tone.

2 Once you've mapped out the position of the features, you can gradually put in more details, such as the spectacles. Loosely hatch shaded areas such as the left cheek; this is simply to delineate the extent of these areas rather than introduce modelling.

3 It's a good idea to lightly hatch or shade part of the area around your subject's head fairly early on in a portrait. Also put in any areas of shade that help you to keep track of where you are in the portrait – for example, in the hair and on the neck.

4 Although you only want to give an impression of the dress fabric, rather than slavishly copy every last detail, you can use elements of the pattern as a guide to the placement of other features. Here, for example, the top of the black pattern just below the neckline is roughly level with the top of the right sleeve. Look, also, for folds within the fabric that cast slight shadows, which suggest the body beneath.

5 Once you've mapped out the figure, decide how much of the surroundings to include and what to change or omit. Although the artist here chose to leave out the television set, he put in a dark background which frames the face and allows the white of the hair to stand out. He also lightly sketched the piles of books, as the sitter's interest in literature is an element of her character he wanted to convey.

6 Begin to define the different planes of the fingers. (Note that the thumb on the right hand is foreshortened: we're looking at the underside of the thumb, with the nail on the very edge.) Put in some shading on the sitter's right arm. There is a strong area of shadow in the underside of the forearm, which clearly shows the muscles of the lower arm. Although you're only establishing the basic lights and darks at this stage, this is the beginning of creating some modelling.

7 To make them stand out more, put in some stronger tones in the facial features – the nostrils, the pupils of the eyes, and the deep creases around the mouth – as well as in the metal rims of the spectacles. Use a kneaded eraser to retrieve any highlights that have been accidentally covered over – for example, on the tip of the nose and within the spectacles. For very fine details, use the sharp edge of the eraser, or mould it to a fine point with your fingertips.

Assessment time

Once you've mapped in the position of the books to the left of the sitter, the pencil underdrawing is virtually complete; now you are ready to begin applying the colour. The underdrawing is relatively detailed and the time and attention you've taken to produce it will pay dividends later, when you come to apply the colour. Although there is not much modelling, you have established the main areas of lights and dark, which you can use as a guide when applying the different tones in watercolour. Most importantly, there is plenty of linear detail in the face, which you will be able to retain in the finished painting.

These pencil lines are strong enough to show through light watercolour washes.

The stacks of books provide a graphic element in the composition without detracting from the figure.

8 Mix a very dilute wash of raw sienna and cadmium orange and, using a small round brush, wash it over the arms and face, omitting only the very bright highlights on the face. Leave to dry. Then mix a blackish blue from indigo and ultramarine blue. Using a medium round brush, wash it over the darkest areas of the background and leave to dry. Note how the brushstrokes of the primer are visible in places, adding texture to the washes.

9 Using a medium round brush, apply a fairly strong wash of cadmium orange over the sitter's dress, leaving a few small areas untouched for the very lightest colours. Leave to dry.

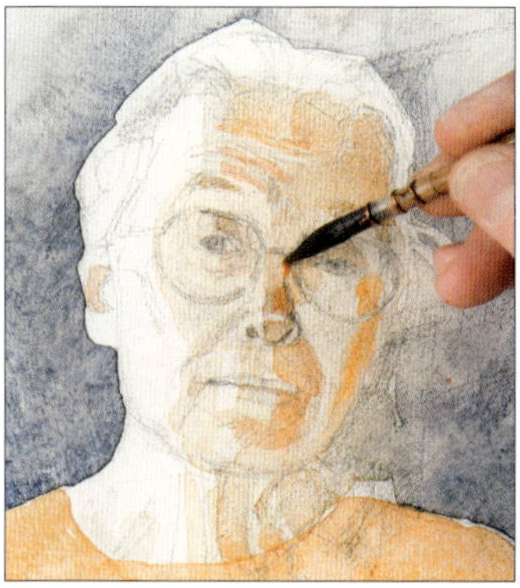

10 Use the oranges from the previous two steps, for the dark and mid tones on the face and neck. The colours are modified a little by the pencil lines that are already there.

11 Mix a warm brown from raw sienna and a little raw umber and put in the pattern of the dress, leaving the underlying cadmium orange showing through where necessary. Leave to dry. Then, using a mix of black and ultramarine blue, put in the darkest tones of the books in the background and the lines of the books behind the sitter's left shoulder, as well as the shadow between the book she is holding and its cover. Allow to dry.

Tips:

- Assess the relative sizes of the various books carefully.
- Leave some of the blue-black mix from Step 8 showing through for pages of the books in the background.

12 Darken the warm brown used for the dress in Step 11 and put in a little more of the mid-to-dark patterning. Continue with the skin tones, using the various tones of the orange and reddish mixes used before and paying attention to the lights and darks. Apply a touch of vermilion to the lips.

13 On the arm and hands, apply dilute washes of vermilion and cadmium orange, singly and together, wet into wet. Using very dilute cerulean blue, 'draw' faint marks on the open book to indicate print and pictures. Wash the same dilute mix over the books to her left.

14 Continue building up the layers on the skin tone, using slightly darker versions of the previous mixes. Brighten the red of the lips with a touch of vermilion. Using the blue-black mix from Step 11 and a small round brush that comes to a fine tip, paint in the metal rim of the spectacles. Darken the pupils of the eyes with the same blue-black mix and wash a very dilute grey into the shaded parts of the hair to create some texture and tonal variation. Be careful not to colour the hair grey, however – your grey shading should, on the contrary, make the white of the hair more striking.

Tips:

- The spectacle rims catch a lot of reflected light, so the outer edge virtually disappears in places. Observe this carefully and leave gaps where necessary.
- If the hair is to read as white in the finished painting, all of the face – except for the very brightest highlights – must have some tone, however dilute.
- Before you make any last-minute adjustments, make sure that your palette and water jars are clean so that you do not risk muddying your colours in the final stages.

15 Use the same blue-black mix for the very darkest patterning on the dress. Don't try to put in every detail, or the pattern will overpower the painting. A general impression is sufficient. At this point you may find that you need to deepen the very pale orange applied in Step 9; if you do, ensure that all other colours on the dress are completely dry or they will blend wet into wet and ruin the effect.

16 You may find that the very dark tones of the dress now dominate and that you need to adjust the skin tones accordingly. Use the same mixes as before, taking care not to lose sight of the overall tonality of the painting.

The finished painting

This is a sensitive portrait that captures the sitter's expression and personality beautifully. Carefully controlled wet-into-wet washes have been used to build up the skin tones and create subtle modelling on the face and neck; the white of the paper has also been exploited to good effect in the highlight areas. The wrinkles and creases in the face, drawn in during the initial pencil underdrawing, add character and expression and show through the later watercolour washes without dominating them. The distracting elements in the background have been reduced to graphic shapes and monochromatic areas of mid and dark tone, against which the figure stands out clearly. The composition and use of light and shade help to convey the lively personality of the sitter.

The patterning of the dress has been subtly painted so that it does not overpower or dominate the portrait.

The wrinkles are conveyed through linear pencil marks.

Note how the very brightest highlights are left untouched by paint.

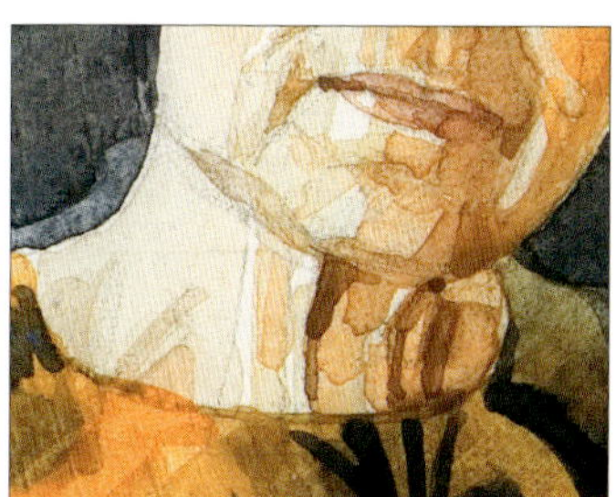

The background has been reduced to a series of graphic, monochromatic elements.

Seated figure in interior

As you have discovered, painting someone in a setting allows you to say much more about them than you can in a straightforward head-and-shoulders portrait. You might include things that reveal something about your subject's interests – a musician with a guitar, perhaps, or an antiques collector surrounded by some of his or her possessions – or their work. In a domestic setting, the décor of the room itself is very often a reflection of your subject's tastes and personality.

The most important thing is not to allow the surroundings to dominate. The focus of the painting must remain on the person. This usually means that you have to deliberately subdue some of the detail around your subject, either by using muted or cool colours for the surroundings, so that your subject becomes more prominent, or, if the setting is very cluttered, by leaving some things out of your painting altogether.

Materials

- *3B pencil*
- *Rough watercolour board*
- *Watercolour paints: raw umber, alizarin crimson, cobalt blue, lemon yellow, phthalocyanine blue*
- *Brushes: medium flat, Chinese, fine round, old brush for masking*
- *Masking fluid*
- *Craft (utility) knife or scalpel*
- *Sponge*

Reference photographs

Here the artist used two photographs as reference – one for the seated, semi-silhouetted figure and one for the shaft of light that falls on the table top. Both photographs are dark and it is difficult to see much detail, but they show enough to set the general scene and give you scope to use your imagination. Instead of slavishly copying every last detail, you are free to invent certain aspects of the scene, or to embellish existing ones.

The highlight on the figure's hair is very atmospheric.

The shaft of bright sunlight illuminates part of the table top while almost everything else is in deep shade.

1 Using a 3B pencil, lightly sketch your subject, making sure you get the tilt of her head and the angles of the table, papers and books right.

2 Mix a warm, pinky orange from raw umber and alizarin crimson. Using a medium flat brush, wash it over the background, avoiding the highlight areas on the window. Add more alizarin crimson to the mixture for the warmest areas, such as the girl's shirt and the left-hand side of the curtain, and more raw umber for the cooler areas, such as the wall behind the girl and the glazing bars on the window. Leave to dry.

3 Mix a very pale green from cobalt blue and lemon yellow and, using a Chinese brush, paint the lightest foliage shades outside the window, remembering to leave some white areas for the very bright sky beyond.

Tip: To enhance the impression of bright sunlight streaming through the window, take care not to paint foliage right up to the edge of the window frame. Instead, allow the white of the paper to stand for the very brightest patches of sky.

Assessment time

Mix a very pale blue from cobalt blue and a touch of raw umber and put in the cooler tones inside the room – the left-hand side, which the shaft of sunlight coming through the window doesn't reach, and the shadows under the table. Leave to dry.

You have now established the warm and cool areas of the painting, which you will build on in all the subsequent stages. Because of her position within the frame (roughly in the first third), the girl is the main focus of interest in the painting, even though she is largely in shadow. Keep this at the forefront of your mind as you begin to put in the detail and as you continually assess the compositional balance while painting.

This area is left unpainted, as it receives the most direct sunlight.

The warm colour of the girl's shirt helps to bring her forwards in the painting.

The shadow areas are the coolest in tone. They recede.

4 Mix a warm brown from alizarin crimson and raw umber and paint the girl's hair. Mix a rich red from alizarin crimson, cobalt blue and a little raw umber and, using a Chinese brush, paint the curtain. Apply several vertical brushstrokes to the curtain, wet into wet, to build up the tone and give the impression that it hangs in folds.

5 Using the same red mixture, paint the shoulders and back of the girl's shirt. Add more raw umber to the mixture and paint the shadow area between the wall and the mirror, immediately behind the girl. Mix a warm blue from phthalocyanine blue and a little alizarin crimson, and paint the dark area beneath the table using loose brushstrokes.

6 Using an old brush, 'draw' the shapes of leaves in the bottom left-hand corner in masking fluid. Leave to dry. Mix a rich, dark brown from raw umber and a little alizarin crimson and, using a fine round brush, paint the darkest areas of the girl's hair.

7 Add a little raw umber to the mixture for the lighter areas of hair around the face. Build up the shadow areas in the foreground of the scene, overlaying colours as before. Darken the girl's shirt in selected areas with the alizarin crimson, cobalt blue and raw umber mixture.

8 Mix a mid-toned green from phthalocyanine blue and lemon yellow and, using a fine round brush, dot this mixture into the foliage that can be seen through the right-hand side of the window. Mix a very pale purplish blue from pthalocyanine blue and a little alizarin crimson and darken the glazing bars of the window.

9 Paint the area under the window in a warm mixture of alizarin crimson and phthalocyanine blue. Mix a dark, olive green from raw umber and phthalocyanine blue and, making loose calligraphic strokes, paint the fronds of the foreground plant. Brush a very dilute version of the same mixture on to the lower part of the mirror. Build up the background tones.

10 Mix a muted green from phthalocyanine blue and lemon yellow. Brush it over the background behind the girl. Because the green is relatively cool, it helps to separate the girl from the background. It also provides a visual link between this area and the foliage on the right.

11 Paint a few vertical strokes on the curtain in a dark mixture of alizarin crimson and phthalocyanine blue. This helps to make the highlight on top of the pile of books stand out more clearly. Mix a warm brown from raw umber and phthalocyanine blue and paint under the window.

12 Rub off the masking fluid from the bottom left-hand corner. Continue building up the tones overall, using the same paint mixtures as before and loose, random brushstrokes to maintain a feeling of spontaneity.

13 Mix a very pale wash of raw umber and lightly brush it on to some of the exposed areas in the bottom left-hand corner. Build up more dark tones in the foreground, using the same mixtures as before.

14 Using a craft (utility) knife or scalpel, carefully scratch off some of the highlights on the bottle on the table. Paint the wall behind the girl in a pale, olivey green mixture of raw umber and phthalocyanine blue.

15 Brush a little very pale cobalt blue into the sky area so that this area does not look too stark and draw attention away from the main subject.

16 Continue building up tones by overlaying colours. Use very loose brushstrokes and change direction continually, as this helps to convey a feeling of the dappled light that comes through the window.

17 Using a 3B pencil, define the edges of the papers on the table. Mix a very pale wash of phthalocyanine blue and, using a fine round brush, carefully brush in shadows under the papers on the table to give them more definition. Dip a sponge in a blue-biased mixture of phthalocyanine blue and alizarin crimson and gently press it around the highlight area on the floor to suggest the texture of the carpet.

The finished painting
There is a wonderful sense of light and shade in this painting, and the loose brushstrokes give a feeling of great freshness and spontaneity. The scene is beautifully balanced, both in terms of its distribution of colours and in the way that dark and light areas are counterposed.

Pale, cool colours on the wall help to differentiate the girl from the background.

The foreground is loosely painted with overlayed colours, creating a feeling of spontaneity.

Sunlight pours through the window, illuminating the books and papers. Much of this area is left unpainted.

Figure in the landscape

When you include the setting in a painting as well as a person, you need to decide how much of the picture space to allocate to each. If you want to create a character portrait in which the person is the main focus of interest, then you need to make that person a large part of the picture as a whole; a mere hint of the surroundings may be sufficient. If, on the other hand, you want to set the figure in context so that the surroundings become an important part of the overall story, then the landscape or interior may well take up the majority of the picture space. Here, the artist decided to include the wider landscape as a way of bringing back memories of a happy family holiday.

In compositional terms, the position of the figure in a portrait such as this is just as important as the overall amount of space it occupies. Although the girl in this painting takes up only a small part of the scene, it is to her that our eyes are drawn. This is partly because the artist has changed the composition of her reference photo and positioned the child 'on the third' – a classic device for leading the viewer's eye to the main point of interest in a painting – and partly because the beach, sea and headland are painted in less detail.

In situ, you could never do more than make a few quick reference sketches of a scene such as this, as young children never stay still for long. This is where a digital camera can prove invaluable; you can fire off a whole series of shots in a matter of seconds and also play back the images immediately to check that you've got all the reference material you're likely to need before you leave the scene.

Materials

- *Watercolour board*
- *Acrylic paints: brilliant blue, yellow ochre, lemon yellow, brilliant yellow green, alizarin crimson, cadmium red, phthalocyanine blue, white*
- *Brushes: large round, medium round, fine round*
- *HB pencil*

The pose

This shot of a little girl playing on a beach is the kind of photo that every parent has in the family album. However, she is positioned so close to the edge of the frame that part of her shadow is cut off. The sea and headland take up so much of the photo that they dominate the composition.

1 Using an HB pencil, lightly sketch the scene, putting in the lines of balance of the figure (the central spine and the tilt of the shoulders). Note how the artist has changed the composition by positioning the little girl 'on the third', including less of the headland and moving the boat to balance the composition and frame the figure.

2 Mix a thin wash of brilliant blue with a little phthalocyanine blue acrylic paint and, using a large brush, wash it over the sky and sea, making the mix a little darker for the sea. Mix a sand colour from yellow ochre and alizarin crimson and wash it over the beach, adding more yellow ochre for the foreground. Use a redder version of the sand mix for the girl's skin.

Tip: Make sure you leave some space above the little girl's head so that it stands out clearly against the blue of the sea. In the photograph her pale hat is too close to the line of the headland.

3 While the paper is still wet, brush a dilute purple (mixed from alizarin crimson and brilliant blue) over the wet sand, allowing the colour to spread wet into wet. Apply a pale wash of the sand colour over the headland. When dry, mix a dark green from phthalocyanine blue, lemon yellow and yellow ochre and dab in the vegetation. Add a little cadmium red and phthalocyanine blue to a thicker mix of yellow ochre and dot in sand and pebbles in the foreground.

4 Mix brilliant yellow green and brilliant blue to give a vivid blue and brush this colour on to the sea along the horizon. Look for different tones of blue and green in the sea and brush them in, using various versions of the vivid blue mix and adding white to the mix in places. For the wet sand along the shoreline, mix a slightly thicker, pale blue violet from alizarin crimson, white and brilliant blue, and apply using a dry brush.

5 Using a fine round brush, put in the white of the little girl's sun hat, bucket and bathing costume. Mix a warm flesh colour from cadmium red, white and a tiny bit of yellow ochre and put in the shaded tones on the little girl's body – mostly on the left-hand side, but also on the inner edges of her right thigh and calf.

6 Use phthalocyanine blue for the bright blue of the little girl's bathing costume, and a pale purple mix for the shaded side of her sun hat. Continue working on the flesh tones, looking for the light and dark tones within the figure. Use variations of the mixes from the previous step for the darker tones and a mix of lemon yellow, white and cadmium red for the sunlit side of the figure, which is warm in tone.

Tip: You may find it easier to judge the shapes if you turn your painting upside down. This helps you to reproduce how things look, rather than following the way your mind says they should look.

Assessment time

The figure requires very little extra work other than adding the cast shadow on the sand. Although the combination of different colours in the sea works well, there is no real sense of the wavelets breaking on the shore.

The boundary between sea and shore can be made clearer by making more of the breaking waves.

Adding a little more detail and texture to the foreground sand will help to bring it forwards in the picture.

7 Brush more colour into the water, using the same green and violet mixes as before. Mix white and the pale blue-violet mix from Step 4 and, using both your fingers and a relatively dry brush and slightly thicker paint than before, dot in the breaking wavelets along the shoreline.

Tip: It's important not to spend too long on one area; instead, keep alternating between the main subject and the background, so that the whole painting moves along at the same pace and you can continually assess the tonal values.

8 Mix a violet shadow colour from the pale blue-violet mix and phthalocyanine blue and, using a fine round brush and fairly thin paint, brush in the shadow that the little girl's body casts on the sand.

9 Using a fine brush, paint the boat in a purplish-blue mix of phthalocyanine blue and alizarin crimson and touch in the light edge of the sail in white.

10 Scumble thicker mixes of yellow ochre and reddish browns into the foreground to create some texture in the sand and pebbles. Paint the sunlit sides of the pebbles in lighter grey-purple mixes.

The finished painting

Acrylic paints are a good choice for a subject such as this as they come in a huge range of colours and can be used very thinly, like watercolour, for delicate areas such as the wet sand, or thickly, like oils, for textural details in the foreground. This painting is full of light and sunshine, and the warm colours on the figure and foreground sand balance the cooler blues and greens of the landscape beautifully, while the composition leads the viewer's eye around the picture, from the figure of the little girl, up to the boat and then across to the headland and back to the girl again.

The modelling on the figure is subtle but effective and conveys the childish plumpness of the figure well.

Note how delicately the reflection in the wet sand has been painted.

Thicker paint, applied both with a brush and with the fingers, is used to give the breaking waves more solidity.

Informal portrait in watercolour

There's no rule that says a portrait has to be formal; a snapshot of a moment in time can be just as effective. Here, the artist took a series of photos of this young couple as they walked along, holding hands, on a sunny autumn afternoon and selected this shot as the one to work from because it was the only one that showed them looking directly at each other, oblivious to the camera. The fact that they are moving also gives the otherwise very static and calm scene more dynamism.

The other thing that makes the scene so appealing is the warm, dappled light. Because of its luminosity and translucency, watercolour is an obvious medium to choose to render the subtle effects of light and shade. Here, you can use wet-into-wet washes to build up the tones of the stonework and create the soft-edged shadows cast on the columns by the leaves. Combine this with wet-on-dry applications for the hard edges of the columns and areas that require more detailing, such as the figures and the foreground leaves. Remember, however, that you cannot apply a dark colour on top of a light one. You have to start with the lightest colour and work up to the darkest.

Materials

- *Heavy HP watercolour paper*
- *Watercolour paints: Prussian blue, raw umber, alizarin crimson, cadmium yellow, cadmium red, Venetian red, yellow ochre*
- *Gouache paint: white*
- *Brushes: large round, medium round, fine round*
- *HB pencil*

The pose

The couple are positioned one third of the way into the picture space – a classic compositional device, as the viewer's eye is immediately drawn to this area. The viewpoint has been chosen so that we are looking back along the row of columns; the line 'linking' the base of the columns seems to slope towards the vanishing point.

1 Using an HB pencil, lightly sketch the couple and their surroundings. Look for anything that you can use as a guide to where things are positioned. Look at the base of the row of columns in particular; as the columns recede into the distance, this line appears to slope upwards towards the vanishing point. Put in the vertical lines of the columns.

2 Continue with the underdrawing until you feel you have put down all the information you may need. The fluted facets of the columns and creases in the young couple's clothing are all things that you can make use of when it comes to doing the painting.

3 Mix a dark olivey green from Prussian blue and raw umber and, using a large round brush, put in the dark tones of the stonework and shadows. Then mix a very dilute reddish orange from alizarin crimson and cadmium yellow and wash it over the sunlit parts of the columns and ground. Use firm, straight strokes for the edges of the columns, otherwise you will get a wobbly effect.

4 Continue painting the columns, with variations on the previous mixes as appropriate. Using a medium round brush, loosely dab in the palest colour of fallen leaves using a dilute wash of cadmium yellow and cadmium red. Mix a flesh colour from Venetian red with a touch of yellow ochre and paint the exposed skin, leaving the highlights untouched. Begin painting their clothes, using Prussian blue with a hint of Venetian red for the jeans and Venetian red for the girl's top.

5 Touch raw umber wet into wet on to the denim jeans to create tonal variation, leaving some areas very pale. For the boy's jacket, mix a dark, purplish black from Prussian blue, alizarin crimson and a little raw umber. Paint the girl's hair in an orangey red mix of raw umber and alizarin crimson, and the boy's hair in a mix of olive green and raw umber.

6 For the darker tones in the girl's hair, use a purplish black mix of Prussian blue and alizarin crimson. Use short, delicate brushstrokes and a fine round brush to build up some texture and detail. Put in the mid-toned leaves using a fine round brush and a reddish brown mix of cadmium yellow and alizarin crimson. Work wet into wet for the background leaves and wet on dry for those in the foreground.

Tip: Having more texture and detail in the foreground than in the background is one way of creating an impression of distance. The viewer's eye assumes that any textured, detailed areas are closer.

7 Apply more warm browns and pinks to the stonework, cutting in around the girl's head to help define her better. Using warmer, slightly darker versions of the previous mixes, begin to build up some modelling on the faces and hair. Darken the clothing, looking for the different tones and creases within the fabric that imply the movement of the limbs beneath.

Tips: Count the columns and their 'flutes' carefully to make sure you put in the right number. Aim for nothing more than a loose impression of the fallen leaves: if you try to put in every single one accurately, your painting will become very tight and laboured.

Assessment time
When you've put in all the basic elements of the composition and established the colours, look for areas that need to be strengthened. This looks a little flat in places, with insufficient contrast between the fore and background. The shadows, in particular, require work. Although the warm and cool colours give an impression of light and shade on the columns, the shadows of the leaves, which add real atmosphere, are missing.

The cast shadows of the leaves, which add real atmosphere to the scene, need to be added.

This highlight area on the girl's neck is too bright.

8 Deepen the shadows on the ground, using dark greys and browns. If you wish you can add a little white gouache to your mixes to create an opaque colour and brush in loose strokes to imply the dappled sunlight on the ground. Using a fine round brush and a range of reddish browns, put in the darkest colours of the fallen leaves.

9 Using short, broken brushstrokes and the same colours as before, build up the tone on the stonework columns. To create a sense of dappled light, add a little white gouache to your mixes for the most brightly lit areas and dab on small randomly-shaped marks for the cast shadows of the leaves.

The finished painting

This portrait exploits the characteristics of watercolour to the full, using wet-into-wet washes of translucent colour while still allowing the white of the paper to shine through. One of the keys to the success of a painting such as this is observing how the figures relate to one another: the time the artist spent on the underdrawing, establishing lines of balance such as the tilt of the shoulders and the angle of the hips, has paid dividends. Although loosely painted, the young couple's animated expressions are clear to see. The beautiful dappled lighting and soft colours give a warm glow to a portrait that is full of charm and life. The diagonal line of the stone columns is a strong compositional device that adds dynamism.

Dabs of opaque gouache, tinted with the appropriate colour, convey the cast shadows on the columns.

The way the light falls across the figures has been carefully observed and rendered, making the portrait atmospheric.

The animated expressions and body language bring the portrait to life, giving it movement and character.

Dancing couple in pastel pencil

When drawing a moving subject, it's helpful to take a photograph to use as reference. You can use a fast shutter speed to 'freeze' the action and risk losing the sense of movement that you wanted to capture. Alternatively, you can use a slower shutter speed so that there is some blur in the photo – but then you risk not being able to see all the detail as clearly as you would like. Here the artist wanted to see the detail clearly and elected to freeze the movement in the reference photo.

The challenge in this scenario is how to create that all-important sense of movement. Sometimes, even when the action is frozen, we know that the subject must be moving because the 'pose' itself is so precarious that we know it simply couldn't be held for more than a second or two. (Think, for example, of a ballerina in mid-pirouette.) Here the dancers have both feet touching the ground and the movement is not obvious at first glance, so you need to find other ways of conveying a sense of movement.

In this drawing the artist used two techniques to give a sense of movement: a 'ghost' image, indicating the position from which the limbs have just moved, and curved lines in the background, which follow the contours of the bodies. The same techniques could be applied just as well to other moving objects, for instance a horse racing at full stretch, or any sporting action.

Manikin
Also called a lay figure, a manikin (available from art supply stores), is a very handy tool for working out the lines of a pose. Use it to help you to work out the 'ghost' image.

Materials

- *Pastel paper*
- *HB pencil*
- *Pastel pencils: brown, spectrum orange, black, light sepia, pale brown, red, orange, pale blue, cream or pale yellow, red-brown*

The pose
Although the action has been 'frozen' in this photo, the woman's flowing hair and the fact that the right foot of both dancers is in the process of lifting off the ground indicate that they are, in fact, moving.

1 Sketch the scene, using an HB pencil. Imagine guidelines running across and down the image to help you: the man's left hand, for example, is roughly in line with his right heel.

2 Block in the man's flesh tones and hair in brown and emphasize the strongest lines of the pose. Using spectrum orange, block in the woman's flesh tones.

3 Block in both dancers' hair in black. For the shaded parts of the man's trousers and shirt and the woman's dress, apply light sepia. Use the same colour to draw the frill around the bottom of her dress.

4 Using the side of a pale brown pastel pencil, block in the background. Begin to put in stronger, curved lines in the background to emphasize the movement of the figures, echoing the curves of the moving arms.

Assessment time

With the same pale brown pencil, put in a 'ghost' image of the moving legs and arms. This, along with the curved lines in the background which echo the shape of the woman's back, helps to give an impression of movement. Now that the main lines of the drawing have been established, you can begin to refine the detail and add some colour to bring the drawing to life.

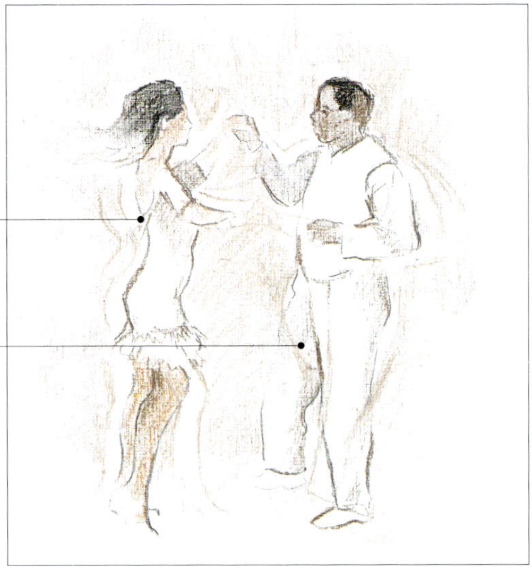

The figures need to stand out more from the background.

Shadows on the inner leg will help give it modelling and help make the dancer's legs a main focus point.

5 Using the same colours as before, darken the flesh tones so that the figures stand out from the background. Block in the woman's dress and the man's waistcoat in red overlaid with orange. (This optical mix of two colours creates a much more lively and interesting effect than a solid application of a single colour.)

6 Using a very pale blue pencil, put in the creases in the man's shirtsleeve and shade his right leg. Block in the shoes in black, leaving the highlights. Working around the 'ghost' image, put in some stronger curved lines that follow the contours of the bodies to enhance the sense of movement.

7 Darken the creases on the trousers and go over the trousers very lightly with a cream or very pale yellow pastel pencil. (Leaving the paper white would look too stark.) Draw the woman's hair, which is streaming out behind her as she moves, with quick flicks of a black pastel pencil.

8 Using horizontal marks, put in the floor. It is on a different plane to the background and using horizontal, rather than vertical, strokes helps to make this clear. Using a red-brown pencil, sharpen the edges of the figures – the hands, faces and the line of the woman's body and legs.

The finished drawing
The sense of movement in this drawing comes as much from the way the background has been handled as from the way the dancing couple has been drawn. The pastel pencil marks are light and free, which gives the drawing a feeling of energy. The synchronized action and engagement of the eyes between the dancers makes this a great study of a relationship. The fact that their whole bodies have been detailed as much (or as little) as their faces is important in a study of a physical activity such as dancing, whereas in a sitting pose the artist may decide to show far less detail in the body than in the sitter's face.

The hair streams out, making it obvious that the dancers are moving quickly.

The 'ghost' images imply that this is the position the figure has just moved from.

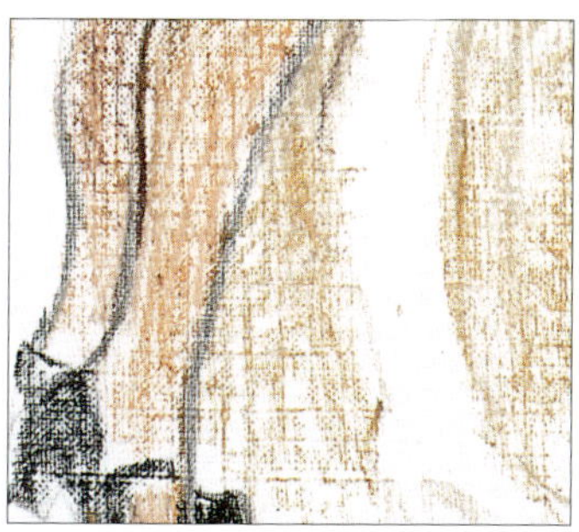

Curved pencil strokes in the background also help to imply movement.

Climber in mixed media

When you're drawing or painting a moving subject, there's obviously a limit to what you can do *in situ*. However, it's always a good idea to try to make a few quick sketches from life, even if you then go home and work up a more detailed drawing and painting later, as it makes you really look at the movements. It also enables you to try out different compositions.

In this project, the artist painted his son practising on an indoor climbing wall. As rock climbers spend time feeling for the next foot- or hand-hold, he was able to make a series of quick sketches and look at the musculature of his subject. He also took a series of photographs to use for reference.

In order to capture something of the energy involved in climbing, he wanted a medium that would allow him to work quickly and vigorously. He drew in the main lines of the body with broad sweeps of oil bar, and then wiped over them with a rag dipped in turpentine to soften the lines and spread the colour. Then he added soft pencil and soft pastel detailing on top, creating lively textural contrasts.

An action scene such as this, where the musculature of the subject is very obvious, is one scenario where a little knowledge of basic anatomy is really useful. You don't need to know the names of the individual muscles, but being aware of where they are and how they contract or extend in order for the limbs to move will make your drawings look more realistic. It also helps if you have some idea of the direction in which the muscles run, as you can imply the muscles beneath the surface of the skin by making your pencil marks or brushstrokes run in the right direction.

Materials

- *Heavy, rough watercolour paper*
- *Oil bars: raw sienna, manganese blue, Naples yellow*
- *Turpentine*
- *Old rag*
- *Graphite pencils: B and 9B*
- *Soft pastels: Naples yellow, burnt sienna, pale blue*

Preliminary sketches made *in situ*

These sketches were all made in around one minute from start to finish so that the artist could work out a composition that appealed to him and get in some practice at looking for the main lines of such a pose.

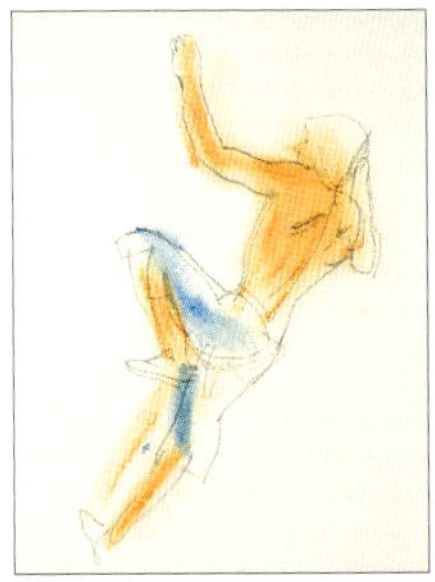

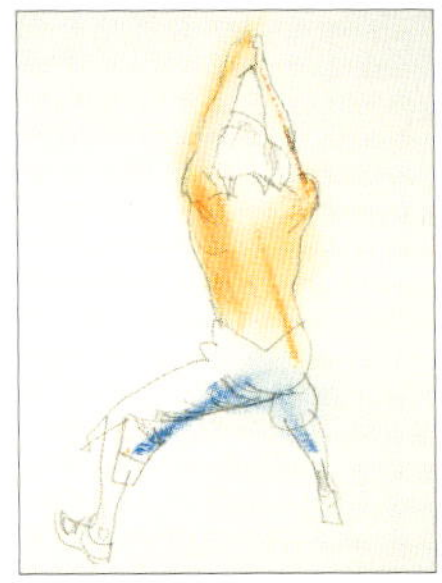

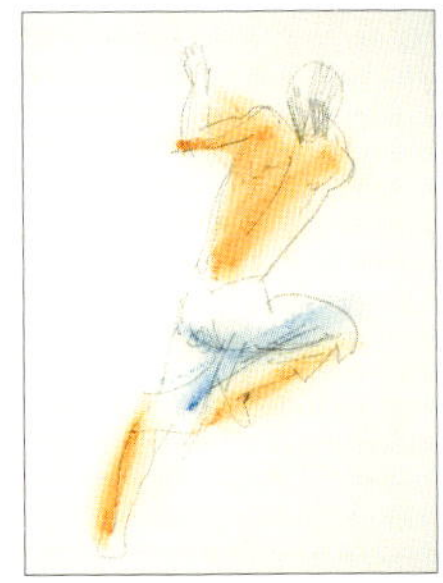

The pose

This is an extreme and unnatural position, so look for where each limb or feature sits in relation to others. The hands, for example, are positioned one above the other and, if you drop an imaginary line down from them, you will see that they align with the left heel. The shoulder and arm muscles are prominent, revealing the amount of effort required for the climber to cling on. There is a strong diagonal line running from the top of the left shoulder down to the left foot, which creates a dynamic composition.

1 Using raw sienna and manganese blue oil bars, put in broad sweeps of colour to represent the climber's back and blue trousers. Dip an old rag in turpentine and wipe it firmly over the oil bar marks to blend them and create the basic shapes.

Tips:

- Tape your paper to a drawing board so that it doesn't slip around.
- Aim for bold, generalized shapes rather than anything precise.

2 Using the raw sienna oil bar, draw in lines to represent the spine, the curve of the shoulder blades, the trapezius (the muscle that connects the shoulders to the spinal vertebrae) and the latissimus dorsi (the muscle that wraps around the sides of the trunk).

3 Wipe over the oil bar lines with a turpentine-soaked rag, as before, but this time do not blend them completely; aim to retain something of the linear quality. Roughly block in the hair with blue oil bar. Using a soft (B) pencil, outline the head and indicate the main muscle masses – for example, around the shoulder blades.

4 Continue using the pencil to put in more detail. Outline the trousers and put in any folds in the fabric that imply the movement of the muscles underneath – for example, under the right buttock and thigh. Use the oil bars to establish the basic shape of the legs, and draw in the feet using the pencil.

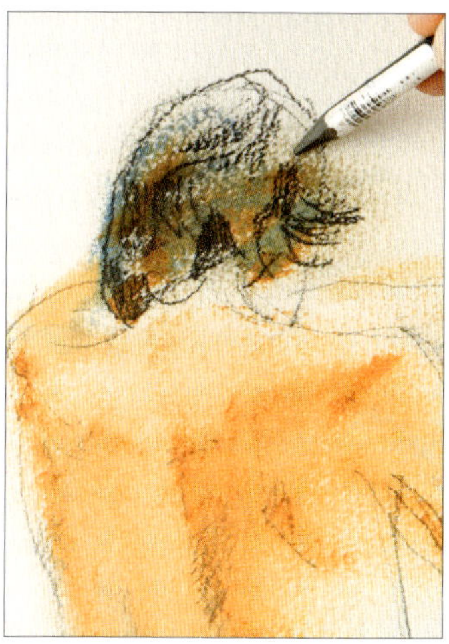

5 Apply raw sienna and a little manganese blue oil bar to the hair and lightly blend on the paper with turpentine to give a dark brown colour. Using a softer pencil (a 9B), put some linear detailing into the hair.

6 Again using the 9B pencil, apply some shading to the back, making closely spaced diagonal lines that follow the direction in which the muscles run. Strengthen the linear detailing on the trousers, again looking for the creases.

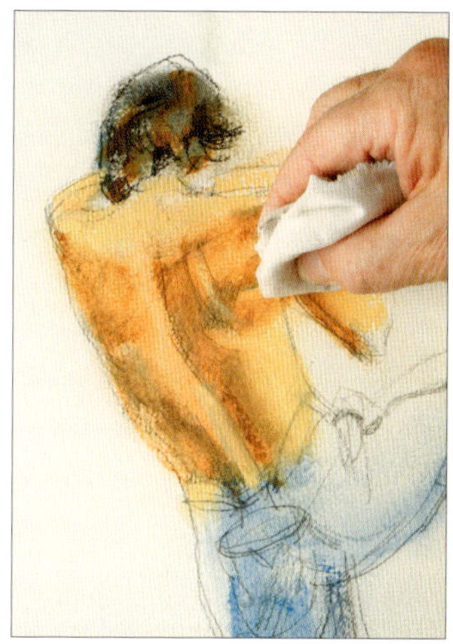

7 Use a Naples yellow oil bar to put in the highlights on the back, then blend the marks with a turpentine-soaked rag, as before. The turpentine will also darken and blur any underlying pencil marks.

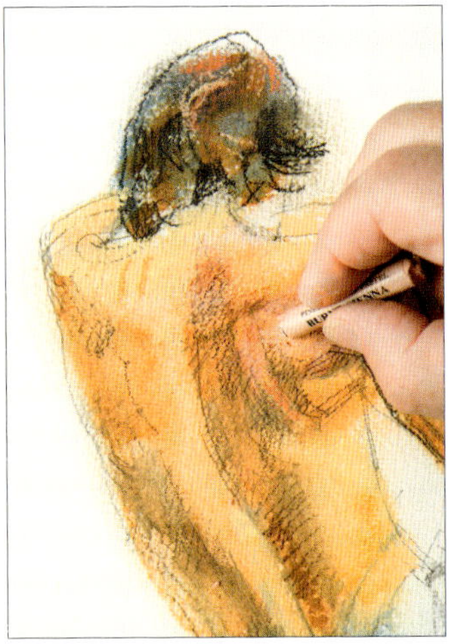

8 Now you can begin using soft pastels to create more texture and variation in the skin tones. Using various shades of Naples yellow and burnt sienna, add more colour and detail to the hair. Apply Naples yellow to the highlit areas of the back, blending the marks with your fingers.

Assessment time

Using a B pencil, sketch in the lines of the climbing wall and the main hand- and foot-holds. This provides a context for the scene without distracting from the figure. All the elements of the drawing are in place and the skin and muscle tones have been nicely rendered, but the drawing could be improved by adding a little more definition and shading over all.

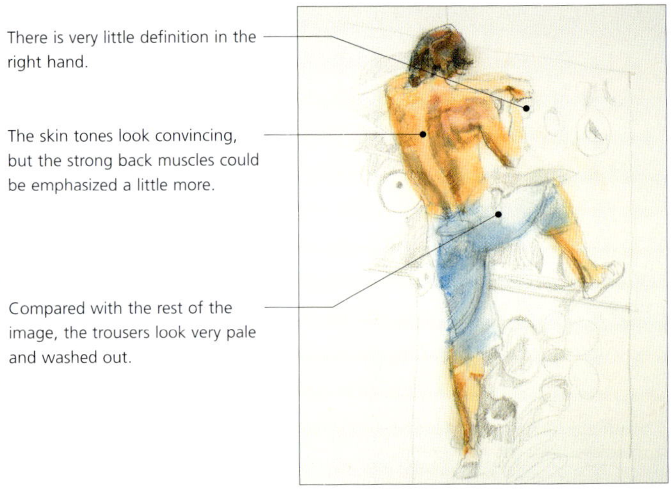

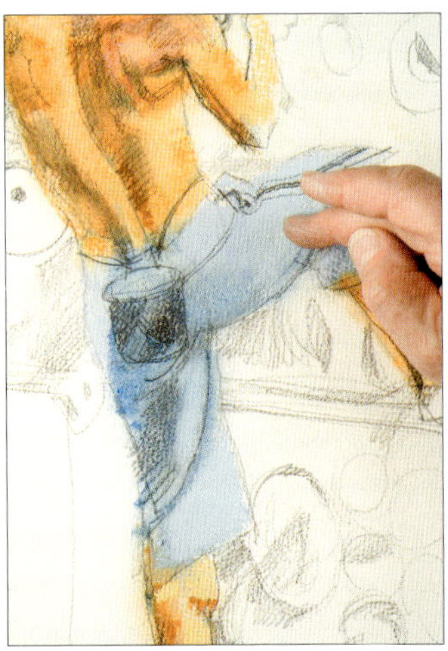

9 Using a 9B pencil, scribble in the chalk bag that the climber has attached to his belt loops. Strengthen the colour of the trousers by applying more blue soft pastel and blending the marks with your fingers.

10 Put in a few more lines of pull on the trousers. You can blend the pencil marks into the pastel with your fingers to create a darker tone in this area. Strengthen the cast shadows on the wall behind the climber.

11 Using a red soft pastel, draw in the red lines on the climbing shoes for a final finishing touch. Red is a very strong colour that immediately draws the eye, so be careful not to overdo it.

The finished drawing

This is a quickly executed drawing that nonetheless captures the figure in motion very well. The feeling of movement comes largely from the fact that the pose appears so precarious: our brains interpret the scene and tell us that the figure is moving simply because we know that such a position cannot be held for long. The taut back and shoulder muscles also reveal the amount of physical effort required on the part of the climber. Artistically, the combination of broad sweeps of colour overlaid with vigorous pencil detailing creates a feeling of tremendous energy, while the soft pastel marks on the skin and trousers create a pleasing contrast in texture. Because the climbing wall itself is not particularly worth looking at, it has only been faintly suggested with rough pencil sketching. This means that all attention is on the muscular tension and form of the climber, as well as the unusual angles of his position.

Oil bar marks blended with turpentine create solid areas of tone that are perfect for conveying the dense muscle masses.

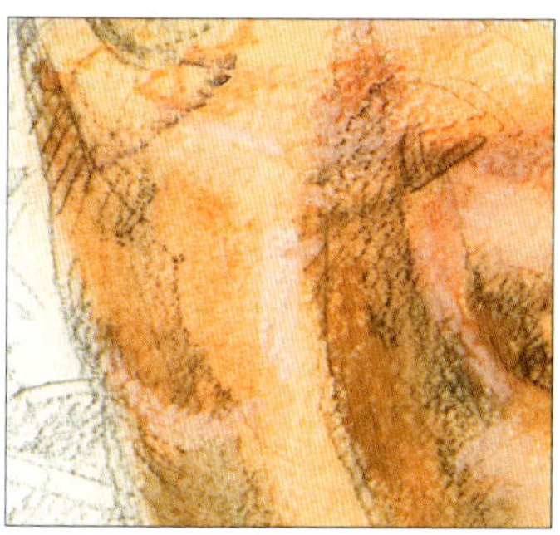

Smudged soft pastel marks create the highlights on the skin and the smooth areas of flesh.

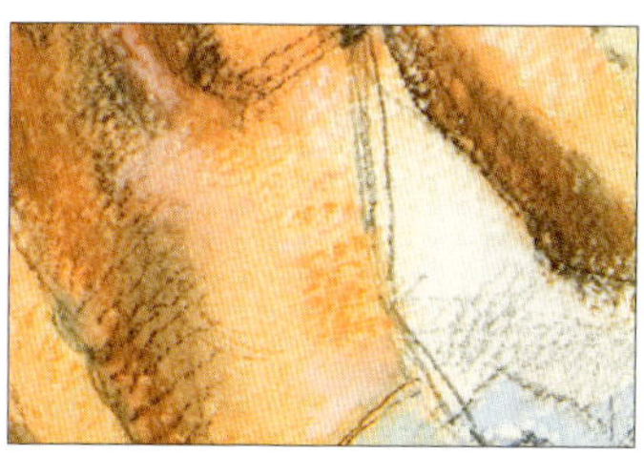

Vigorous pencil marks show how the fabric is being stretched and imply the movement of the limbs beneath.

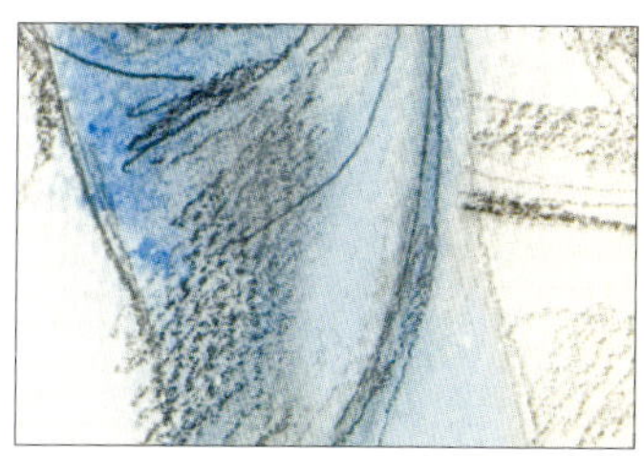

Glossary

Additive
A substance added to paint to alter characteristics such as the paint's drying time and viscosity. Gum arabic is a commonly used additive in watercolour painting.

Alla prima
A term used to describe a work (traditionally an oil painting) that is completed in a single session. *Alla prima* means "at the first" in Italian.

Blending
Merging adjacent colours or tones so that they merge into one another. In dry, powdery drawing media, such as charcoal or soft pastel, blending is usually done with your fingers or by using a torchon.

Body colour
Opaque paint, such as gouache, which can obliterate underlying paint colour on the paper.

Charcoal
Charcoal is made by charring willow, beech or vine twigs at very high temperatures in an airtight kiln. Charcoal is available in powder form and as sticks. It can also be mixed with a binder and pressed into sticks of 'compressed' charcoal, creating a form that is stronger than regular stick charcoal and does not break so easily. Charcoal pencils, made from sticks of compressed charcoal encased in wood, are also available.

Below: Coloured pencils

Colour
Complementary: colours that lie opposite one another on the colour wheel.
Primary: a colour that cannot be produced by mixing other colours, but can only be manufactured. Red, yellow and blue are the three primary colours.
Secondary: a colour produced by mixing equal amounts of two primary colours.
Tertiary: a colour produced by mixing equal amounts of a primary colour and the secondary colour next to it on the colour wheel.

Colour mixing
Optical colour mixing: applying one colour on top of another in such a way that both remain visible, although the appearance of each one is modified by the other. Also known as *broken colour*. Optical colour mixes tend to look more lively and interesting than their physical counterparts.
Physical colour mixing: blending two or more colours together to create another colour. Physical colour mixes tend to look duller than their optical counterparts.

Cool colours
Colours that contain blue and lie in the green-violet of the colour wheel. Cool colours appear to recede.

Composition
The way in which the elements of a drawing are arranged within the picture space.
Closed composition: one in which the eye is held deliberately within the picture area.
Open composition: one that implies that the subject or scene continues beyond the confines of the picture area.

Conté crayon
A drawing medium made from pigment and graphite bound with gum. Conté crayons are available as sticks and as pencils. They create an

Above: Waterproof ink

effect similar to charcoal but are harder, and can therefore be used to draw fine lines.

Drybrush
The technique of dragging an almost dry brush, loaded with very little paint, across the surface of the support to make textured marks.

Eye level
Your eye level in relation to the subject that you are drawing can make a considerable difference to the composition and mood of the drawing. Viewing things from a high eye level (that is, looking down on them) separates elements in a scene from one another; when viewed from a low eye level (that is, looking up at them), elements tend to overlap.

Fat over lean
A fundamental principle of oil painting. In order to minimize the risk of cracking, oil paints

Below: Oil pastel sticks

containing a lot of oil ('fat' paints) should never be applied over those that contain less oil ('lean' paints) – although the total oil content of any paint mixture should never exceed 50 per cent.

Fixative
A substance sprayed on to drawings made in soft media such as charcoal, chalk and soft pastels to prevent them from smudging.

Foreshortening
The illusion that objects are compressed in length as they recede from your view.

Form
See **Modelling**.

Format
The shape of a drawing or painting. The most usual formats are landscape (a drawing that is wider than it is tall) and portrait (a drawing that is taller than it is wide). Panoramic (long and thin) and square formats are common.

Glaze
A transparent layer of paint that is applied over a layer of dry paint. Light passes through the transparent glaze and is then reflected back by the support or any underpainting. Glazing is a form of optical (or broken) colour mixing as each glaze colour is separate from the next, with the colour mixing taking place within the eye of the viewer.

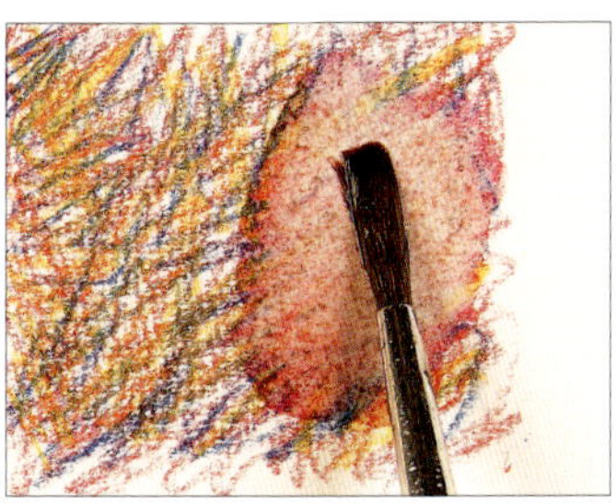
Below: Blending watercolour pencils

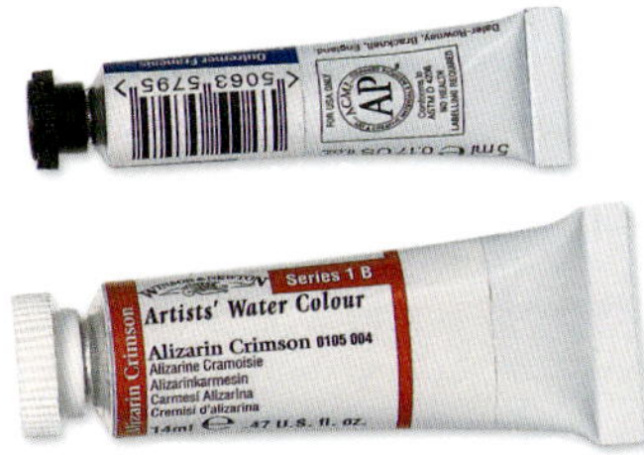

Above: Tubes of watercolour paint

Gouache
Opaque paint which can hide underlying paint on the paper.

Graphite
Graphite is a naturally occurring form of crystallized carbon. To make a drawing tool, it is mixed with ground clay and a binder and then moulded or extruded into strips or sticks. The sticks are used as they are; the strips are encased in wood to make graphite pencils. The proportion of clay in the mix determines how hard or soft the graphite stick or pencil is; the more clay, the harder it is.

Ground
The prepared surface on which an artist works. The same word is also used to describe a coating such as acrylic gesso or primer, which is applied to a drawing surface.

Hatching
Drawing a series of parallel lines, at any angle, to indicate shadow areas. You can make the shading appear more dense by making the lines thicker or closer together.
Cross-hatching: a series of lines that crisscross each other.

Highlight
The point on an object where light strikes a reflective surface. Highlights can be added by leaving areas of the paper white or by removing colour or tone with a kneaded eraser.

Hue
A colour in its pure state, unmixed with any other.

Impasto
Impasto techniques involve applying and building oil or acrylic paint into a thick layer. Impasto work retains the mark of any brush or implement used to apply it.

Line and wash
The technique of combining pen-and-ink work with a thin layer, or wash, of transparent paint (usually watercolour) or ink.

Manikin
A jointed wooden figure that can be moved into almost any pose, enabling the artist to study proportions and angles. Also known as a *lay figure*.

Mask
A material used to cover areas of a drawing, either to prevent smudging, stop marks from touching the paper underneath, or to allow the artist to work right up to the mask to create a crisp edge. There are three materials generally used for masking – masking tape, masking fluid and masking film (frisket paper). You can also simply cover up the relevant part of the drawing by placing a piece of paper over it.

Medium
The term has two very different meanings in art techniques:
(1) The material in which an artist chooses to work – pencil, pen and ink, charcoal, soft pastel and so on. (The plural is 'media'.)

Below: Blending pastel pencils

Above: Liquid acrylic ink

(2) In painting, 'medium' is also a substance added to paint to alter the way in which it behaves – to make it thinner, for example. (The plural in this context is 'mediums'.)

Modelling
Emphasizing the light and shadow areas of a subject through the use of tone or colour, in order to create a three-dimensional impression.

Negative shapes
The spaces between objects in a drawing, often (but not always) the background to the subject.

Overlaying
The technique of applying layers of watercolour paint over washes that have already dried in order to build up colour to the desired strength.

Palette
(1) The container or surface on which paint colours are mixed.
(2) The range of colours used by an artist.

Perspective
A system whereby artists can create the illusion of three-dimensional space on the two-dimensional surface of the paper.

Aerial perspective: the way the atmosphere, combined with distance, influences the appearance of things. Also known as atmospheric perspective.

Linear perspective: this system exploits the fact that objects appear to be smaller the further away they are from the viewer. The system is based on the fact that all parallel lines, when extended from a receding surface, meet at a point in space known as the vanishing point. When such lines are plotted accurately on the paper, the relative sizes of objects will appear correct in the drawing.

Single-point perspective: this occurs when objects are parallel to the picture plane. Lines parallel to the picture plane remain so, while parallel lines at 90° to the picture plane converge.

Two-point perspective: this must be used when you can see two sides of an object. Each side is at a different angle to the viewer and therefore each side has its own vanishing point. Parallel lines will slant at different angles on each side, accordingly.

Picture plane
A imaginary vertical plane that defines the front of the picture area and corresponds with the surface of the drawing.

Positive shapes
The tangible features (figures, trees, buildings, still-life objects, etc.) that are being drawn.

Primer
A substance that acts as a barrier between the board or canvas and the paint, protecting the support from the corrosive agents present in the paint and the solvents. Priming provides a smooth, clean surface on which to work. The traditional primer for use with oil paint is glue size, which is then covered with an oil-based primer such as lead white. Nowadays, acrylic emulsions (often called acrylic gesso) are more commonly used.

Recession
The effect of making objects appear to recede into the distance, achieved by using aerial perspective and tone. Distant objects appear paler in colour than those close to the observer.

Above: Gouache paint

Resist
A substance that prevents one medium from touching the paper beneath it. Wax (in the form of candle wax or wax crayons) is the resist most commonly used in watercolour painting; it works on the principle that wax repels water.

Sgraffito
The technique of scratching off pigment to reveal either an underlying colour or the white of the paper. The word comes from the Italian verb *graffiare*, which means 'to scratch'.

Shade
A colour that has been darkened by the addition of black or a little of its complementary colour.

Sketch
A rough drawing or a preliminary attempt at working out a composition.

Below: Gouache paint

Above: A tub of oil paint

Solvent
See Thinner.

Spattering
The technique of flicking paint on to the support in order to create texture.

Sponging
The technique of applying colour to the paper with a sponge, rather than with a brush, in order to created a textured appearance.

Stippling
The technique of applying dots of colour to the paper, using just the tip of the brush.

Support
The surface on which a drawing is made – usually paper, but board and surfaces prepared with acrylic gesso are also widely used.

Thinner
A liquid such as turpentine or citrus solvent which is used to dilute oil paint. Also known as solvent.

Left: Acrylic glaze

Tint
A colour that has been lightened. In watercolour a colour is lightened by adding water to the paint.

Tone
The relative lightness or darkness of a colour.

Tooth
The texture of a support. Some papers are very smooth and have little tooth, while others – such as those used for pastel drawings – have a very pronounced texture.

Torchon
A stump of tightly rolled paper with a pointed end, using for blending powdery mediums. Also known as paper stump or tortillon.

Underdrawing
A preliminary sketch on the canvas or paper, which allows the artist to set down the lines of the subject, and erase them if necessary, before committing to paint.

Underpainting
A painting made to work out the composition and tonal structure of a work before applying colour.

Value
See Tone.

Vanishing point
In linear perspective, the vanishing point is the point on the horizon at which parallel lines appear to converge.

Viewpoint
The angle or position from which the artist chooses to draw his or her subject.

Warm colours
Colours in which yellow or red are dominant. They lie in the red-yellow half of the colour wheel and appear to advance.

Above: Three different grades of pencil

Wash
A thin layer of transparent, very diluted watercolour paint.
Flat wash: an evenly laid wash that exhibits no variation in tone.
Gradated wash: a wash that gradually changes in intensity from dark to light, or vice versa.
Variegated wash: a wash that changes from one colour to another.

Wet into wet
The technique of applying paint to a wet surface or on top of an earlier paint application or wash that is still damp.

Wet on dry
The technique of applying paint to dry paper or on top of an earlier paint application or wash that has dried completely.

Below: Bars of oil paint

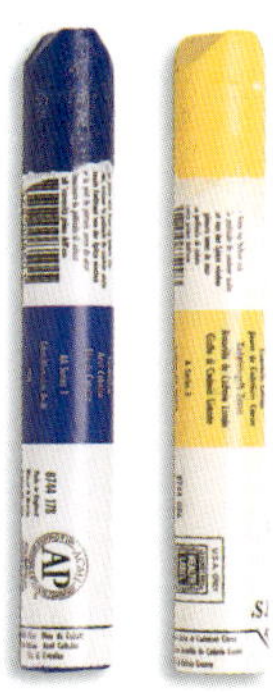

Suppliers

Manufacturers
Daler-Rowney UK Ltd
PO Box 10
Bracknell
Berkshire RG12 8ST
United Kingdom
Tel: (01344) 461000
www.daler-rowney.com

Derwent Cumberland Pencil Co.
Greta Bridge
Keswick
Cumbria CA12 5NG
United Kingdom
Tel: (017687) 73626
www.pencils.co.uk

Sennelier
Max Sauer S.A.
Z.I. 2, rue Lamarck BP 204
22002 St-Brieuc Cedex
France
Tel: 02 96 68 20 00
Fax: 02 96 61 77 19
www.sennelier.fr

Winsor & Newton
Whitefriars Avenue
Wealdstone
Harrow
Middlesex HA3 5RH
United Kingdom
Tel: (020) 8427 4343
www.winsornewton.com

Stockists
United Kingdom
Art Express
Design House
Sizers Court
Yeadon LS19 6DP
Tel: (0113) 250 0077
www.artexpress.co.uk

Atlantis Art Materials
7–9 Plumbers Row
London E1 1EQ
Tel: (020) 7377 8855
www.atlantisart.co.uk

Ken Bromley Art Supplies
Curzon House, Curzon Road
Bolton BL1 4RW
Tel: (01204) 381900
Fax: (01204) 381123
sales@artsupplies.co.uk
www.artsupplies.co.uk

Dominoes
66 High Street, Leicester
Tel: (0116) 2533363
Fax: (0116) 2628066
info@dominoestoys.co.uk
www.dominoestoys.co.uk

Hobbycraft
Hobbycraft specialize in arts and crafts materials and own 20 stores around the UK.
Freephone (0800) 027 2387
www.hobbycraft.co.uk

Jackson's Art Supplies Ltd
1 Farleigh Place
London N16 7SX
Tel: (0870) 241 1849
www.jacksonsart.co.uk

Paintworks
99–101 Kingsland Road
London E2 8AG
Tel: (020) 7729 7451
shop@paintworks.biz
www.paintworks.biz

Stuart R Stevenson
68 Clerkenwell Road
London EC1M 5QA
Tel: (020) 7253 1693
info@stuartstevenson.co.uk
www.stuartstevenson.co.uk

The Studio Art Shop
13 Crawford Arcade
King Street, Stirling FK8 1AX
Tel: (01786) 446454
info@thestudioartshop.com
www.thestudioartshop.com

Turnham Arts & Crafts
2 Bedford Park Corner
Turnham Green Terrace
London W4 1LS
Tel: (020) 8995 2872
Fax: (020) 8995 2873

United States
Many of the following companies operate retail outlets across the US. For details of stores in your area, phone the contact number below or check out the relevant website.

Art Store
Website: www.artstore.com

The Art Supply Warehouse
5325 Departure Drive
Raleigh
NC 27616-1835
Tel: (919) 878-5077
Fax: (919) 878-5075
www.aswexpress.com

Dick Blick Art Materials
PO Box 1267
Galesburg
IL 61402-1267
Tel: (800) 828-4548
www.dickblick.com
Hobby Lobby
www.hobbylobby.com

Madison Art Shop
17 Engleberg Terrace
Lakewood
New Jersey 08701
Tel: (732) 961-2211
Fax: (732) 961-1511
mail@madisonartshop.com
www.madisonartshop.com

Michaels Stores
8000 Bent Branch Drive
Irving
Texas 75063
Tel: 1-800-6432-4235
www.michaels.com

New York Central Art Supply
62 Third Avenue/11th Street
New York
NY 10003
Tel: (212) 473-7705
Fax: (212) 475-2513
sales@nycentralart.com
www.nycentralart.com

Rex Art
2263 SW 37 Avenue
Miami
FL 33145
Tel: (305) 445-1413
Fax: (305) 445-1412
www.rexart.com

Canada
Colours Artist Suppliers
10660-105 Street
Edmonton
Alberta
Canada T5H 2W9
Tel: 1-800-661-9945
E-mail: info@artistsupplies.com
Website: www.artistsupplies.com

Curry's Art Store
490 Yonge Street
Toronto
Ontario
Tel: 416 967-6666
info@currys.com
www.currys.com

Island Blue Print
905 Fort Street
Victoria
British Columbia V8V 3K3
Tel: 250-385-9786
Fax: 250-385-1377
info@islandblue.com
www.islandblue.com

Kensington Art Supply
132 10th Street NW
Calgary
Alberta T2N 1V3
Tel: 403-283-2288
Fax: 403-206-7095
info@kensingtonartsupply.com
www.kensingtonartsupply.com

The Paint Spot
10516 Whyte Avenue
Edmonton
Alberta T6E 2A4
Tel: 780-432-0240
Fax: 780-439-5447
E-mail: info@paintspot.ca
Website: www.paintspot.ca

Australia
Art Materials
Website: www.artmaterials.com.au

The Artists Warehouse
65 Sheridan Street
Cairns
QLD 4870
Tel: (0740) 316-947
sales@artistswarehouse.com.au
www.artistswarehouse.com.au

Oxford Art Supplies Pty Ltd
221–225 Oxford Street
Darlinghurst
NSW 2010
Tel: (02) 9360 4066
Fax: (02) 9360 3461
Website: www.oxfordart.com.au

Oxford Art Supplies Pty Ltd
145 Victoria Avenue
Chatswood
NSW 2067
Tel: (02) 9417 8572
Fax: (02) 9417 7617
www.oxfordart.com.au

Premier Art Supplies
43 Gilles Street
Adelaide
SA 5000
Tel: (618) 8212 5922
Fax: (618) 8231 0441
www.premierart.com.au

New Zealand
Draw Art Supplies Ltd
PO Box 24022
5 Mahunga Drive
Mangere Bridge
Auckland
Tel: (09) 636 4989
Fax: (09) 636 5162
www.draw-art.co.nz

Fine Art Supplies
PO Box 58018
18 Neil Park Drive
Greenmount
Auckland
Tel: (09) 274 8896
www.fineartsupplies.co.nz

Art Supplies.co.nz
312 Ti Rakau Drive,
Botany, Auckland
Tel: (09) 273 9450
www.artsupplies.co.nz

Index

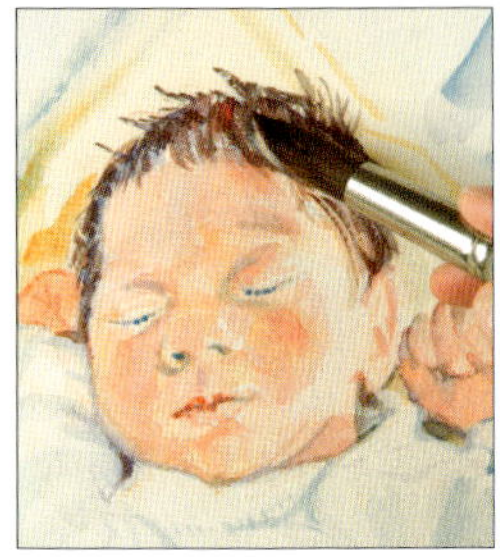

Notes

Notes

Notes

Notes

NOTES

Notes

Notes

Notes

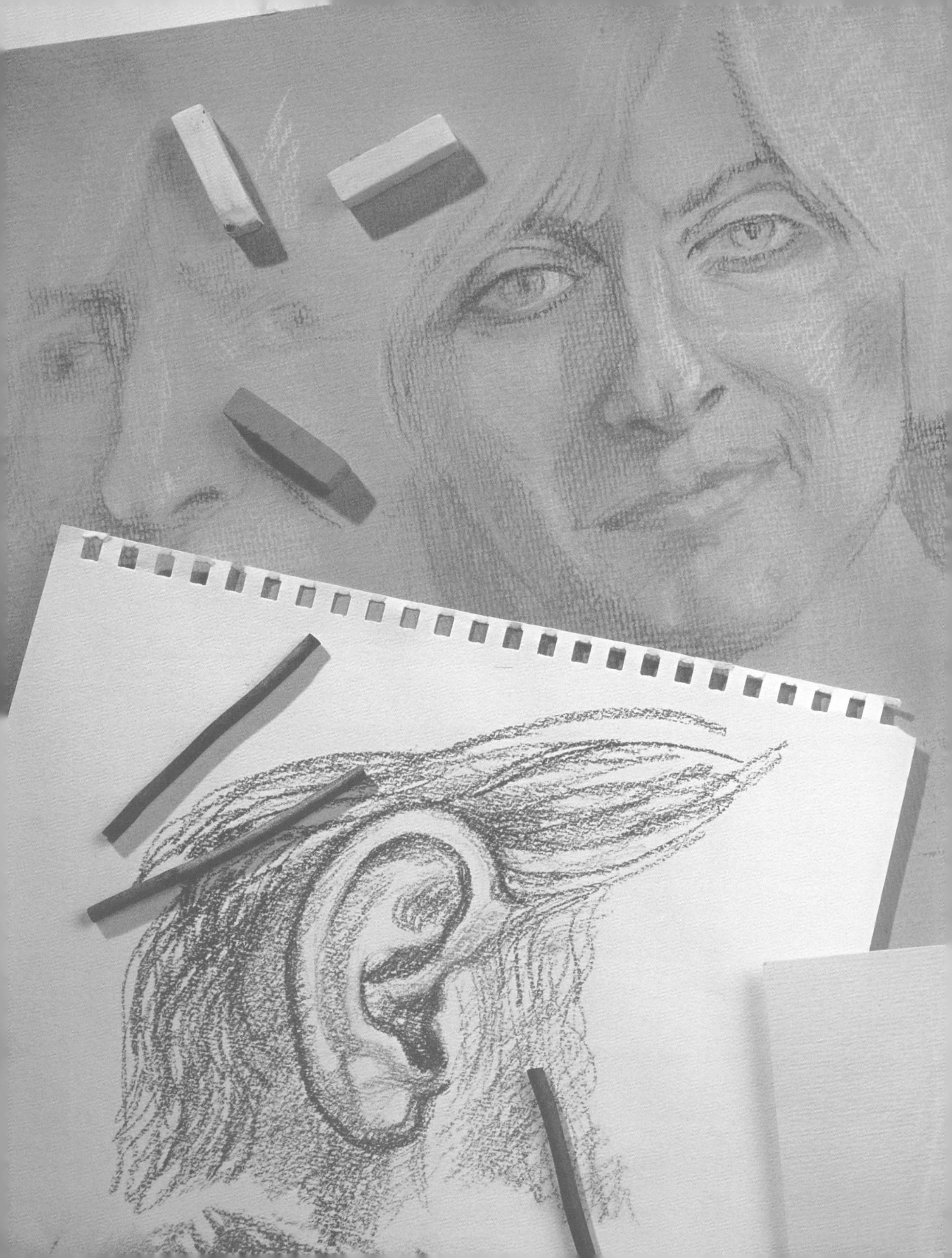